CLINTON
&
ME

CLINTON

&

ME

MARK KATZ

miramax books

HYPERION

NEW YORK

For Molly

Contents

CLINTON
&
ME

PROLOGUE

The Bravest Thing I've Ever Done
(The Egg Timer)

HE OPENED THE DOOR AND I JUMPED TO MY FEET. WATCHING THE president of the United States enter the room is always a startling sight. Of course, the sight he encountered might have caught him off-guard too: a nervous guy in a tuxedo, standing in a dimly lit holding room with a stack of pages in one hand and an egg timer in the other.

I had been waiting for him for nearly half an hour, deep inside the brass and mahogany Capitol Hilton, all alone but for a bowl of fruit that had been placed on a table by an aide. In the minutes before he arrived, I expended my nervous energy pretending to greet him with the salutation "Hey Prez!," entertaining myself by practicing it aloud numerous times to the empty room. Its breeziness and brazen familiarity made me laugh each time, and I wondered if the purpose of our meeting gave me the liberty to say it. We were there to rehearse a humor speech, after all. But as he entered the room, something about him made me lose my nerve.

"Good evening, sir!" I offered instead. The president nodded in my direction but offered no audible response. I was instantly deflated. I had been hoping for a warm, high five of a greeting. The last time I had seen him was seven months before, on a triumphant night at the White House Correspondents' Dinner. A photograph taken immediately after that speech—a pleased president towering over me as the first lady literally patted me on the back—evoked images from my bar mitzvah album. But on this night the only reason I assumed Bill Clinton even remembered me at  all was that he didn't look at me and immediately ask, "Who the hell are you?"

A few steps behind the president was the first lady, in a formal evening dress. Her greeting was silent—not even a nod. Mrs. Clinton posted herself near the door and deliberately outside of our conversation, waiting for whatever this meeting was to be over.

I hoped my unilateral enthusiasm might at least jump-start some jocularity. I held up the prop in my hand. "You know, Josh King had to go to three different stores to get an egg timer with a dial. Evidently egg timers have gone digital." I thought I might engage him by recounting the lengths the advance staff had gone to in procuring the speech's central prop, but he was not amused.

Perhaps I had failed to consider that the seven months since we'd last met might have dampened his mood. That summer, the Clinton health care plan had gone down in flames, the midterm elections in the fall had rebuked him severely and with the new year came the cringe-inducing reality of House Speaker Newt Gingrich and his Contract-with-America Congress. In January 1995, a presidency that had started with such promise seemed halfway toward ending with one failed term. Maybe that's why this was not shaping up to be a "Hey Prez!" kind of a meeting.

Although this was the fifth humor speech I'd written for Clinton since he'd taken office, we were having our very first one-on-one conversation. The occasion was a speech he was about to give that night to the Alfalfa Club, the least known of the four annual

Washington humor dinners that take place from January through April—collectively known as the "Silly Season." I was there in my capacity as presidential joke writer, an adjunct member of the White House speechwriting staff on retainer by way of the Democratic National Committee. Normally, a meeting with the president is attended by the maximum number of aides who can lobby their way into the room. But on this snowy Saturday of Super Bowl weekend, every White House speechwriter and communications aide was eager to have the night off. The Alfalfa Dinner came four days after the State of the Union address, the Super Bowl of presidential orations and the culmination of an exhausting process that began in the previous calendar year.

The president would have preferred to take the night off as well. His dislike for the Alfalfa Club was common knowledge among his schedulers. Unlike the other annual humor dinners, the Alfalfa Club is attended not by the press but by a fraternity of corporate CEOs, federal power brokers and other establishment stalwarts all gathered for an event that could easily double as the Winter Ball of the Trilateral Commission. Clinton regarded its members as the fat cats who had voted against him once and couldn't wait to do it again. I had heard repeated reports of the effort required to convince him to attend. The long history of presidents who had made the eight-block trip from the White House to the Capitol Hilton was not sufficient to make the case; this year, it had taken a personal plea from Clinton's close friend and Alfalfa Club member Vernon Jordan for him to RSVP.

Abandoned by his staff, the president was stuck in a place he did not want to be, holding in his hands a draft of a speech now covered with his cross-outs and scribbles. His first full sentence to me in the holding room torpedoed the speech's very premise: *"You can put that egg timer away."*

The egg timer, as you've waited patiently to learn, was the comic answer to that week's weekly crisis. It was born in the aftermath of the State of the Union Address, otherwise known as

"SOTU," the acronym written on the thousands of drafts and memos that helped create it. Clinton's first two SOTUs were widely regarded as far too long. This, his third, was his longest yet. The speech was clocked at one hour and twenty-one minutes, a fact pundits were using as a metaphor for an undisciplined, flailing presidency. In the news cycles that followed the State of the Union, everyone from David Brinkley to David Letterman had something to say about its oppressive length.

As far as I was concerned, this "disaster" might as well have been hatched in heaven itself. Suddenly the largely overlooked Alfalfa speech had a reason to be relevant. Prior to that speech, my draft had been a mishmash of jokes on the prevalent, if familiar, topics of the day: the new Republican 105th Congress and its Contract with America, the ascent of Gingrich and the questionable details of his $4.5 million book deal and the GOP's assault on the Public Broadcasting System. Less seismic topics included a recent decision by the U.S. Supreme Court's chief justice, whose latest opinion held that the robe of the highest-ranking justice ought to be adorned with decorative stripes—judicial activism at its silliest.

From the Friday I arrived at the White House right up to the State of the Union, I had assembled a growing list of jokes on those subjects. With the speechwriting and communications staff crunching on the State of the Union, I was all but left alone in a temporarily vacant office in the Old Executive Office Building to assemble a draft. I spent my days at my laptop and on the phone, trading jokes with friends and reliable joke writers eager to pitch in. By Wednesday, the list included these:

I see Chief Justice Rehnquist is here. He's the one wearing the tux with the tasteful gold stripes.

You know these are strange days on Capitol Hill when the Republicans are playing good cop/bad cop—and Bob Dole is the good cop.

I think history will show that I've had the best relationship with Congress of any southern president since Jefferson Davis.

Dick Armey and Phil Gramm both taught economics. Evidently, they taught it to each other.

Ronald Reagan. George Murphy. Fred Grandy. Fred Thompson. Sonny Bono. Don't any good actors become Republicans?

But the SOTU rearranged the humor landscape. The consensus molded in the post-speech punditry of Tuesday night had been set in the kiln of the next day's news. Of all the facts crammed into the SOTU, only one resonated by Wednesday morning: the president's speech had been far too long. Yet the White House refused to concede that characterization. Every authorized spokesperson in the building was quick to point out that overnight polling revealed that approval ratings of the speech had come in at 83 percent.

That detail, while true and even interesting, did not strike me as a strong premise for humor. But a guy about to give a speech as he was still being mocked for the length of his last speech—now that seemed fertile with comic potential! As the president's joke writer, my job was to mine this premise in a way that would allow the president to score points with the room. As the most obvious solution, the egg timer joke presented itself first. It was a simple idea made funnier by juxtaposing a kitschy kitchen device with a presidential podium brimming with gravitas.

By Thursday morning, the egg timer had been fleshed out into the speech's opening and running joke. The stage direction of the draft instructed the president to approach the podium, pull the egg timer from his pocket, set it to five minutes and greet the audience. That was sure to start the room laughing while also setting up a better joke to come: once the timer expired, he was to add as many minutes as he wanted, as often as he wanted. (Not only did Josh King really have to go to three stores to find an analog egg timer, but he also returned with extras so we could choose the one with the most resonant and comic bell. Advance staffers—especially good ones like Josh—are as detail-oriented as plutonium-licensed nuclear physicists.)

I had no doubt that the egg timer gag would deliver a strong laugh to start his remarks before a word was spoken—except that in the only rehearsal of an imminent speech, this particular egg timer had just been excised by a presidential executive order.

"No egg timer?" I asked. His mood notwithstanding, I hoped he was joking.

"The egg timer's a joke on my State of the Union, right?" He seemed only about 83 percent sure.

"Yes it is," I said, choosing to ignore for the moment what else he might think the egg timer could possibly refer to.

Before responding, the president diverted his attention to the bowl of fruit placed there for him by advance staffers. As he poked through the red grapes and green apples and dried figs, he seemed as pleased with the selection as he was with the egg timer.

"Well, forget it," he said, still rifling through the bowl. "They've been on me for four days straight about that speech." His hand dug deeper into the bowl to bring up the contents from the bottom, but there he found only more of the same. Not only was the president cranky about his speech, he was hungry for a snack—and neither I nor the bowl was giving him what he wanted. What he wanted was for me and my speech to go away, and to find something else in that bowl besides fruit. Something with protein. Something more like a chicken parm sandwich.

Done with the bowl, he returned his attention to me. His eyes narrowed and his lower jaw became jutted and tight. "Eighty-three percent of the American people thought I gave a *helluva* speech. Only here inside the bubble did the reporters have trouble sitting still for more than twenty-five minutes."

He was making a substantive political argument to his joke writer—which I appreciated, I guess. But I had a hard time imagining how to fold that fact into the speech. More to the point, at this moment in his presidency the benefits of self-deprecating humor were not evident to him. Alone in a room with an angry president, abandoned by the aides skilled at negotiating his moods and poorer instincts, I was left on my own to make the case.

"That's exactly why you should do it!" I blurted. The tone of my voice suggested a matter of global consequence or moral imperative. In fact, that may have been the first time I'd ever said something to him that was not plainly deferential or a clearly marked joke. I gave him my best advice with heartfelt urgency, as though I were speaking to a stubborn or misguided friend. As I saw it, this joke traded away nothing (conceding the obvious) for something (approving laughter and applause). Yet he saw it differently. The reason he was not inclined to engage in charming, self-effacing humor on this subject was that he was simply not willing to concede the point. I doubt very much that he thought that speech was too long; he probably still missed the paragraphs and pages deleted by pleading staffers. And it's a safe bet that the detailed poll reports of approving responses were still on his Oval Office desk, dog-eared and red-inked. Which is probably why he did not appreciate the egg timer, or the many other jokes on the topic of the burdensome, mind-numbing speech that refused to end. Here are a few that probably made him pretty mad:

I'll admit my speech could have used a good editor. In fact, it could have used a bad editor.

I got some good feedback the next day. Senator Byrd called to ask if he could read it at his next filibuster.

I suppose there is something to be said for a short speech. You know what they say: brief comments that get straight to the point are the heart and soul of penetrating witticisms. Or something like that.

. . . Hey, if you don't like these jokes, I can always read the unfinished half of the State of the Union. [REPEAT AS NECESSARY]

No, he probably didn't care for any of those. So by the time I finished making my case for the egg timer, he had dropped his head and was giving me the full measure of his glare. For the first time, the president directed his anger at me. I was petrified, yes, but also aware that he was wrong and I was right. (I knew for a fact that his speech was too long: I had procured from a friend in Legislative Affairs a standing-room-only guest pass to the House Gallery, and I had watched it on my feet.) It is an awesome responsibility to offer advice to a president when your expertise on a subject exceeds his. In this knee-buckling moment, I was John Dean, making the case for a funnier form of conceding the truth.

Having heard my best advice on the matter of the egg timer, the president gave a nonverbal response that could not have been louder. In one swift and startling motion, his arm bridged the distance between us and his hand removed the egg timer from my grasp; swinging his tuxedoed torso ninety degrees, he placed the timer on a mantelpiece a long reach away. It was a maneuver an exasperated parent might pull on a willful child. The egg timer part of our conversation was over, he seemed to be saying. He returned his attention to me. "What else?"

The organizing principle of the speech had just been forcefully vetoed. There really wasn't that much else to talk about.

This meeting was not going as I had hoped. To be honest, at that moment this president was not all that I had hoped. For eight days, I had been staring into a computer screen imagining the ways that humor might enable Bill Clinton to be bigger than his current circumstance. I wanted to find the laughs that would reassure those in the room who wished him well and unnerve those who did not. I listened for the voice of candor that conveys perspective, confidence and self-awareness. But I guess I was also imagining a president who would make these words his own, adding more grace and courage and wisdom than I could conjure. Maybe the president I had in mind was my idealized version of a president. Come to think of it, the words I had spent that week typing on the screen echoed in my mind with a rhythmic telltale cadence. The president I had in mind, somewhere deep in the back of my mind, was John Fitzgerald Kennedy.

Growing up, I had come to regard the many Time-Life books on Kennedy's "Camelot" that lined the bookshelves in our shag-carpeted den as alternate family albums. And when I graduated to picking up books with words instead of pictures, I came across another published tribute, a well-known compendium called *The Kennedy Wit*.[1] The book captured not only a moment in time but also a man with a charismatic verbal style, its pages filled with an engaging, irrepressible, impromptu, hyper-ironic and recklessly self-effacing wit. *(A question from a young boy: "How did you become a war hero?" Kennedy: "It was absolutely involuntary. They sunk my boat.")* John Kennedy was many things to many people, but what made him a hero to me was the sense of humor he brought to the sense of possibility. (It is my strong belief that Kennedy's sense of humor helped send a man to the moon. But for the grounded sanity evident in his self-directed humor, a manned mission to the moon might have sounded like the deluded musings of a callow, cocksure cowboy—you know, like a Missile Defense Shield.)

Somewhere inside that book was my very favorite Kennedy line. Appropriately enough, it was something he had said at this very hotel, upon this very same dais, to a room filled with powerful and important people in their most formal attire. The year was 1958 and then-Senator Kennedy was already at the front of the pack for the Democratic presidential nomination two years away. There were many people in that room who dismissed him as the brash son of a wealthy, powerful and unscrupulous man for whom he was both pawn and proxy. But that did not stop John Kennedy from opening with a joke that night that was nothing less than audacious. Only a moment after watching a skit that mocked him for having a father eager to bankroll his upcoming bid for the

---

1. A name you won't find in *The Kennedy Wit* is Ted Sorensen. Sorensen was the aide-de-camp, master wordsmith and first-rate wit of the Kennedy White House. According to legend, were you to ask Ted Sorensen if he was the author of JFK's Inaugural Address, he'd halt you with the broad side of his hand and reply, "Ask not."

White House, Kennedy held up what he said was a telegram from his "generous daddy" and read it aloud:

Jack—Don't spend one dime more than is necessary. I'll be damned if I am going to pay for a landslide.[2]

Every time I read that line, I could practically hear a tsunami of laughter overtaking a room. With a wink and a smile, John Kennedy gave everybody a good laugh about his willingness to subvert democracy itself. Yet the president standing right in front of me was adamantly refusing to comically concede that he had given a speech that dragged a little.

Forgive me for putting to paper my own *Profile in Courage,* but what happened next is without a doubt the bravest thing I have ever done. (I'm hard-pressed even to think of a runner-up.) I've told this story on dates to impress women and already arranged for it to be repeated at my funeral one day as a testament to my high and unyielding principles. My boat having been sunk beneath me, what came next was less of a decision than a response: I reached across the three feet that separated my hand from the egg timer, so demonstrably banished, and returned it to the sphere of our conversation. And then I said,

"In case you change your mind . . ."

The words stunned him. The look on his face was either awe or contempt, I honestly couldn't tell. After his unequivocal message, my impudent response was like Christina Crawford inquiring of her mom, "Are you *absolutely sure* you don't want me to use a wire hanger?"

---

2. This joke took on greater significance two years later, when some accused Kennedy of Election Night chicanery that tipped the scales in Chicago precincts, earning him Illinois' electoral votes and, supplying the margin of victory of what was until recently, the tightest (and most disputed) presidential election in history.

At this crucial moment, I made one last effort to make eye contact with Mrs. Clinton. My silent plea went out: *Hello, health care lady! I'm hemorrhaging over here!* It went unanswered. I continued on, erasing the line between brave and stupid, hoping I could make him see the humor that had eluded him so far.

"The funniest part is, after the egg timer goes off, you just keep adding more time." I demonstrated by dialing another minute onto the prop. "For as many times as you like." *Tick-tick-tick-tick-tick-tick-tick-tick.* The room was tense enough already, and now I had introduced the sound effect of a time bomb.

"The joke gets funnier each time," I promised. There was a panicked tone to my comic pitch, like Morey Amsterdam at gunpoint. I returned the dial to zero, using the metallic clang of the bell to punctuate the punch line.

The bell had tolled for me. The president turned on his heels and headed for the door. The first lady preceded him but turned around once before she left as if to memorize my face. The one ear she had used to listen to the conversation probably could not believe what it had heard. Two steps from the exit, the president stopped and turned around. Had he changed his mind about the egg timer he'd left behind? Did he have an encouraging word to leave me with? No. He reached for an apple and left for good, leaving me to stare at the back of his head as he marched out the door. *'Bye, Prez.*

I felt many different things at that moment, and one of them was exhilaration. I felt like a guy with the courage of his convictions, even though they were expressed as a joke. I left the room and handed the egg timer, now basted in palm sweat, to an advance aide with these instructions: "The president needs this to be at his seat on the dais." In the interest of expedience, I did not tell him that the president might kill or imprison the person who returned this object to his field of vision.

Having made my way from the holding room to my assigned ballroom seat far from the dais, I nervously picked at my meal, distracted by Clinton scribbling furiously on my draft—never a promising sign. Occasionally he'd lift his head to engage in polite conversation with the dais dignitaries around him. Former President Bush, Chief Justice Rehnquist and New Jersey governor Christine Todd Whitman were to his right. Former Speaker Tom Foley, new Speaker Gingrich and the first lady were to his left. The rest of the head table was filled out with various cabinet secretaries, four-star generals and the former high-ranking officials of a Republican administration in exile.

The evening went on too long, as they always do. The night's program included humorous speeches by Senator Bennett Johnston, Senator Pete Domenici and former Secretary of Everything James A. Baker. Each was well received and each took good-natured jabs at the president sitting in their midst. And with every remark directed at him, I could see him jot down another note on the draft now heavy with ink.

The president's turn to speak arrived sometime close to midnight. Upon reaching the podium, he replaced the self-deprecating egg timer opener with this bon mot:

> President Bush, you don't have to put up with this crap anymore. Why are you here?

Then came a second impromptu grace note:

> It's a beautiful night tonight. The snow is on the ground and as Hillary walked out of the White House, she looked so pretty as she got in the car I felt almost as if we were young again and on a date. We got out of the car here and I thought of that wonderful Robert Frost poem—you know, in the woods in the snowy evening, two roads diverge in the woods nearby and I took the one less traveled by—and wound up in *this damn place.*

I was disappointed but not surprised that the president had not had a change of heart on the egg timer. Also, I was concerned that he had just confused two of the world's most beloved poems and combined them into a singularly less than gracious remark. Having thanked his hosts for inviting him to this "damn place" for some "crap," the president proceeded to translate pages of gentle, self-directed humor into a hostile drive-by diatribe. I listened intently for material or topics I recognized but heard things like this instead:

> I'm under a lot of pressure tonight. Newt Gingrich is looking over my shoulder for the second time this week, [he] only laughs at the jokes that are politically correct in the counter-counterculture.

> There's going to be a new movie out called *Newt's World* in which it is more blessed to receive than to give.

> ... And where Adam Smith knows more about human nature than Thomas Jefferson and Sigmund Freud put together.

> ... In which Bert and Ernie are elitist and those guys who give to GOPAC who want to buy them so they can make a profit are the populists.

Only about two-thirds of what he was saying made any sense to me at all. Aside from the dry, nervous grunts I was emitting, none of it made me laugh, either.

He continued with a meandering speech, settling scores one minute *("I'm glad Bennett Johnston is [Alfalfa Club] president now—maybe I'll get a chance to vote against his budget")* and wallowing in self-pity the next *("We deserved to lose in November. All we did was a good job").*

He segued into an ardent defense of his economic plan *("Of all the bad press I got, I beat the press once. We are the first administration in the history of the country to cut taxes on 15 million working families and keep it a total secret")* and offered a few potshots for good measure *("You guys like to dish it out but you don't like to take it. I noticed that about all of you").*

The room generously offered feigned laughter whenever it sensed that something he said was intended as a joke. Otherwise the response was a collective, incredulous gape. Somewhere along the way, the president found a moment to make this inquiry of Senator Pete Domenici: *"Do you dye your hair?"* Senator Domenici was one of five hundred people in the room at a loss as to what to make of that.

This would-be humor speech was so nakedly hostile, it was unsettling to consider that within fifty feet of this seething president a military aide trained to follow orders held the nuclear football. To watch him give that speech was to suspect that this person would be very mean when drunk. At some point during the speech, I stopped hoping to hear familiar words from the draft; no longer did I want my handiwork to be associated with what was coming out of his mouth. Now, it was every man for himself. Only when the room's response had been reduced to near silence did Clinton reach for the object behind the *In-Case-of-Emergency-Break-Glass* sign in his mind. He pulled out the egg timer from his pocket and placed it on the podium, eliciting one of the few authentic laughs of the night—despite the fact that it was all but out of context by the time he did it.

He finished a speech punctuated by ad hominems and non sequiturs with a seemingly sincere call for cooperation, invoking FDR's fireside chats and becoming suddenly somber. By the time it was done, the speech's only saving grace was that it had been relatively short. A few Alfalfa rituals later, the evening was mercifully over. I left the hotel as quietly and quickly as I could, purposefully avoiding a path that might intersect with the president in his departing entourage. I took an early train back to New York the next morning, and by Sunday afternoon I was safely ensconced among good friends at a traditional Super Bowl party with my high school buddies and their growing families. Instead of watching the hideous halftime show, I regaled the room with this very story. Later that day, I retold it once more over the telephone to Don Baer, the head of White House speechwriting, giving an account of the speech that sounded more like a casualty report.

"I probably should have been there," he said.

As it turned out, the Alfalfa speech, not the State of the Union, was the real disaster speech of the week. White House honchos were horrified by the report on the front page of the Style section of Monday's *Washington Post* under the headline "The Reverent Bill Clinton" with this subhead: "Instead of Cutting Loose, He Falls Flat at the Alfalfa Dinner." Inside the article, dinner attendees marveled at the ill-humored, off-pitch tone of his would-be humor speech. An internal transcript of the speech absolved me from direct guilt: my draft and the president's verbatim remarks contained very few of the same words, to say nothing of premises and punch lines.

Scarring as it was, that speech might have been a turning point in my relationship with President Clinton. No doubt, he enjoyed that Alfalfa Dinner even less than I did. No one can read a room like he can, and his internal alarm sensors must have been flashing red as the speech progressed. On that night, his instincts had not served him well, and he had to have known it. Among his regrets for that night might have been his reaction to a petrified writer trying his hardest to help him, despite the fact that he was in pretty far over his head. The only solid evidence I have that our relationship changed that night is that in the years after this debacle, each time I entered a room to meet with him, he greeted me with some version of "Hey Mark, how ya doin?" It wasn't anything too effusive, but more than once I heard him say it and remembered how much I preferred that to the blank stares and angry glares I received that snowy Saturday night in January 1995.

I'd wager he woke up the morning after the Alfalfa speech hoping the groggy details of a terrible night were just the residue of a nightmare. The day after that, he had the opportunity to relive it all again when he read the *Washington Post*'s horrific account of his failed attempts at humor. I'm sure that on Monday morning, the president was eager to forget that the speech had ever happened at all. He could have jumped into any one of the pressing issues on his desk and left it all behind. But he didn't. He took a minute to revisit a dreadful evening and write a personal note that arrived in the mail later that week.

Dear Mark–
Thanks for your help with the Alfalfa Dinner. You are a funny man.
The egg timer was great. Best, Bill Clinton

CHAPTER ONE

Growing Up Kennedy

MY FIRST CONNECTION TO A PRESIDENT CAME BY WAY OF THE UMBIL-
ical cord.

I don't remember much about that terrible day in November,
but here's what I've been told: by the time the third shot was fired
from the book depository behind the grassy knoll, the phone was
already ringing in my parents' Brooklyn apartment. My mother,
eight months pregnant and prone to hysteria, was watching the
horror happen on live TV. On the other end of the phone was my
Grandma Rose, a can-do matriarch calling from her home on
Avenue U, not six blocks away. The tone of her voice had the
calm, cool resonance of a hostage negotiator.

"Adrienne, listen to me. This has nothing to do with you. Now
turn off the television and go lie down. I'll be over in five minutes . . ."

Like Camelot itself, my family's history with the Kennedy
administration may have been somewhat mythologized.[1] But

---

1. Contrary to my mother's vivid memory, the arrival of the presidential motorcade into Dallas was not televised live in the New York metropolitan area—which
means she must have had a satellite dish.

this story was repeated year after year, usually over a Carvel ice cream birthday cake. In our house, the birthday child was traditionally regaled with the details of the day we arrived, perhaps slightly embellished with each retelling, and mine always began with this incident from when I was minus five weeks old. The next beat of this time-honored tale takes place two days later: a nearly identical phone call from Grandma Rose that rang at the moment Jack Ruby was being wrestled to the ground. For the second time in those frightful forty-eight hours, my grandmother managed to successfully reason with my mother's uterus.

These details from the weeks before my birth only hint at the effect that the Kennedy era had on a child born in its aftermath. And like the birth itself, this was mostly due to a determined effort by my mom.

This was also the period when the legend of Camelot was born.[2] According to a popular anecdote from the annals of public opinion, by 1965, nearly 80 percent of Americans surveyed recalled having voted for Kennedy in the razor-close 1960 election that squeaked him into office. I don't doubt for a minute that Mom recalls correctly when she says she cast her first-ever presidential vote for JFK. And except for a few tense weeks in October of '62, when my father was eligible to be recalled to active Air Force duty during the Cuban Missile Crisis, I'm sure she was prepared to vote for him again, had she been given the chance. But in the months after Kennedy's assassination, my mother developed such a strong emotional attachment to all things Kennedy that by 1965, she was probably telling pollsters about the get-well-soon cards she'd sent to Jack after the sinking of *PT-109*.

Mom's ex post facto fixation began in earnest with the arrival

---

2. Interesting historical fact: This reference to the Kennedy era was coined in 1964 when, Theodore H. White made the connection between the Broadway musical and this presidency cut short. During the actual years of the Kennedy administration, the only person that a reference to "Camelot" conjured was Robert Goulet.

of the Kennedy memorial issues of magazines like *Life* and *Look* that began piling up in the living room of the split-level house we moved to in the summer of 1964. Page after page featured photographs of John and Jackie, John-John and Caroline—impossibly attractive, naturally stylish people in saintly repose—and flipping through them elicited the sort of aching lifestyle yearnings that would later be exploited by the makers of the J. Crew catalog. Before long, these magazines became for my mother easy-to-follow, how-to manuals for creating a little Camelot of her own. And in my first five years, those between Dallas and the moon landing, I was raised in a suburban enclave of Kennedy culture entirely of my mother's making.

Phase One began innocently enough before I was born, when my mom was one of millions of women taking fashion cues from America's fashionable first lady. In the Jewish fashion week otherwise known as the high holidays, she started showing up at synagogue in Oleg Cassini knockoff dresses, her bouffanted hair beneath a pillbox hat. Young, slender and pretty, she carried off the look better than most, but might have elicited fewer stares had Nixon won in 1960 and she had just worn a respectable Republican cloth coat. Instead, one by one, the dresses in her closet had their buttons replaced with larger, more pronounced ones, and each was accessorized with a coordinating wrap. And if there was a tailor who could have lengthened her neck or widened the distance between her eyes, she might have done that too.

Phase Two focused on my father. She set out to refashion a short-but-sturdy, round-faced dentist with sparse, flaccid hair into a chiseled, toothy Kennedy. Dentists are notoriously bad dressers, and my father was color-blind to boot. Dad proved immune to the Jack Kennedy accents she added to his wardrobes: thin ties, tie clips, crisp shirts and athletic-cut sport jackets with narrow lapels. Clothing that looked effortlessly good on JFK looked belabored on him. One Father's Day, she gave him monogrammed handkerchiefs, but the embroidered "JSK" protruding from his pocket seemed more than just one letter off. By the time this experiment was abandoned, she took solace in having successfully replaced his many print madras shirts with neat, button-down oxfords. Her efforts also had positive effects in the local dental community: the guys my father met for lunch on Tuesdays followed his lead and began wearing socks that matched their pants.

But Phase Three, the real and constant focus of my mother's compulsion for Kennedy makeovers, was me—the child she nearly delivered the day he was shot and whom she hugged through her belly the day he was buried. When I arrived, five weeks into the Johnson administration, my life began as my mother's very own living, breathing, crying, pooping John-John doll.

I make no apologies for the fact that I was a stunningly beautiful child. My eyes were big and blue, my hair was golden and silky, and I'll be damned if my face wasn't cherubic. Later in life, I'd stare at the photographs that only partially captured my beauty and curse the ravages of puberty. But at the time, my mom gazed upon a baby prince and set out to raise a John-John of her own, the templates for which were right there in the pages of the magazines on the coffee table.

It wasn't just her. She had a team. She was in the unique position to fashion a child to her will because both of my grandfathers were professional clothiers. Her father, my Grandpa Joe, was the proprietor of Joseph's, a children's clothing store well-known to those who lived in Sheepshead Bay, Brooklyn. My Grampa Max was a tailor and the man behind the counter at his Parkway Cleaners in St. Albans, Queens, where his only employee was my Grandma Ida. At my mother's behest, they worked in tandem to customize, to her specifications, the finest children's clothing on the market: velvet jackets with embroidered crests; knit jumpers in regal purples, reds and blues; and short pants lined with satin that hung from matching suspenders. Each morning I was bedecked anew, and from my earliest days I was soiling some of the finest garments to adorn a child since the Sun King was a toddler.

As if the princely wardrobe weren't enough, she put the telltale Kennedy imprint on my feet. The first pair of shoes I ever wore were red, open-toe, faux-leather Stride-Rite sandals—near-perfect replicas of the pair John-John wore the day of the poignant salute. When my feet grew, I was issued a new, larger pair. Before I was enrolled in nursery school, I had outgrown a half-dozen pairs of those shoes, but none went to waste. Sixteen months after I was born came my brother Robby, reared as a spare John-John, dressed in my hand-me-downs. Now my mother was raising a twin pair of red-shoed princes.

But of all of my mother's attempts to mold her sons, my very first haircut had the most lasting effect. She took me to the stripe-poled barbershop in the local shopping plaza and asked the old Italian gentleman for "a John-John." His perplexed look prompted her to pull out a collection of photographs from her handbag, showcasing the front, side and back of John-John's head. She explained in exact detail the hairstyle she sought: bangs pushed forward for the effortlessly tousled look—perfect for a vigorous lifestyle of roughhousing and touch football. The sides should be trimmed above the ear and the back left longer and fuller. The nice old man promised to do his best, but as he lifted the electric clipper to my head to give the only haircut he knew how, my mother snatched me from his chair and took me back to the car. On the way home, she stopped off at the pharmacy and picked up a new pair of stainless steel scissors, long and slim with a Q-shaped finger rest. This was the day I received my first Mom-administered haircut. It was also around this same time that I was christened a Yankee fan, as I sometimes needed a cap to cover her handiwork.

This perfectly cute story took a dark turn after my mother moved along the learning curve of a self-taught haircutter toward the realm of obsession. She began to take great satisfaction in the money she was saving on the hair maintenance of all of her children, and she began amassing a sizeable collection of scissors, combs, clippers, thinning shears, plastic aprons and hair tonics (the kind of equipment the state requires one to have a license to use on the general public but somehow is available for purchase over the counter). Every six weeks or so she would open the bathroom cabinet where the haircutting arsenal was kept, and one by one, my brothers, sister and I would go in for our turn in our home-style barber chair—a sturdy upholstered chair that started its life as part of a dining room set. Having your  hair cut by your mother in the bathroom is not necessarily a bad thing; it was just an uncommon practice this far from Appalachia. But the sad fact was that none of the Katz children had a professional haircut by a licensed barber until we went off to college. And even then, the positive effects of professional hair care were largely undone over Thanksgiving break. Most people pleasantly associate getting their hair cut with the smell of talc and astringent, but to this day a waft of L'Air du Temps makes the hair on the back of my neck stand on edge.

On a drizzly Sunday morning in the fall of 1994, I got a call from my friend Mitch Brill, once a regular in the after-school driveway basketball games of my suburban youth and now a Manhattan assistant district attorney.

"Hey, a bunch of guys from work are playing touch football in the park. If you want to play, come by Sheep Meadow at around noon."

"It's raining out," was my response, but I'd have been just as likely to beg off on a crisp, sunny day. Football has always been my least favorite sport to play, as it is premised on speed and size, both of which I lack. To make matters worse, I can only throw a wobbly spiral, and passes thrown directly at me have a way of bouncing off my chest. But Mitch added the detail that he knew might overcome my lack of interest:

"My buddy John is supposed to show."

He knew that I knew whom he meant.

An hour later, I arrived at Central Park in sweatpants and a slicker, along with another good friend from high school, Rich Rosenthal. We hopped the fence that was supposed to keep people from playing on the recently reseeded lawn and approached some guys tossing a football around. As I got closer, I could see that the one wearing the backward Jets cap was John F. Kennedy Jr. I was about to play touch football with John-John and I could almost smell the chowder.

Quick introductions were made among the dozen or so players and I took my cue from the group when we all pretended that John was just another one of the guys, no different from all the Daves, Steves and Mikes. We chose up sides and I was assigned to John's team. Mitch and Rich were on the other, not-John team.

When we lined up on defense for the first time, John pointed to my friend Rich—six foot, skinny, with longish, blond curly hair—and announced, "I got Goldilocks." And just like that, "Goldilocks" was inscribed into the lexicon of nicknames that never *ever* gets forgotten.

On offense, John played quarterback while I quietly assigned myself the task of trying not to be an obvious detriment to our team. As we played in the cold, light rain, I noticed some photographers huddling on the other side of the fence. From that point on, I stayed close to John in the huddle, mindful that the expression on my face might be seen in the next day's *Daily News*. He was so classically handsome, I would have to describe my response to him as a heterosexual crush. I wanted to play well so that he would like me, but that was unlikely, as I had never played well in my life. As the game went on, the team on defense quickly learned that I was the weak link on our offensive line and they assigned larger, quicker players to line up against me to get to our quarterback. I was reassigned out of necessity to be one of two or three eligible receivers but never tried terribly hard to break free from my defender. This gave John little choice but not to throw to me and he seemed happy to oblige—except on the one occasion when the guy covering me slipped on the wet grass as I left the line of scrimmage, leaving me wide open as I ran down the field. John spotted me as I broke free, pumped once, twice, and then released a tight spiral, thrown with some zip, as I waited near the end zone for it to arrive. The ball hit me like a pre-cordial thump, bounced off my sternum and went two feet up in the air, giving me a chance to drop the same ball twice, which I did. It was the last pass he threw to me for the rest of the game. There was no way I was going to be invited to Hyannis Port now.

As the game disbanded and the East Siders headed east and the West Siders headed west, I worked my way into the circle of sweaty rain-soaked guys who surrounded John. We had met once before, I reminded him, at the White House Correspondents' Dinner, and segued sharply from there to tell him a story I thought he might find amusing: that once upon a time my mother cut my hair to look like his and that was the reason for a childhood of home haircuts. He smiled graciously at my anecdote, as he must have had a lot of practice listening patiently to random people's disparate connections to his very public life. After all, his mother had raised him right. Then he had a question for me.

"Does your mom still cut your hair?"

"No."

"Good for you."

CHAPTER TWO

Anti-Nixon Youth

A RECENT FREEDOM OF INFORMATION ACT INQUIRY REVEALS THAT I never made it onto the Nixon Enemy List. Neither did my brother. I was ten, he was nine, and as I think about it now, the omission strikes me as a blatant case of age discrimination. Nixon was our #1 enemy just the same, and if Ehrlichman was really the diligent henchman everyone says he was, then he really should have been familiar with the names KATZ, MARK and KATZ, ROBBY.

From the spring of 1973 through the summer of 1974, hating Richard Nixon took up a fair amount of time for Robby and me, a hobby we happily shared and one that sublimated normal sibling rivalries for hours on end. On school days, we'd race home from the bus stop, throw down our book bags and rush to the rec room, where the second of our family's two televisions was kept. We'd spin the dial to channel thirteen, twist the antenna until the black-and-white image congealed, and set ourselves down on an orange plaid couch to watch PBS's live coverage of the Senate Select Committee on Presidential Campaign Activities—better known as "the Watergate Hearings." For the next few hours, we'd hoot and holler at the screen the way other kids our age watched professional wrestling. And once the gavel concluded each day's testimony at around 5 P.M., Robby and I might have been the only two viewers in America who stayed tuned to PBS for that day's episode of *Zoom!* Neither of us knew exactly why we hated Richard Nixon so much. We only knew it was fun.

As is the responsibility of older siblings, I introduced Robby to this particular pleasure of life. Yet to describe myself as Robby's big brother is not quite accurate. Robby arrived just sixteen months after me, and if only for reasons of convenience, my parents effectively raised us as twins. For as far back as I can remember, Robby and I were a tandem, a duo, a collective unit assigned a single proper noun: *markandrobby*.[1] Not only did we

 share a room and its content of toys, we shared a wardrobe. Whenever we went anywhere in public, my mother dressed us in identical outfits, because when one of us inevitably got lost, she would grab the other and announce, "He looks like this!" (As bad as this arrangement was for me, it was even worse for Robby. At least when I outgrew a shirt or a sweater or, even worse, a leisure suit, I was done with it forever. He first had to outgrow his and *then* outgrow mine.)

Nor did Robby take well to the role of baby brother. He was always eager to show that he was not my subject but my peer. We didn't look the same, but we certainly looked like brothers. His dark brown eyes and determined look were the counterbalance to my big blue eyes and *who, me?* countenance. And while this was only a working theory at the time—one later verified by standardized testing—Robby was smarter than I was, which made it that much harder for me to meet my older-brother obligation to manipulate and outwit him. But working together, we were a dangerous force, regarded by others as a two-headed monster that

---

1. Also: *Heckle&Jeckle, MoronOne&MoronTwo* and *The Two Schmendricks*.

romped around as one. That might explain the initial shock I felt on the early fall day in 1968 when I was sent off to Robin Hill Nursery School all by myself.

These were the early years of the Nixon administration, but that fact failed to permeate the largely apolitical atmosphere of prekindergarten. Sometime during the first term, I'm sure I must have known a man named "Nixon" was the president, but the idea of "president" was unclear to me and seemed roughly equivalent to "principal." Not until the complexity of my world expanded to include multiplication tables and cursive penmanship did Richard Nixon begin to penetrate my consciousness. By the fall of 1972, I had turned one of life's corners from which there was no turning back.

Eight is an early age to be thrust into the arena of national politics. I was in the third grade when I was assigned to represent George McGovern in a mock debate against designated Nixon stand-in Gretchen Gillis. The next day, somewhere between my bus stop and the classroom, I lost the list of reasons to vote for McGovern that my mother helped me compile. Forced to free-associate in front of the room, I asserted that my candidate shared a first name with George Washington and tried to suggest that the "Govern" of his last name was a credential unto itself. When all the ballots were counted, McGovern lost the election in Mrs. Carr's class by a two-to-one margin, slightly worse than he was doing in the national polls. (Only later in life did I confront the obvious question: did the Nixon goons break into my cubby and steal my notes?)

From that day on, I felt guilty about George McGovern's lack of support, both in Mrs. Carr's class and in the rest of the country. Having failed McGovern, I felt connected to him and hoped that in victory we might both be redeemed. With Election Day just a week away, I began asking questions over dinner about presidential politics, and I expressed an interest in helping McGovern in the days ahead. My parents, who were both born to FDR-worshiping families and later became teenage Adlai Stevenson supporters, encouraged my interest and liberal leanings and helped me enlist Robby in the cause as well. My older brother Bruce, in his early teens, was uninterested in politics per se—although, as one already engaged in a lifestyle of sex and partying, he was at the very least a latent Democrat. My sister, Ruthie, still in a high chair, seemed unengaged by the political dialogue, preferring to concentrate on smushing the tuna noodle casserole on her plate into a paste with her fork.

On the Saturday before Election Day, my father took Robby and me to the local Democratic office to pick up a campaign button and bumper stickers. Seeing McGovern's name embossed and shimmering against a backdrop of red, white and blue made the election seem real in a way the classroom debate had not. I immediately placed a button on the front of my Mighty Mac jacket, where it stayed pinned until Robby finally outgrew it sometime in 1975. Robby and I eagerly took as much paraphernalia as the nice lady behind the desk would give us, and when we got back to our car, we proudly affixed one of the bumper stickers to the back of my dad's royal blue '68 Mercury Cougar. I stared at it, proud that my initiative was now making a tangible impact. I felt empowered.

On Monday, I took the better part of our stash to school and met Robby at recess for some grassroots campaigning. With Rob starting at one end and me at the other, we worked our way through the entire parking lot, placing a McGovern bumper sticker on the right rear chrome of each car. No one had explained to us that bumper stickers were different from, say, windshield flyers, and that, as a rule, people like to put bumper stickers of their own choosing on their cars. I know this for a fact because Mr. Stein, our principal, repeated this to us in stern tones in his office later that afternoon. The next day, Election Day, we were back in his office being admonished again, this time for approaching registered voters on their way to cast their ballots in the cafeteria and beseeching them to vote for McGovern.[2]

Our enthusiasm for McGovern was apparent, but the more we expressed it, the more our parents tried to prepare us for the outcome they knew was inevitable. I was aware McGovern was behind in the polls, but all week long I clung to the idea of a late-inning, come-from-behind victory—the kind that anyone acquainted with national politics would know was impossible, but that a kid who watched a lot of Yankee games could easily imagine. On the Tuesday morning of Election Day, I arrived at the kitchen table and found that day's newspaper. On the front page was a picture that set the tone for the day and has stayed with me for life: George McGovern in a dimly lit hotel room reading a newspaper and hovering over a bowl of cereal, spoon in hand. The photo's caption specifically mentioned that there was no milk in the bowl, an odd detail but one that captured my attention. Staring into the photo as I consumed my milk-soaked King Vitaman cereal, I felt more connected to McGovern at that moment than I ever had or ever would. In fact, it might have been my first encounter with empathy.

Like most children that age, I had a special love for breakfast cereal, and like most emotionally stunted adults, I still do. Cereal was more than mere packaged foodstuff: it was a passion. In a world of assigned classroom seating and prepicked matching outfits, cereal offered a treasured realm of free will. The cereal aisle of Waldbaum's supermarket was where I learned to become a consumer, a rational decision maker exposed to a dizzying array of choices, responding consciously and subconsciously to the hundreds of Saturday morning television commercials meant to mold

---

2. Let's recap: in the first week of my fledgling political career, I blew a debate, committed an act of inept vandalism, broke a federal law against electioneering at a polling place and had my heart broken by a noble candidate with zero chance of winning. How hard was it to predict that one day I would go on to become a professional Democratic party operative?

my mind and forced finally to pick just one. (Actually, two. Working in concert with Robby, we could select a set of cereals that complemented each other while doubling our options.) The only constraint was that the cereal not have "sugar" as its first listed ingredient, a mandate issued more out of fear that one of my father's patients would spot us buying Super Sugar Smacks than out of genuine concern for our teeth.

This obsessive relationship with breakfast cereal was why the Election Day image of it on the front page of the newspaper was tattooed onto my consciousness that day. A ten-year-old knows of no worse way to start a day than to fill a bowl with cereal, open the refrigerator, reach for the milk and immediately sense the weightlessness of the carton. Complaints registered with my mother only brought the suggestion of opening a packet of Carnation Instant Milk—a fate worse than a bowl of Wheatina. On this day, George McGovern was about to lose the election *and* he had no milk! But the longer I stared at the picture, the angrier I got with Nixon. In my mind, Nixon was somehow responsible for McGovern's joyless breakfast of dry flakes—as though Nixon were the one who had finished off the last of the milk. Of course, this made no sense, but it was not the product of a brain's rational response; this was the viscera of a third grader speaking, and clearly, I hated Nixon.

Or was it just fear? I was certainly scared of Nixon. Almost everything about him scared me: the way he looked, the way he talked, especially the way he smiled. His was the uneasy smile that came from practicing in a mirror, exuding the kind of fake sincerity that children and dogs can almost always detect. But more than anything, it was his hair that scared me. Not just his famous five o'clock shadow—which to my eye looked like the time was actually closer to midnight—but even the hair on his head. He had mean-old-man hair. It was combed not to the side, as with most adult men, but straight back and flat, as though it were trying to run away from his face.

My attention to his hair was directly related to the fact that I was at the onset of puberty, and hair was becoming an increasingly important facet of my life. Behind locked bathroom doors, I was experimenting with various hair-care products that belonged to my mother: Short & Sassy conditioners, Final Net hair spray, Alberto VO5, and Dippity-Do. I studied the effect each had on my hair, longish bangs worn in a style that might best be described as latter-day Brady Brunch. I was in the vanguard of my peers who carried black rubber combs in their back right pockets. More than that, hair was helping me to understand the world around me, a visual clue that corresponded to personality types. All on my own, I had deciphered the lesson of the 1960s: the world was divided into two kinds of people—the fluffy and the unfluffy. The people I liked were almost uniformly fluffy. So were my television role models, among them David Cassidy, Joe Namath, Ron Blomberg[3] and Bob McAllister,[4] people whose defining characteristics came in the form of hair and sideburns and Fu-Manchus and Afros, even if they were white. I responded to people with this kind of hair—buoyant, unabashed hair that wasn't afraid to flow, curl, bounce or catch the wind. For hours, I would stare at the portraits of the Beatles on the inside of *Sgt. Pepper's,* whether the album was spinning on the turntable or not. Then there were the flat-hair people: vice principals, unpleasant neighbors and people who smelled like Aqua Velva. Their hair was unfluffy, overmanaged, repressed and almost apologetic for the fact that it existed at all. The kind of hair that was deadened with Brylcrccm and a fine-tooth comb. Although I didn't understand it in partisan terms, the distinction I had instinctively arrived at was the dividing line between Democrats and Republicans.

* * *

3. A Jewish Yankee!
4. The host of *Wonderama!*

It was around this time, when the Watergate scandal was brewing, that my Nixon nightmares started. The most persistent involved Nixon trying to break into our house. This dream always began with him stealing something—our television, a car, my homework—and usually ended with my being blamed for it. Soon Nixon was showing up in almost all of my dreams. As my gym teacher. A cousin at a family wedding. The guy driving the ice cream truck. One nightmare was so unsettling that I still remember it vividly: it was the first day of a new school year, and Nixon was my bus driver. Each day the bus got less and less crowded until I was the only one left, at which point he turned onto the highway and the bus started to fly. We flew in the bus to Long Beach Island, New Jersey, where our family rented a house for two weeks each August. I told Nixon I was hungry, so we stopped off for a hot dog. I excused myself to go to the bathroom to make a number two, and when I sat down on the toilet, a family of hermit crabs that lived in the back of the tank crawled into the bowl and started nipping at my testicles. (There's a chance that last part may not have been exclusively rooted in my fear of Nixon.)

This odd adolescent affliction of Nixonphobia could have easily sent me down a different and dangerous path, one that would have ultimately left me more fearful than funny. And but for my Uncle Al, it might have.

Uncle Al was not really my uncle. He was the sitcom-perfect wacky neighbor-type who was my father's best friend from dental school. His wife, my Aunt Gloria, was not really my aunt, but she was my mom's best friend. And their son Charlie was our nominal "cousin" and absolute favorite playmate, introduced to Robby and me in the mid-sixties when he was plopped down next to us in a crib. They lived one town over, and given our families' symmetry, it's no wonder that they spent a lot of time at our house and we were frequently over at theirs.

Uncle Al was a renegade dentist and counterculture renaissance man, both funny[5] and contrary[6] by nature. The fact that he walked with a limp from a motorcycle accident made him seem like a hulking giant, even though he was maybe five foot five. His den was our favorite playroom, seemingly immune to disruption because it was already a mess. The room was alive with books and magazines, musical instruments, high-end stereo equipment, piles of LPs and reel-to-reel tapes of everything from Bach to Bachman-Turner Overdrive. There was also other paraphernalia lying about that we were probably too young to accurately identify. I don't believe it is an overstatement to say that his collection of comedy albums changed my life. Robby, Charlie and I spent hour after hour sampling George Carlin, Robert Klein, Woody Allen, Bill Cosby, Richard Pryor, Tom Lehrer, Vaughn Meader and—the Rosetta stone of Jewish humor—Mel Brooks and Carl Reiner's *2000-Year-Old Man*, as well as its second tablet, *The 2013-Year-Old Man*. We'd play the albums and repeat the punch lines to each other, only a small percentage of which we fully understood. Especially George Carlin's.

Not all of the reading material in Uncle Al's den was intended for children, either. Fortunately, Charlie knew the secret place where Uncle Al's *Playboy* magazines were stashed—in the back of a file cabinet beneath a thick pile of sheet music.[7] Once the den door was secured and the literature was retrieved, we'd form a semicircle around the *Playboy* altar—three boys staring at naked ladies and engaged in conversation consisting mostly of prepubescent nouns like "tushy," "woo-woo," and "bazoombas," and the all-purpose adjective "Nice!"

---

5. He liked to brag that he was the one dentist who dissented from the other four by recommending *sugared* gum for his patients who chewed gum.

6. He gave me the cast album to *Jesus Christ Superstar* as a gift for my bar mitzvah—a fact that to this day elicits a disapproving look from my mother.

7. Later in the decade, when my parents sat us down to tell us that Uncle Al and Aunt Gloria "no longer loved each other" and were getting divorced, I immediately thought: "Uh-oh. Aunt Gloria found the *Playboys!*"

Of course, the fact that Uncle Al maintained a tasteful adult library now seems perfectly normal. The truly telling detail about my Uncle Al was that he was a grown man with a subscription to *MAD* magazine. These were kept out in the open, and in some ways, the cartoon covers were more engaging than near-naked ladies with bunny ears. Alfred E. Newman is the very face of irreverence and a role model for the would-be wiseass. It was in the pages of *MAD* magazine that I found the cure to my irrational fear of Richard Nixon.

By the time Watergate had become a full-blown scandal, the topic had received extensive coverage in the pages of *MAD*, although in a decidedly different manner than in *Time* or *Newsweek*. The face that twisted into a demonic mask in my sleeping mind's eye seemed positively inert when transformed to comic caricature. Inside Uncle Al's den of subversive culture, I came to understand that Nixon was not a monster but a cartoon character, no more worthy of dread than my cereal-box-monster breakfast companion, Count Chocula. My relationship to Nixon was forever changed. I still hated Nixon because he was Nixon, but I discovered that I loved hating Nixon because it was fun.

In the aftermath of this breakthrough, Nixon remained in the front of my mind but no longer inhabited the dark corners of my subconscious. Instead, I began to incorporate the lessons learned in the pages of *MAD* magazine and in the grooves of George Carlin albums into a brand of adolescent Nixon comedy. I delighted in each new funny fact I learned about him. He was a Quaker. In my breakfast-cereal-centered mind, that prompted an image of the Quaker Oats guy, and so my mind's eye conjured Nixon's smiling-at-gunpoint face beneath the white powdered wig. His vice president was named Spiro Agnew, and that name was funny in itself, but the day I learned that Nixon's best friend was named Bebe Rebozo, I lit up just as brightly as when I first heard of the existence of Lake Titicaca. Just saying "Bebe Rebozo" made Robby and me giggle with delight. Knock-knock jokes that had

"Bebe Rebozo" at the door ended in guffaws before anyone inquired *"Bebe Rebozo who?"* We could also crack ourselves up just as hard by making the signature Nixon poses, peace signs waving over hunched shoulders as we flapped our jowls from side to side.[8] Of the stray facts we knew, one truth stood out: Richard Milhous Nixon was a comic playground where the sun never set.

Our delight and infatuation with all things Nixon soon put Robby and me on the front row of the Watergate scandal. We knew that Nixon was guilty from the beginning, even before we understood what he was guilty of. As the televised Watergate hearings became part of our daily routine, we were barraged with new facts about Nixon and responded with new jokes. Jokes we were quite certain were very clever.

Q: Why did Nixon cross the road?
A: Because he was across the street from the Watergate Hotel.

Q: What did Ehrlichman say when he walked into the Oval Office and saw Haldeman?
A: Testing. Testing. One, two, three.

Knock! Knock!
Who's there?
Nixon.
Nixon who?
Wait a minute, I'll rewind the tape.

We incorporated Nixon references into our everyday routines. I referred to my meager treasury of coins and dollar bills as "the slush fund." Every time we passed a Howard Johnson hotel in the

---

8. Of course, we were not imitating Richard Nixon as much as we were imitating Rich Little imitating Richard Nixon.

car, one of us would say, "Speak up—the Republicans can't hear you."[9] We began collecting all of our jokes and lines and skits on the GE cassette tape recorder Robby got for his ninth birthday. And as the scandal grew, so did our tape. However, perhaps the single most productive day we had for producing Nixon jokes was the day we discovered the happy coincidence that Nixon's nickname corresponded exactly to a popular colloquial term for "penis." A discovery like this can rock the world of a ten-year-old. We started with the obvious *(Nixon—what a Dick!)* and kept going until we arrived at *Dick Nixon—you said it, not me!*

The hearings themselves were endlessly entertaining. Of course, we didn't really follow them on a substantive level, nor did we have anything more than a rudimentary understanding of the grave issues at hand. Mostly we just repeated breathless phrases ("assault on Democracy," "constitutional crisis" and "cancer on the presidency") without knowing what the hell we were talking about. But we knew whom we liked (Sam Ervin, John Sirica, John Dean[10]) and whom we didn't (Haldeman, Ehrlichman, Colson et al.). Around that time, there was a television commercial on the air for a carpet company named Dean. It featured a catchy little jingle, *"Dean-Dean, Dependable . . . Dean!,"* with the tagline: *"You can't spell 'dependable' without D-E-A-N."* Once we understood that Dean was saying things that the White House didn't want him to, we danced around the room singing that song. *"Dean-Dean, Dependable . . . Dean!"* and intoned the tagline to sing his praises.

---

9. Nixon's Republican operatives were located at the Howard Johnson's Motor Lodge across the street from the Watergate complex, where they listened in to the bugged conversations from Room 723, perhaps munching on room service Tendersweet clams.

10. My only recollection of my brother Bruce's interest in the Watergate hearings was when John Dean testified. Not because he cared about the testimony, but because Dean's very attractive wife was in the shot sitting directly behind him.

Other catchphrases that we incorporated into our vernacular included these answers to almost every question then asked of us:

Mark, did you finish your homework?
"I do not recall."

Mark, will you stop teasing your sister?
"Not at this time."

Mark, would you like me to strangle you with my own hands?
"Not as such."

Perhaps our favorite pastime was imitating the impenetrable North Carolina accent of that self-styled simple country lawyer, Sam Ervin, exhorting taciturn White House witnesses to *"Answer the question, puh-LEESE!"* At the dinner table, in the car, on the playground, Robby and I pushed the limits of preadolescent obnoxiousness by responding to any question unsatisfactorily answered with this scream, usually in unison:

"Answer the question, puh-LEESE!"

This wonderful time of our life came to its inevitable conclusion while Robby and I were away at sleepaway camp in the summer of 1974. Knowing we were unable to follow the hearings on a daily basis, my mother sent us occasional clippings from the newspaper to keep us abreast of major developments. But the fact was, I was otherwise distracted by softball games, art shack projects, instructional swim, Wendy Zolt and making sure that whatever T-shirt I was wearing that day did not match Robby's. Then came August 9, the day Nixon resigned. The impact of this news at camp was mitigated somewhat by the fact that it broke on the last day of Color War. But I remember hearing it from a counselor and immediately running to find Robby, who was preparing to engage in an egg-eating contest on behalf of the Blue team. I interrupted to tell him the news.

We didn't scream or jump up and down or exchange high fives. Something strange happened: we hugged. It was probably the first time we hugged outside of the familial peacekeeping auspices of our parents. Later that night, the more raucous celebration began as we raced in, around and through our bunks wearing nothing but underwear with rolls of toilet paper threaded by a plunger unfurling in our wake, chanting "NIXON *IS* A CROOK!" "NIXON *IS* A CROOK!" Robby and I celebrated Nixon's resignation as if it were our own accomplishment, as though I were Woodward and he were Bernstein—that other dangerous duo.

CHAPTER THREE

Portrait of the Wiseass as a Young Man

TO ANSWER YOUR QUESTION, YES, WE HAVE MET BEFORE. I WAS THE kid who launched jokes from the back row of your ninth-grade English class.

Of course, it's a comedy cliché: every half-wit who ever went to high school cut his teeth on the cheap laughs of classroom impropriety, and most of them will eagerly recount for you their glory days as a classroom cutup. In fact, this person—now a fully realized, self-aggrandizing jerk—will probably make you listen to the story of the first time they were thrown out of a classroom, whether you care to hear it or not.

Mine came in the seventh grade.

Miss Nussbaum[1] was my very first English teacher and the oldest grown-up I had ever addressed as "Miss." But only in the classroom. In the corridors of Felix V. Festa Junior High, she was better known as "Nussie" and was infamous for her severe looks and cruelty. In a world where teachers were placed in one of two cate-

---

1. Some names and details in this chapter have been changed in an attempt to ward off lawsuits. But not "Nussbaum." Come and get me, Nussie.

gories—those who gave homework on Fridays and those who did not—Nussie assigned book reports over midwinter break. She was the personification of the new world order of junior high, where every forty-three minutes shrill buzzers demarcated eight periods a day, none of them recess.

In fourth-period English, Nussie's permanently pinched face seemed to suggest that someone in the room had just passed gas, and her verbal style was just as off-putting. She spoke in stilted, complete, well-conjugated sentences with punctuation you could practically hear. Her response to an inquiry was never "yes," "no" or "in a minute." Instead, it was, "The answer to your question, Mr. Katz, is 'negatory.'" "Negatory" is a good example of her diction. For an English teacher, she used a lot of non-English words. Many were Latin, some were archaic English and others were just of her own invention. I specifically remember that she was very fond of the word "quizzical," a word that—much like its meaning when used correctly—is curious. But Nussie did not use it correctly. Once a week, she would announce upcoming exams like this: "Class, tomorrow there will be a spelling *quizzical,*" or, "Monday there will be a literature *quizzical.*" Each time I heard it, the word hit my ears hard. For a week or so, it floated in my brain, unresolved, like a cerebral sneeze that never came to be. Until the day that Nussie announced a comprehensive vocabulary quizzical, and suddenly I lit up at the culmination of a thought my subconscious had been toiling over all this time. I could barely contain my glee as I raised my hand to ask:

Figure 1: "Nussie" (artist's rendering)

"Excuse me, Miss Nussbaum—will that be a quizzical or a testicle?"

I had generated classroom laughter before, but this was different. This laughter arrived in waves, gaining strength just when typical laughter recedes into smiles. All heads swiveled in my direction, each face a various expression of hysterical convulsion.

Cool guys looked at me with approving eyes and pretty girls looked at me longer than they ever had before. This was the kind of moment your mind begins to relive even as it unfolds in real time, and I would have savored it even longer but for the screaming woman at the front of the room. Nussie had risen to her feet and was radiating anger. Her arm shot sideways, and a bony finger protruded from her clenched fist, pointing toward the door:

"Get out!"

She repeated "GET OUT! GET OUT!" louder and louder until I found myself on the other side of the door. This being the first time I had been thrown out of a classroom, I did not know that implicit in the "GET OUT!" was ". . . AND GO TO THE PRINCIPAL'S OFFICE!" Once outside the room, I did not know where to go, so I went to the cafeteria and had an early lunch—hardly the punishment Nussie had in mind. All I wanted to do was find someone, anyone, to tell what had just happened. This exchange, which completely unhinged Nussie, had exhilarated me. If ever a single joke altered the course of a life, this was it. To suggest that I have spent the years since subconsciously trying to relive that glorious moment would miss the point that my efforts have been entirely conscious. And they began the very next day.

News of the incident spread through the halls and into my other classes, earning me the junior high version of celebrity status. The legend grew as it went from lunch table to lunch table; according to one version, Nussbaum fainted and had to be carried to the nurse's office by John Kung and Linda Millman, two notorious teachers' pets. Later that week, a kid in my gym class asked me if I was the same Katz who had mooned the principal.

In the first days and weeks after the "quizzical" joke, my classmates would break up at almost any offering I made. This was the golden age of my humor career, when I was the beneficiary of a "laugh-first, figure-out-why-it's-funny-later" policy that all but begged me to interject at will. As any behaviorist would predict, my unsolicited comedy output increased dramatically, from about three jokes per class to seven or eight, depending of course on the class. Social studies and English lent themselves to wisecracks more than science or math[2]—while health class lent itself to a microphone and a two-drink minimum.

The pressure to perform increased again when my friend Kanef began charting my jokes per class, with the number of jokes on one axis and their humor value on a scale of one to five on the other. Soon I was mass-producing comic lines with diminishing concern for the quality of each offering. Now the name of the game was quantity, as if laughter were scored cumulatively and three half-hearted clucks were just as good as one full-throated cackle. Before long, I was offering cheap callbacks to the once-glorious line, asking unprompted questions like, "Will this be on the quizzical?" Within two months of my magnificent "quizzical" moment, I had turned into a relentless comic hack who had not yet been bar mitzvahed.

My enthusiastic class participation soon became the subject of parent-teacher conferences. Upon their first invitation, my parents were eager to meet Miss Nussbaum, if only to see how she compared to my descriptions of her. My worst fears came true when they returned from the meeting with a favorable impression of Nussie, applauding her style of discipline and threatening to have her babysit on weekends.

However, the most memorable parent-teacher meeting involved my social studies teacher that year, Mr. DeSilvio. Mr. DeSilvio was a burly, balding, no-nonsense autocrat who was biding his time teaching kids about Manifest Destiny until he could fulfill his dream of becoming a henchman vice principal. DeSilvio did not care very much for my class contributions either, and he kept his eye on me. Before too long, he had moved me up to the front row, the desk closest to his, knowing that this created a logistical hurdle.

---

2. You try doing a joke about the value of x when y is an integer greater than or equal to 9.

Now my classroom contributions had to be broadcast a full 360 degrees, as opposed to my 180-degree hemisphere of the back row. (See diagram.) With an adjustment in volume and the angle of my chair, I soldiered on—but soon enough, DeSilvio too put me on notice to curtail my comedy during his class. Even that didn't prepare me, though, for the day he caught me off-guard and extended the gag order to include the minutes before class started as well.

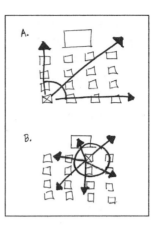

A moment before the bell rang one day, DeSilvio entered the class and saw a crowd of kids huddled around my desk. I was showing off my latest project, a notebook filled with unkind renderings of my nemesis Nussie under equally mean-spirited headlines, many done up in the style of movie posters:

Return of the Loch Nuss Monster

The Wicked Witch of the East (Wing)

You can re-create the A-Bomb.
You can re-create the H-Bomb.
But you can't re-create the Nuss-Bomb!
[mushroom cloud]

Reminder to Nussbaum students:
It's not polite to stare.

It's 10 A.M. Do you know where your children are?
[Picture of scared children in Nussie's class]

Like any good despot, DeSilvio was suspicious of laughter and crept behind the crowd to examine its cause. A moment later, he swooped down, seized the notebook and instructed me to follow him. He walked briskly down the corridor with me in his grasp until we arrived at an empty room in the principal's office, whereupon I was seated in a chair and interrogated. A transcript might read like this:

DESILVIO: Do you think these pictures are funny?
ME: [No response]
DESILVIO: Do you think Miss Nussbaum would think they are funny?
ME: [No response]
DESILVIO: I repeat. Do you think Miss Nussbaum would think they are funny?
ME: Well, she really doesn't have a good sense of humor.
DESILVIO: I think Miss Nussbaum has a fine sense of humor. You know what? I think we ought to show these pictures to her and see if she laughs.

With that, DeSilvio had broken me. I was dangerously close to crying but fought back the tears as best I could (and not very well), if only to deny him the satisfaction. I needed backup. I told him I wanted to call home and he nodded toward the phone on a gray metal desk. My throat was so tight, I could barely get out a plaintive "Hello?" when my mother picked up the phone.

"Mark, is that you? Mark? Mark? Are you all right?"

I finally was able to dislodge words from my throat on my second or third attempt.

"How's Aunt Clara?"

This was the distress signal of Katz family code. Just a year or so earlier, when my parents began allowing me to attend Saturday night parties at the homes of kids whose names they had never heard before, they made me promise that if I was ever in a "situation" (a.k.a. there were drugs in the room) from which I needed to be rescued, all I needed to do was call home and ask about Aunt Clara[3]—saving me the humiliation of having to say "I'm scared. Come and get me!"—and they would know that I was scared and come and get me. I started to tell her the situation when she told me to put the teacher on the phone. DeSilvio hadn't gotten much further in the explanation than I had when she told him not to do a thing until she arrived. Not twenty minutes later, all ninety-nine pounds of my mother strode through the door of my holding cell armed with nothing but a pocketbook.

Upon seeing the evidence and hearing the circumstance of my arrest, my mother's response to DeSilvio's actions was outrage. In an increasingly loud voice, she demanded that the school principal be summoned and, once Mr. Hession arrived, gave my social studies teacher a lesson in civics with special attention paid to the First Amendment, right of assembly and illegal search and seizure. She then threatened a lawsuit if the notebook were delivered to Miss Nussbaum. I heard it all from outside the door and the lump returned to my throat as my mother the lioness roared back the jackals to protect me, her precocious cub. Mom did such an outstanding job as my attorney that day that no one would have ever suspected that her formal academic training was in dental hygiene.

That night at dinner, we celebrated our victory over DeSilvio and recounted it in full detail for the rest of my family. Listening most intently was my father, who had a special insight into my situation and the burden of a brain that generates impudent impulses.

The working assumption in my family was that I had inherited my sense of humor from my father. This was arrived at by process

---

3. I had never even met my Aunt Clara. She was my father's aunt—and his least favorite relative—who taunted him as a child with nasty comments about his family's poverty. He and my Uncle Stanley were raised in a dingy apartment with a bathtub in the kitchen that was the backroom of my Grampa Max's cleaning store in St. Albans, Queens—a fact my siblings and I were reminded of each time we complained about a particularly burdensome aspect of our spoon-fed suburban life.

of elimination, as my mother, God bless her, was born without one. As a breed, dentists are smart and funny, but not so smart as to make them medical doctors and not so funny as to be lured away from the dentist chair to entertain paying audiences. Most practitioners of dental humor get by for their entire career with the same dozen jokes. ("This isn't going to hurt me a bit.") My father is an insult-comic orthodontist with many hundreds of jokes in his repertoire,[4] honed on the thousands of eleven- to fourteen-year-olds who have sat in his treatment chair since the early sixties. And in the event his material fails to elicit a laugh, he's not above squirting a patient in the crotch with the dental console spritzer and admonishing them for poor bladder control.

Not surprisingly, my story prompted my father to recount his formative days as a classroom smart-ass. He told a story hauntingly similar to mine, how he came close to getting thrown out of dental school when he lent a friend, Jesse Gedzelman, his pharmacology notes with margins filled with sketches of the widely hated Professor Neuwirth in compromising positions. This was the night I learned my proclivity for public humor was not a character flaw but a genetic predisposition.

Most important, my father suggested we think about ways to rechannel this energy of mine into something more positive, something that might cut down on the parent-teacher conferences. After some collective brainstorming, my mom or dad (I don't

---

4. Joseph S. Katz D.D.S.'s Greatest Hits:

- "Try not to scream too loudly. My last patient nearly broke my eardrum."
- "Not to worry: these braces worked great on the last kid who wore them."
- "If you get blood on my new carpet, I'm going to be really angry."
- "The cement comes in two flavors: disgusting and monkey vomit."
- "I've never used this procedure before, but if it works on you, I am going to try it on humans."
- "This appliance I'm about to use is so painful, it's illegal in many states. Fortunately, not in New York."
- [as he's tightening the braces] "I hope you like yogurt. No? How about mashed bananas?"

remember who, but it certainly wasn't me) suggested I find more suitable forms of written humor, such as the school newspaper. We all agreed it was a good idea.[5]

It wasn't long before I published my first humor article in *The Ram's Horn*. More accurately, the "article" was a collection of jokes about the proliferation of designer jeans commercials on television, focusing mainly on the images of denim-covered asses sashaying to disco music that flashed across the TV screen every ten minutes, a new phenomenon in these days before MTV. The name of the article was "Jeans Cover Screens," and it was about as subtle as the "Jordache Look" and no funnier than what you'd expect from a kid mining a trite topic for obvious jokes. But that was almost beside the point. My words were in print, and the printed word marked a new chapter in my humor career.

As it happened, this was an excellent time for me to pull back on my aggressive pursuit of classroom attention, because I was just hitting the most unfortunate stage of adolescent awkwardness. My mid-teens found me with a mouth full of braces and rubber bands (applied by Dad) and a shiny, blemished face only partly obscured by increasingly pronounced peach fuzz. The hair on my head grew thick and coarse, and with every week since my last home haircut, my head looked more and more like a Q-Tip. These were my "growth spurt" years, during which I shot up from five foot three all the way to five foot seven—while my nose, chin and eyebrows enlarged erratically without bothering to consult the rest of my face. The only constant in this distressing era was the blue polyester Adidas warm-up jacket I put on for the first day of eighth grade and didn't take off until the end of my sophomore year,[6] so well worn that it was not even handed down to my brother Robby.

---

5. My writing career began as a plea bargain. I got into writing the same way Michael Milken got into public service.

6. What else would you wear with a pair of ink-stained Lee jeans, maroon suede Puma Clydes, knee-high tube socks and a first-generation digital wristwatch that required pushing a button to learn the time?

While I continued to offer salient classroom commentary, I discovered mild restraint, still shouting out my best offerings but swallowing lesser material. (If nothing else, writing had taught me the value of editing.) I devoted the remainder of my comic energy to my humor articles. *The Ram's Horn* allowed my byline to speak more for me, and every few weeks I'd pump out another article: hallway etiquette, report card day, weird gym sports, excuse notes from home, my secret life as a slob, meaningless everyday expressions, a restaurant review of the school cafeteria, pep rallies, bake sales and an homage to my locker. No subject was too obvious to be overlooked. And had I known that Dave Barry would one day win a Pulitzer Prize, I might have written even more.

In high school, when you spend your free time voluntarily doing something most kids hate, that's what you become known for—and I became known as a "writer." This reputation led to other opportunities—namely, to write for others—and before my high school career was over, I had written speeches that elected a half-dozen student council members and essays that were admitted to Penn, Swarthmore and Tufts and wait-listed at Brown.

The political ghostwriting started out with simple sloganeering, first for my brother and then for my friends. By the time my brother Robby got to junior high school a year after me, he was going by the name "Rob."[7] Rob decided the best way to make a name for himself was to run for student office. He came up with his first slogan on his own: ROB WILL DO THE JOB. The slogan did not do the job. Rob finished third, just a few votes ahead of Tracy Lonzar, a known carrier of cooties.

Undeterred, Rob ran again the next year—but this time, he consulted with me about his strategy. Rob was of the strong opinion that high school elections were nothing more than popularity contests, a widely held belief that I ascribed to also. I pitched him an

---

7. This was his name of choice for the next six years, until he got into Harvard and began introducing himself as "Robert."

idea that, to his credit, he was brave enough to approve. Within forty-eight hours, the corridors were plastered with signs that read:

Tired of elections that are just popularity contests?

ROB KATZ.

He's not popular at all.

The result: Rob Katz. Student Council Representative.

My next assignment was on behalf of a kid who had moved to New City just the year before and quickly established himself as a rival for back-of-the-class comments. Fisher and I might have become rivals, but instead we became friends. Our alliance formed the nucleus of a half-dozen smart, funny, slightly mean-spirited guys who were my closest friends throughout high school and beyond. The roster read like the roll call at a yeshiva: Rosenthal. Fisher. Scheff. Katz. Kanef. Berkin. Brill. Together we comprised a gang of Marx Brothers anarchists who flagrantly broke the laws of decorum but, by and large, stayed within the boundaries of federal, state and local ordinances.

One day Fisher handed me a stack of pages on the bus. "Katz, you're a writer—look at this." It was a speech he was planning to give in his bid for sophomore class president. I spent an entire study hall period doing a major rewrite. Later that week, against a backdrop of nerveless competitors squeaking about "improved school spirit" and "making this the best sophomore year it can be," my mouthpiece stepped up to the PA system microphone to deliver his two-minute public pitch, all of which was a preamble to this memorable sound bite: "And if elected, I vow to make

Clarkstown North a nuclear power." That was the day I learned firsthand that all politics is local: Fisher lost the election to Dawn Magaletta of the "Longer Lunch Period" party.

Other memorable speeches written in the chalk-dust-filled back room of high school politics included an alliterative speech for Gary Rohrbacher in his bid for homeroom representative: "It's high time people whose last name begins with R had as their advocate someone who was responsible, respected and resourceful—not radical, rancorous or racketeering."[8] Most notable of all was Mitchell Halpern's impassioned "I have a dream" speech for youth group president of Temple Beth Shalom, in which he prophesized about a social circumstance wherein Jason Coopersmith—an obnoxious kid with hygiene issues—might no longer be a virgin. And thanks to that speech, Mitch Halpern delivered Jason to the Promised Land (with no small help from Rona Temkin).

My senior year of high school brought the only election that had every person in the building wishing to be on the ballots: senior superlatives. Most Likely to Succeed, Best Looking, Class Flirt, Personality Plus—these were the only yearbook distinctions that maintained any currency after graduation. While I publicly downplayed my interest in the title, I secretly wanted to be voted Class Comedian, if for no other reason than I considered myself the funniest of my five hundred classmates. But the fledgling politico in me had surveyed the electoral landscape a hundred times over and had me losing each time. Even assuming that I was the funniest and most deserving (my working assumption), my constituency was one-fifth of the student body: for four years I had earned my laughs among the kids in honors classes and those who bothered to read *The Ram's Horn*. To make matters worse, I shared that constituency with

---

8. Somehow echoes of Spiro Agnew's "nattering nabobs of negativism" notions got knocked into the nethers of my noggin.

Fisher, and he was sure to siphon votes. But from
the tenth grade on, I knew that I would eventually
lose Class Comedian to Warren Zenna.

Warren Zenna was a genuinely funny kid who
had a number of insurmountable advantages over
me. First, sharp as he was, his test scores placed
him in the meaty part of the bell curve that put
him in regular (non-honors) classes. Every day, day

Warren Zenna

in and day out, he was getting guffaws from a wider spectrum of the
student body. He was Johnny Carson, and I was Dick Cavett. Second, he had raw comic skills that I lacked—specifically, the ability to
do impersonations, dialects and sound effects (mostly tire squeals
and fart noises). Third, and most important, Zenna was impossibly

Fisher

good looking. Both girls and guys liked Zenna in
equal measure. He was tall and lanky and had perfect feathered hair that would make Scott Baio jeal-
ous. His dark skin was set off by the white puka
beads he wore around his neck. (I wore puka beads
once, and I was mocked so severely in homeroom
by Kanef that I removed them before my other
caustic friends could feast on me during lunch.) For

all these reasons, as I had long anticipated, I finished comfortably
behind Zenna in the vote for Class Comedian. What really hurt was
that I finished behind Fisher as well.

My consolation prize was "Class Writer"—a category I didn't
know existed until the ballot sheet arrived on
my homeroom desk and I filled in my name in
the blank. Upon learning of the honor, I was
informed of the responsibility it entailed: the
head of the yearbook committee asked that I
work with Zenna to write the senior luncheon
award presentation where the winners were to be
announced.

Mark Katz

The senior luncheon was an awards ceremony second only to the prom in high school rite-of-passage events. Carload by carload, the entire class showed up in their best clothes and already intoxicated for lunch at a local catering hall that was a step up from the high school cafeteria. Zenna and I spent two consecutive afternoons cracking each other up generating the material we would use to present each award, and he brought the finished product with him to an after-school meeting with the yearbook staff—a meeting I could not attend, for one reason or another. He called me at home that night to tell me the bulk of our material had been rejected as too racy. The school principal, Dr. Bonnamo, had made a surprise showing at the meeting, asked to see Zenna's notes and redacted them with a thick black Magic Marker. Bonnamo was there to make sure the luncheon observed proper decorum, and he was not pleased to learn that I was the co-emcee. I had come to his attention during my short stint as the school's morning PA announcer, when I hawked tickets for the senior class play, *The Miracle Worker*, with this pitch: "Come see the play that Helen Keller couldn't." In what turned out to be my last day of that assignment, one of his vice principals, Mr. Speranza, wrestled the microphone from my hands.

It was unlike Dr. Bonnamo to show up at the senior luncheon meeting. His stewardship as principal had a ceremonial air. He walked the hallways of Clarkstown High School North as though he were above it all, and he largely left the dirty work of chasing down kids and doling out punishment to his arsenal of Speranzas, who seemed to genuinely enjoy it. Terecizio Bonnamo was six foot, gray-haired, strong-chinned and carefully coiffed and manicured. He dressed with a lot of style, all of it bad: matching cuff links and tie clips adorned shiny shirts and suits with patterns that might be described as bold, if you were determined to describe them kindly. He looked like Troy Donahue reared in the Lucchese crime family. But to take in the full comic effect of Dr. Bonnamo, you had to hear him speak. His swallowed mumble might have been mistaken for a Marlon Brando impersonation but for a noticeable distinction, a piercing teakettle whistle that squeaked with every "S" word that crossed his tongue. That's why the easi-est laugh to be had in my high school was the mere mention of his name: "Tere*sizzzzz*io Bonnamo."

As far as I could tell, Dr. Bonnamo knew only one adjective—"very"—and liked it so much, he usually used it twice. When spo-ken in his distinctive dialect, however, "very, very" sounded like *"ve-ve."* "Ve-ve" was quickly incorporated into my most heavily rotated catchphrase jokes, as evidenced by the fact that nearly half of the inscriptions in my high school yearbook include some ver-sion of "I'm sure you'll do *ve-ve* well in college."

At the award luncheon, I tried to stick to the approved script, but I could only avoid temptation for so long. How could I offer up lesser material when I knew much better jokes were going unused? Upon handing out the award for "Most Musical" to Jen-nifer Mishkin, a sweet, pretty, wholesome girl who was in fact an accomplished musician, I introduced her by saying:

"Everyone knows that nobody blows the oboe like Jen." Lifting my face heavenward, I added: "Dear God, why couldn't you have made me an oboe?"

I was working blue, as they say in the business, not my usual hue. But I was standing in front of an audience of drunken seventeen-year-olds and the joke was there to be made. Not surprisingly, the line was received with the mindless hoots and hollers of raucous morons. When I returned to my seat on the dais, Laurie Reeder, the yearbook editor and event coordinator, was panicked.

"That wasn't in the script!"

I was one of the few people in the room who was not drunk, but at that moment I was feeling no pain: "There's a script?"

At the luncheon's end, I made a quick exit to duck Bonnamo, only to find my friend Scheff in the parking lot throwing up in the bushes behind Bettina Matalon's black Camaro.[9]

---

9. He probably had food poisoning. I'd hate for the impressionable kids who currently call him "Rabbi" at the Orangetown Jewish Center in Rockland County, New York, to think otherwise.

The following Monday, I arrived at my first-period English class and gladly accepted the kudos of my classmates—but had a lingering feeling that the long weekend had not erased the possibility of repercussions. A few minutes into the class, the door opened and a bespectacled, plain-looking ninth-grade girl who worked in the principal's office entered the room.

"Is Mark Katz in school today?"

A hush fell over the room as all eyes turned toward me. My teacher, Mrs. Scalera, immediately gave me up:

"Yes, he is."

"Okay. Thank you."

I looked to Fisher, whose gestures assured me not to worry. (On his notebook, Fisher sketched a picture of a cat with a noose around its neck and flashed it to Rosenthal, who began to snort in laughter.) In the next few minutes, I would look over to Fisher for reassurance, which he gave me each time. (And in the interim between my glances, he drew a picture of a cat being run over by a bus, a cat strapped into an electric chair and a cat frying in a skillet. And each one made Rosenthal crumble anew.) Five minutes later, the office drone returned.

"Dr. Bonnamo would like to see Mark Katz."

The blood drained from my face. Fisher saw his opening: "He probably wants to tell you he thought you were *ve-ve* funny." I exited the room on the Fisher-induced guffaw.

I followed the diminutive office servant to the doorway of the principal's office. Bonnamo called me in and gestured that I should sit. "Sit, Katz." He pronounced my name as though it were the plural of "cot," but I decided this was not the right time to correct him. "I'm gonna have to suspend you, you know. Insubordination. You violated our little understanding not to say anything not in the script." It all sounded pretty serious to me, despite the whistle in his words and the red-and-black plaid jacket he was wearing with a bright yellow shirt. I considered a number of avenues I might try to use to get myself out of this one. For some reason, I went with snotty sarcasm.

"Dr. Bonnamo, I know kids telling jokes is a big problem in this school, but may I point out that there are guys smoking joints right outside your window?"

Bonnamo shot a look outside. In fact, there was a cluster of badasses in the parking lot passing something in plain sight, but he paid them no attention. Then he said something I'll never forget:

"Lemme tell you something. There are plenty of kids out there carrying all kinds of weapons and contraband. They don't scare me. There's a prison cell upstate waiting for every one of them. But you and your pals, you scare me. Because you've got a brain. I got news for you, Katz: in my book, you are the most dangerous student in this school."

My face broke out in an aw-shucks smile as I took in a compliment greater than I had a right to expect from someone about to suspend me. But this remark was also my first glimpse of the man behind the caricature that I had helped foster.

We had arrived at an honest moment of mutual respect, which I was happy to exploit: "Listen, I understand why you would have to suspend me if I directly disobeyed you. But I wasn't at the meeting where you gave the order. I only heard it secondhand from Zenna. I didn't hear it from you, so I didn't directly disobey you."

He followed my desperate, legalistic reasoning but wasn't prepared to buy it yet. Instead, he bought some time to think it over.

"Maybe you directly disobeyed me and maybe you didn't. But as of now, your suspension is pending. I'll come for you at the end of the day and let you know what I decide."

Bonnamo never came to find me that day and I didn't look too hard for him. In fact, I spent the final weeks of my high school career avoiding him, just in case. Later that month, I graduated from Clarkstown High School North knowing that whatever I went on to do with my life, my suspension would always be pending.

CHAPTER FOUR

How I Didn't Become an Orthodontist

CAREER PLANNING IN MY FAMILY OPERATED LIKE THE OLD SOVIET economy: begin with the predetermined results and work backward from there. While never announced at dinner or posted on the refrigerator, somehow the message was communicated that out of the four kids, we needed to produce at least one real (i.e., medical) doctor, as well as one orthodontist to inherit my father's practice. Bruce, the firstborn, was the first premed candidate until his freshman year at Franklin & Marshall College, when his grades in organic chemistry made him a borderline candidate even for podiatry school. The medical school onus skipped me and landed on the sure bet, Robby—who by then had scored in the 99th percentile of every test he ever took. My test scores suggested I was at least smart enough to be a dentist, so, for a short time, I became the family's orthodontic-designate.

I was twelve or so when my apprenticeship began. My father brought me into his office on Saturday mornings, where my most important assignment involved sterilizing the stainless steel torsion tools used in kids' mouths. But as I peered over my father's shoulder while he twisted wires to move teeth through jawbones, the only question I could think to ask was, "Can I wait outside?" My evident lack of interest, combined with a personality that was growing increasingly obnoxious, got me reassigned to law school while I was still in junior high. My sister, Ruthie, then only in the fifth grade, began sterilizing dental instruments on Saturday mornings.[1]

My legal ambitions brought me to the best school I got into— Cornell, a pressure cooker of a college with an alarmingly high rate of matriculation to top graduate schools—a condition only exacerbated by the "Am I better off yet?" Reagan eighties. Once an East Coast epicenter of 1960s social activism for civil rights and black power, the Cornell I attended was a petri dish for Yuppie scum. I was no better than any of them. By now my determination to be a lawyer was so thoroughly internalized that the poster for *The Paper Chase* pasted to the wall of my freshman dorm was more motivational device than decoration. Yet my ambitions had nothing to do with social justice, a public agenda or my concern with the plight of the working man; my political impulses were little more than a collection of well-imbued, standard-issue middle-class liberal prejudices. At what should have been the apex of idealistic youth, all I really wanted in the world was to get into a top-tier law school, make a lot of moolah, consume conspicuously and drive a fully loaded, fire-engine red Beemer convertible, Dolby-B cassette deck and all.

I killed time during the four-year run-up to my true calling by majoring in government. As it happened, though, I found that I had a genuine interest in the American political system, political theory, history and creative writing, and I was pleased to fill my schedule with that kind of coursework. (As for my science requirement, I found out what the Cornell hockey players usually took and signed up for two semesters of astronomy.) But somewhere

---

1. And like the Soviet planned economy, the plans backfired and resulted in ruin: both Bruce and Rob went to law school. Bruce has his own practice and specializes in litigation, and Robby (now Robert) is a professor of law who helps inflict legal careers on the young. Ruth is a marketing maven involved in endeavors unrelated to teeth in any way.

along the way, I lost my zeal for being a lawyer and yet lacked the kind of imagination that could summon an alternative to law school. Long conversations with my parents did not help: in my family any career plan that did not chart a clear path to professional school was received as though you'd just announced you were running away to join the circus.

By senior year, I had watched just about every non-premed I knew apply to law school, too many of whom arrived at their decisions not because they wanted to be lawyers but for lack of a better idea. One of my best friends who had spent four years studying hotel management begged me to write his law school application essay for him, so bereft was he of actual reasons to study law (aside from the fact that he did not want to take a job as a bellhop). I tried to do him an even bigger favor—talking him out of it—but he found his own argument more convincing: "What the hell else am I going to do?" I winced as his words hung in the air, as it was the same damn question that was keeping me up at night, too.

Law school was the Vietnam of my generation, a quagmire where promising young lives were needlessly wasted or damaged forever. By the time the Reagan eighties were over, I'd lost two brothers and most of my closest comrades to law school, all victims of the upscale lifestyle showcase, lawyer-as-hero myths and the infectious theme song they were exposed to each week on *L.A. Law*. As for me—an argumentative, obnoxious, politically aware, government-major careerist for whom law school seemingly made perfect sense—I somehow managed to dodge the Tort Offensive. Despite having been preordained as an attorney since junior high, by my senior year in college I had no intention of re-upping for law school. At my own college graduation, which my parents attended with a sense of dazed alarm, I had no idea what I wanted to do with myself. The event that really marked a turning point in my life was Robby's graduation a year later.

* * *

"Dukakis? What's a Dukakis?" my Grampa Max asked, in what was for him a whisper, adding some *ccchhh* noises in the middle for comic effect. The people who occupied the folding chairs a row in front of us smiled to each other at the funny grandfather asking the funny question.

"He's the governor of Massachusetts," I answered, in a real whisper. "He's running for president."

"The president of what?" he wanted to know.

"America," I told him. He was genuinely surprised.

"Jewish?" he asked, causing the shoulders of the people in front of us to vibrate with silent laughter.

"No. Greek."

"What? They got no Jews in Greece?" This comment generated audible laughter from the next row, but by now he was probably just playing to the crowd.

"Shh!" my mother reprimanded. Somewhere before us, in a sea of crimson, my brother Robert was about to be awarded a bachelor's degree from Harvard and Mom wasn't just experiencing the day, she was committing it to long-term memory.

On this perfect June day, Governor Mike Dukakis stood at the podium to give the Class Day address to the graduating seniors of Harvard's class of 1987. His speech commanded special attention from the crowd because a small wave of positive press had recently made the name "Dukakis" the least unknown of the many unknown or implausible Democratic presidential candidates (Babbitt, Biden, Gephardt, Gore, Simon and the Reverend Jesse Jackson) angling to assume the mantle of "front-runner" that Senator Gary Hart had recently dropped on his testicles.

Like most people not from Massachusetts, I had never heard Dukakis speak—and as a fledgling politico, I was analyzing the speech in real time, under the aggrandizing belief that I possessed the critical insight to size up presidential timber. His speech called upon young people to reject the self-interested ethos of the Reagan revolution and embrace the "ask not what your country can do for you" idealism that makes liberals like me well up in tears. At one point in the speech, as he congratulated the Class of '87 on their achievements, he made special mention of a particular subset:

. . . Especially those of you who live in Iowa and New Hampshire who—I can tell just by looking at you—are already among the most promising and able leaders of your generation.

The crowd gave him an obligatory laugh, but I did not give mine up so easily. It struck me as the type of joke unfunny people tell, the kind of recycled [insert-something-funny-here] joke told at Kiwanis Club podiums. Still, as belabored as it was, I had to at least give him points for trying.

Like the speaker, the speech was short and to the point. Dukakis left the podium to appreciative applause, having sufficiently impressed an audience that seemed to want to be impressed. As others nodded approvingly to those around them, my grandfather picked up where he had left off.

"Dukakis? That's his real name?"

I answered his question with a question: "You think he changed his name to Dukakis?"

"I never heard of it."

"It's a funny name," I said. "Two *K*'s. If it had a *P* in it, it would be even funnier."

"What's this? He spells Dukakis with a *P*?" he asked.

My Grampa Max, usually sharp as a needle, did not pick up my reference to one of the great lines from *The Sunshine Boys*.[2] He didn't have to: he *was* one of the Sunshine Boys. Max Katz was the funny old Yiddish man from central casting, the kind of character

---

2. "Words with a *K* are funny. 'Pickle' is funny. 'Cockroach' is funny. Not if you get 'em, only if you say 'em."—Scene Three

who inspired almost every person he met to remark: "He's quite a character." Five foot nothing with a crown of clean scalp, he wore heavy glasses that hung from oversized ears and rested on the bridge of a good-sized nose. He was Mr. Magoo with the mumbled cadence of Jackie Mason. During winter months, his face was framed by a dark plaid Stetson hat that had been out of style for thirty years but looked like it had been invented for him. His hands smelled like presmoked tobacco, because a doctor once  told him he should cut back on smoking and he had carefully ripped his cigarettes in half ever since. He made conversation by asking people he had just met how much they had paid for the garment they had on—and then, with sixty years of tailoring under his belt, detailing the specific ways in which corners were cut in its manufacture. Over time, he acquired the family nickname "Mister," the salutation with which he addressed the world: "Hey *Mister*, can I ask you a question?" Only "Mister" was "mist-eh" and "question" was "qvestion?" and the question wasn't really a question at all: it was a Socratic device intended to deliver an opinion and spark a bantering dialogue. (This guy was quite a character.)

A Harvard commencement ceremony might have been the least likely event a self-taught Yiddish Yoda would ever attend, but even I was taken aback by the events of the day. My graduation from Cornell the year before could have been the model for mass Moonie weddings, but Harvard's commencement was a ritualistic pageant reminiscent of a royal coronation or the investiture of a Pope. After the last bit of Latin voodoo ritual mysticism, my family made its way to find Robert at the designated meeting place outside Littauer Hall, home of the government department and its graduation reception. After hugging Robert nearly to death and then snatching his diploma for safekeeping, my mother openly wept. (At my graduation, I only recall my parents' complaining about the heat.)

A few yards away, I spotted the other man-of-the-hour. Mike Dukakis had been invited to the government department ceremonies, and soon the Katzes were on a receiving line to meet the governor and the dean of the department. When our turn came, Robert did the introductions, beginning with my parents and my grandfather. Upon making eye contact with the governor, my grampa put the question to him directly:

"You're sure you're not Jewish?"

While my family emitted a collective nervous laugh, I trained my eyes on Dukakis. What I had heard was a perfectly teed-up setup line, and for some reason I thought he was about to hit it out of the park. Mike Dukakis gave off all the visual cues of a guy with a good sense of humor. He was short. He was ethnic. He had Groucho Marx eyebrows. Basically, he looked like me. And in that split second, I silently projected a few suggested replies:

I'll have my staff look into it.

If you must know, my mother had me circumcised so I'd be less prone to infection.

Not only am I a goy but my daughters are shiksas.

Instead, Mike Dukakis said in a manner that would have been deadpan had he been telling a joke: "No, I am Greek."

A moment passed, as if we were all waiting for the funny line to follow. Again, my mind offered up a few suggestions:

. . . the OTHER short, swarthy big-nosed people.

. . . we invented math but not accounting.

. . . the Romans screwed us pretty good, too.

But Dukakis offered up nothing, so on the second beat of silence my grampa filled in a punch line for him:

"Okay, if you say so . . ."

If only to stop my grampa from saying whatever he was about to say next, Rob introduced me to Governor Mike Dukakis.

"Governor, this is my brother Mark. He is an aide to Senator Moynihan."

"Pat Moynihan is one terrific senator. Tell me your name again?"

"Mark Katz."

"Well, Mark Katz, please be sure to give your boss my very best."

"I certainly will," I replied, with eye-to-eye gravitas. With that exchange, I went from being the ancillary brother of the guy in the crimson gown to an appointed emissary, conveying personal–possibly coded–messages from a Democratic presidential candidate to a powerful Democratic senator. The conversation started replaying in my head even as my family and I were dumped out at the end of the receiving line. Then my grandfather said out loud the very thought that was racing through my head: "Hey!–that guy could be president and he knows your name!"

But the more I thought about it, the more I realized what had really happened in that exchange. Of *course* he was not actually sending his regards to Daniel Patrick Moynihan; one look at me would have informed him that I hadn't been a registered voter long enough to be anything more than what I was, a low-level staffer. Mike Dukakis said what he said to make me look like a player as my parents and grandfather looked on. This insight was confirmed over the course of the rest of the day, as my parents mentioned it several more times. That's when it occurred to me that, sense of humor or not, this guy was good.

The fact that Dukakis knew my name stood in stark contrast to the fact that my current boss called me "Mike." Daniel Patrick Moynihan, America's self-styled philosopher/legislator, was my home state U.S. senator, and working in his Manhattan district

office was my first job out of college. My duties as his "special assistant" included, among other things, tending to him during his not-
infrequent trips to New York City. Moynihan, well accustomed
over his decades in public life to being the smartest person in the
room, was a very hard person to correct. After a few failed attempts
to inform him that my name was not Mike, I learned to answer to
a proper noun with many of the same consonants as my own.

The job started well enough, offering a front-row seat to the
rudimentary lessons of workaday politics. I was with him at a private fund-raiser at the Upper East Side home of a wealthy con-
tributor when I came back from the bar with a martini that was
not to his liking.

"Come with me, young Michael."

He arrived at the bar with me in tow and relieved the amateur
bartender from his post. "Watch carefully, Mike. This is a task you
may be called upon to perform," he said, checking the cabinets
for a silkier vodka and a more substantial shaker.

"One—must—use—a—shaker—with—sufficient—heft—if—the—ice—
is—ever—to—be—cracked," he clucked in his inimitable style, which I
can only partly capture on the written page. (Of Moynihan's many
achievements, most overlooked is the invention of a whole new
dialect of English spoken only by him, where every word brings the
sentence to a halt, only to be resumed forcefully with a wind generated from his upper palate on the next staccato beat.) Not two
months after I had received an undergraduate degree in government, there were probably a million pearls of knowledge that
Daniel Patrick Moynihan, among the most dazzling social thinkers
of the twentieth century, might have imparted to me. On that night,
I learned that the secret to mixing the perfect martini is to drain the
brine from the olive jar and marinate its contents in vermouth.

On another occasion, the thinking man's senator flew up from
Washington for an extended stay without having packed any under-
garments. My assignment that day: take the senator's American
Express card, go to Brooks Brothers and purchase his necessaries.

When I presented the Am/Ex card engraved **D P MOYNIHAN** (Member since '62) at the cashier counter to purchase six pairs of size 40 pima cotton boxer shorts, I aroused suspicion. (In 1962, I wasn't old enough to be a zygote.) A few tense moments later, I was explaining to the men's accessories manager and a security guard that I had not stolen Sen. Daniel Patrick Moynihan's credit card. Nor, I wanted to add, despite the intimate apparel I claimed to be purchasing on his behalf, was there anything untoward about the nature of our relationship. A clerk returning from a break validated my story by confirming the waist size and undergarment preference of the esteemed Brooks Brothers customer from the state of New York, bringing to an amicable end a situation that might otherwise still be on my record.

As time went on, I began to feel less like a young politico and more like a butler. One day, I went to drop off the senator's dry cleaning and have it delivered to his suite at the Carlyle Hotel. This was an errand I had run many times before, and the man behind the counter said, "Good afternoon, Mr. Katz." Moynihan's dry cleaner knew my name and Moynihan didn't. (By now, Moynihan had even lost track of my wrong name and had taken to calling me "Mitch.") I realized maybe it was time to move on and began to consider other options. In my shoulder bag was a copy of that week's *New York* magazine with a cover story written by Joe Klein. Inside was a lionizing profile of "The Democrats' Hottest New Face": my old friend Mike Dukakis.

In October 1987, I arrived at the Dukakis campaign headquarters in Boston as an uninvited, unpaid volunteer. The campaign occupied the basement and first three floors of what was once a perfectly nice corporate workspace at the margins of a corporate neighborhood just a few blocks from the heart of downtown. By the time I got there, it had become a sprawling-yet-cramped triage unit on a block located on the wrong side of the subway tracks. Interior walls were covered with a collage of printed "Dukakis for President" signs and well-stuffed manila message folders, and the air was filled with the blaring of ringing phones and internal pages—"*Scheduling, pick up on six-two. Scheduling, pick up on six-two.*" Dukakis headquarters at 105 Chauncey Street was a chaotic but purposeful ant farm set up to generate money, messages and marching orders twenty-four hours a day.

Within a minute of my arrival, I was embarrassed to be so obviously overdressed. I was wearing my Senate aide getup, a dark gray suit with a standard-issue red tie, but I kept my jacket on so as not to reveal what was underneath: a white oxford shirt with my initials monogrammed on the pocket, an unsubtle emblem of someone who had arrived positively determined to make a name for himself.[4] In my briefcase was a reasonably thick stack of newspaper clips and humor columns under my byline from the pages of the *Cornell Daily Sun*, and a few (unaccredited) articles I had writ-

---

4. The reasons for the MSK on my shirt were many and complicated. A year and a half earlier, my mother had purchased a dozen such shirts from the Lands' End catalog as a gift, so that I could start my first real job with crisp new shirts in all the standard colors and stripes. I did not request the monograms, but I will admit they appealed to me at the time. This was still the Reagan eighties age of conspicuous consumption, and conspicuous initials had become the family fashion, in part for the practical reason that with four short, thick-necked men of the same approximate size, monograms made it harder for one brother to steal the shirt of another. But the fact that there were four monogrammed men in our family was also partly an ode to JFK, or at least a vestige of my mother's longing to bring a bit of Camelot to the Katz clan. More specific to me, the MSK may have also been an unwitting ode to APK (Alex P. Keaton), as my size, ambition, political agenda and clean-cut cuteness made me a liberal counterpart to a contemporary sitcom character made famous by Michael J. Fox. Whatever its origin, the shirts created an initial bad impression for me on the Dukakis campaign. In my first weeks, the MSK on my pocket earned me the nicknames "Senator Katz," "Ms. Katz" and MMK—for "Monogrammed Mark Katz." Which would have been fine if these were the kind of nicknames assigned in good-natured, ice-breaking joshing. Unfortunately, they were not. I know this because I only learned in the course of writing this chapter that these were my nicknames, used to deride me when I was out of earshot. Thanks, Mom.

ten during a junior-year semester's internship with the Washington bureau of the *New York Times*. Before I could pull out my bound, 125-page honors thesis analyzing the media coverage of the 1984 Democratic primaries, the volunteer coordinator was already escorting me three flights up to the press office, distinguished from the other frenetic, makeshift offices by a handwritten sign on a manila folder that read PRESS OFFICE.

The first person I met greeted me like a long-lost friend. Instead of initials on his chest pocket, he had initials where his name should have been. J.B. wanted to know everything about me: where I came from, where I went to college and so on. We even figured out some people we knew in common. And then he asked: "Hey, how would you like to get involved in radio actualities?"—as if I knew in actuality what an "actuality" was. Too new to risk being impolite, I expressed a modicum of interest.

Eighteen hours later, my second day as a volunteer on the Dukakis campaign began in the predawn hours of a brisk fall day, and the first person I spoke to that morning was the news director of a radio station somewhere in New Hampshire. Actualities, as it turned out, were prerecorded sound bites from our candidate that were then fed, via telephone, from our tape recorder to radio stations in early primary states, in the hope that the clips might get some airtime in the morning news cycle. (Although I cannot recall the specific message of that morning's actuality, it's a decent bet that it mentioned "good jobs at good wages," the well-mocked economic mantra of the guy running for president as the manager of the "Massachusetts Miracle.") I repeated the process for the next few hours as I worked my way down the list of every radio station in Iowa and New Hampshire. By 10 A.M. I had finished, and J.B. was just arriving after his first good night's sleep in recent memory. J.B. had taught me an important lesson: campaigns operate like pyramid schemes, predicated on the fresh flow of new suckers so that others may advance. After two weeks of predawn cold calling, I greeted the next new volunteer to arrive at the press office like a long-lost friend.

There was no shortage of overeager people on the Dukakis campaign, all motivated equally by common purpose and personal agendas. The press office I had joined was such a perfect portrait of young go-getters, we might as well have been picked by the same casting director who assembled the cast of *Friends*. The half-dozen staffer/volunteers who had arrived in the weeks and months before I did all came with similar profiles to mine: top-tier college credentials and the means to eat regularly and live comfortably in pricey Boston without the benefit of a weekly paycheck.[5]

Infinite possibility is the oxygen of fledgling presidential campaigns, and each of us quietly imagined that we might be the White House press secretary in Dukakis's second term. John was six foot something with preppy good looks, a skillful, penetrating wit and a degree from blue-blood Williams College. Keith, quieter but just as sharp, was a recent Dartmouth graduate and collegiate track star who was on the 400-meter relay team that, as of this printing, still holds the school record. He was also one of only a handful of African-Americans in the building, which, in the realpolitik of constituent-conscious campaigns, made him an even stronger candidate for the fast track. J.B. was a year or two older than the rest of us and considered himself more senior to the group, a status the others delighted in denying him. He was also entrepreneurial and a gifted operator—and, like an operator, attached a headset to the phone on his desk years before workplace ergonomics made it fashionable.[6]

The three women in the office had just as much going for them, plus they were pretty. (Around the campaign, they were known collectively—and unimaginatively—as "the press babes.") Joan was a blue-chipper from Yale who was so self-assured that I assumed

---

5. I was able to stay afloat mainly due to a grant from the Joseph and Adrienne Katz Foundation for the Pursuit of Professional School Studies, approved at a kitchen-table waiver hearing earlier that fall.

6. Now I realize that the nickname "Headset," which even I called him behind his back, must have been used a lot like "MMK" when I was out of the room.

incorrectly for weeks that she outranked us all. Pam was smart, able and hardworking and made friends easily because she was a self-effacing cutie-pie. Kim had many of the same professional qualities and personal charms, but that fact took longer to discern, as most people focused on the fact that she was stunning to look at—a five-foot-ten Texan with long Jaclyn Smith hair and wide-set Jacqueline Kennedy eyes. Kim had joined the campaign just a month before I had and had already escaped the J.B. trap. But she had also become ensnared in an infamous incident that was, at the time, above-the-fold, page-one news, but is now merely an asterisk.*

Just a few weeks ahead of me on the seniority chart, Kim was my partner in my second campaign assignment, a predawn ritual known as "the clips." The clips were a thick compilation of published news-

---

*On September 10, 1987, Dukakis's campaign manager, John Sasso, instructed his assistant to find someone in the press office to complete a task. Kim was standing by a file cabinet when she was handed two VHS tapes. On one tape was an impassioned, eloquent speech by British labor leader Neil Kinnock; on the other, a nearly word-for-word unattributed rendition of that memorable speech by Dukakis-rival Senator Joseph Biden. Per Sasso's second-hand instructions, Kim combined the two tapes into one for easy back-to-back comparisons and covertly sent it to a handful of reporters in an "off-the-record" fashion. Two days later, the plagiarism "scandal" was big news—and a day after that, a disgraced Biden dropped out of the race. The tape became a red-hot topic, spurring fevered speculation about its origin. Having initially denied any role, Sasso and his deputy, the late Paul Tully, hunkered down and waited for the storm to pass. It did not. As the pressure mounted, they even went so far as to compound the lie with one even more desperate, quietly pointing to the rival Gephardt campaign as the real culprits. Dukakis, assured by Sasso that the campaign was not involved, unwittingly lied to the press corps by denying the allegation that it had been. Finally, after a barrage of persistent truthful evidence, the Dukakis campaign issued a retraction/admission—adding yet another example to the adage that the cover-up is usually worse than the crime. In this case, a very smart man had made the ultimate and unforgivable mistake. Sasso had put his candidate on the record—and on the news—strenuously telling a provable lie. On September 30, Sasso and Paul Tully resigned, which was seen by the political community as a potentially lethal body blow to the nascent campaign—all because Sasso had lied about being behind a tape that was made, in fact, by Kim. Kim had done nothing wrong and everybody knew it, but for the rest of the campaign she had to pretend not to hear when people walked by and one whispered to the other: "That's her."

paper articles about politics, and their assembly and circulation combined basic arts and crafts skills with assembly-line production. Once nine newspapers–everything from the *Wall Street Journal* to the *Boston Herald*–were edited with scissors and tape into a pile of legal-sized pages, copies had to be run off on the Xerox machine and delivered to the desks of senior staffers before they got to their offices. Rare was the morning when the copy machine did not jam, run out of toner or blow a gasket. Inside of a week, panicked deadline necessity taught me to become an adept Xerox mechanic. The final product, fastened with an industrial-strength stapler capable of penetrating the Yellow Pages of a medium-size city, was distributed throughout the campaign offices before the 7:30 A.M. senior staff meeting in the third-floor conference room.

The clips involved the same unholy hours as actualities (sometimes worse[7]), but it was a job with real advantages to the more-seasoned eye. For nearly every person on the campaign, each day started with the clips, and producing them was a direct connection to the central nervous system of the headquarters. Volunteers like me were not paid in dollars but were offered instead the opportunity to advertise ourselves, and each time a warm stack of clips was handed directly to a campaign honcho before he had yet to take off his coat, an unspoken message was also delivered: *I am young and eager and willing to set my alarm clock for 5:15 A.M. What else do you have for me to do?* Such is the currency in the subtle economy of campaign underlings.

Two weeks into my new assignment, I arrived at first light to learn that my recently assigned key to the front door was still in the pockets of yesterday's pants. In search of a pay phone, I entered

---

7. On the days that Mike Dukakis was at home in Brookline, he liked to have the clips faxed to him before he set off on his 6 A.M. power walk. At least that's what we were told. But I still don't see how a person even as famously competent as he could walk briskly with weights in each hand and still read 193 faxed pages of newsprint.

the lobby of the building next door, where the floor was in the process of being mopped by the building's custodian, a large man with crooked teeth and untamed hair. On his uniform I could see his name in scripted letters: *Tex*. I don't know if he caught the monogrammed **MSK** on mine, but he already had a pet name for me and my colleagues.

"Hey you, *Duk-asshole*! Get out!"

With one glance it was clear that Tex was a man at the margins of self-sufficiency. Recognizing this, I responded with an extra dose of human kindness to this challenged but obviously agitated person. With sweet tones and disarming smiles, I tried to explain that I just needed to make a quick phone call and I'd be out of his way. But he would have none of it.

At this point, I already knew something that Tex did not. I knew that there was no way in the world I was about to walk through Boston's unforgiving Combat Zone at six in the morning looking for a pay phone when I could *see* the phone booth just on the other side of his bucket of soap. As deferential as my tone was, I hardly broke stride on my way past him. This made Tex even angrier.

"Hey you, goddamm *Duk-asshole*!" He seemed to enjoy the word *"Duk-asshole"* and shouted it a few extra times.

"I'll just be a second! I promise."

"I'm calling the cops, goddamn you!"

"I'm almost done!" I shouted back, the sweetness in my voice replaced by the kind of assertive tone one would use to keep a snarling dog at bay. I dialed up to Kim and asked her to come down to open the door and let me in.

"What's all that screaming?" she asked.

"I'll tell you later. Just hurry!"

That's when I heard a door slam behind me, followed by the *ka-chunk* of a lock. A moment later, Tex was at the pay phone next to mine. He dialed 911 and began explaining as best he could that he had an intruder trapped in the lobby of 98 Chauncey Street.

Tex might have been smarter than I'd thought, but I had not yet been outfoxed. I hung up with Kim and dialed 911 myself.

"Hi. Yes. Hello. I am the hostage being held against my will in the lobby of 98 Chauncey Street. Could you tell the patrol car you just dispatched to please hurry!"

By this point Tex and I were equally enraged. Having made the mistake of leaving the relative security of the enclosed phone booth, I spent the next minute or so in a screaming match, with our faces so close I could smell the ketchup he had poured on his breakfast. But before the squad car could arrive, Kim was banging on the door, yelling over the ruckus.

"Tex! Tex! Tex!" she screamed from the other side of the locked glass door. Tex turned his head and melted at the sight of her. Either Tex had a little crush on Kim or she had once removed a thorn from his paw. Either way, she was about to save my life.

"Tex! Can you please open the door for me?"

Tex unbolted the door without hesitation.

"Hiya, Kim."

"Hiya, Tex. He's okay. He's with me."

"I told him to go away but he won't listen."

"Yeah, he can be obnoxious," she said. Her Houston accent was more pronounced than I had ever heard it before. "He's from New York, you know."

Tex, calmer now, turned back to me. "You shoulda told me you work with Kim. Kim's my friend."

"We're both from Texas!" Kim expounded.

The fact that I was still catching my breath and mopping the perspiration off my neck kept me from responding and, in all likelihood, from saying some wiseass thing that would have restarted the screaming.

Back on the third floor of the campaign offices, I called the police back to tell them the situation had been resolved, and Kim and I rushed faster than usual to meet our 7:30 deadline. What I did not know was that a reporter for the *Boston Herald* had been monitoring the police radio and had heard the dispatches. The next day, at 6:15 A.M., I was back in the office, scissors in hand. Only this time, I wasn't just doing the clips, I was in them ("Duke Aide Dukes It Out with Building Worker").

The clips continued to define my day for a few intense but unnewsworthy weeks after that. In early January, word got out around the press office that Keith was going to Iowa for the next two months. The status quo was about to change, and the unspoken question among the rest of us was, who would inherit his duties as the author of the campaign's press releases? The campaign generated as many as a dozen a day, mostly predigested news of endorsements or campaign maneuvers. Unlike clips, it was a job that allowed a person to show off skills that had been acquired after elementary school, and I wanted it. The next morning, I quietly left a manila folder on the chair of our campaign press secretary, Mark Gearan. Inside was a collection of newspaper articles with my byline. Gearan came to find me soon after that.

"Here, I think you lost these," he said. "Good thing someone put them on my chair."

As the warm blush of embarrassment drained from my face, I found comfort in the fact that Gearan took obvious pleasure in tormenting me—a trait that is the common denominator with every friend I've ever had. Gearan had a special talent for making every person he came into contact with feel like they had just made a great new friend, and he intuitively knew how to connect with me. Aside from his corner office, there were no other visual clues that would have indicated he was our boss and a member of the campaign brass. In a building full of buttoned-downed Harvard boys, Gearan, then thirty-one, looked like he'd just arrived at Dunster House for freshman year of college. Later that day, he called me into his office and, with a freshly minted press release in his hand, instructed me that he needed it to be faxed ASAP to the networks, the wires and the *New York Times.*

"Oh, yeah," he added as he handed it to me, "also the *Rockland County Journal News.*"

That one got my attention. The *Journal News* was the local paper that had landed on the doorstep of the house in which I grew up. I looked down to read the headline: "Dukakis Campaign Appoints Mark Katz as Official Press Release Writer." As much as Gearan enjoyed the delight that registered on my face upon learning the news, he treasured even more my crestfallen response upon hearing that the press release need not, in fact, be released to the media. The very next day, January 29, I wrote my first release—DUKAKIS PICKS UP KEY SOUTHERN ENDORSEMENT[8]—and for the first time since I'd joined the campaign, I felt worthy of my own monogram.

Being the press release guy put me directly in the loop, a cog in the message-making process that had me assembling, in simple-to-read sentences, the who/what/when/where details of the campaign's bid to break into that day's news cycle. Newspaper endorsements. Political endorsements. New policy initiatives. Campaign roster announcements. Monthly FEC filings. Updated delegate totals. Each day's assignment had me knocking on the doors of higher-ranking staffers in every department as I hunted down the details of the would-be news. The final product, trumpeted FOR IMMEDIATE RELEASE, was printed out on a clean page of Dukakis-for-President stationery and sent to every news organization via the fax machine. But the job that I inherited from Keith also came with an afterthought duty that, much to my surprise, soon came to rival preparing press releases. My daily responsibilities now also included the midmorning task of printing out and distributing something called *The Hotline.*

The Hotline was an emerging phenomenon in campaign culture, daily Cliffs Notes of the morning papers and network news plus a scorecard of tracking polls and the campaign schedules of opposing candidates. It was an echo chamber for buzz, spin and dirt, and

---

8. The attorney general of Louisiana. Trust me, you never heard of him.

by 11 A.M. each day, it was in the hands of campaign spinmasters and political news editors alike. At the time Keith handed off the distribution duty to me, *The Hotline* was not yet—but was just becoming—the hottest commodity in the building. Two weeks into the job, I watched as assistants to top campaign aides grabbed the first dozen copies or so right as they landed in the Xerox collator. Being in charge of *The Hotline* at campaign headquarters, I soon discovered, was like being in charge of the stash at a Dead show.

The Hotline was also a technological marvel. By 1988, science fiction had given way to the science fact of PCs with hard drives the size of ten floppy disks, fax machines capable of automatic redial and mobile phones that could comfortably fit inside carry-on luggage. But with *The Hotline*, paradigms were shifting beneath our feet. Every day at quarter after ten, I would go to the computer services office on the second floor to use the one computer in the building that was connected to the telephone system, of all things. (In 1988, the idea of connecting a PC to a phone wire made as much intuitive sense as hooking your sneakers up to your stereo system.) There may have been three modems in all of Boston at that time, and the other two were at MIT. Keith had left me with a three-page instruction manual on the M-DOS commands that activated the magic box with the blinking lights, and somewhere near the bottom of page two, it began binging and bonging like an answering machine in epileptic seizure. Although I knew the machine had dialed a phone number in Alexandria, Virginia, the process was as goose-pimply as trading photon-beam radio transmissions with neighboring star system Alpha Centauri.

My duties as the press release person and *The Hotline* person overlapped in *The Hotline*'s back pages, where each campaign was invited to submit a 200-word report comprised of whatever it wished. Mostly the space was used as a supplemental outlet for yesterday's press releases or that day's schedule. But I had another idea: counterprogramming. I was determined to put my own stamp on my little fiefdom, so each day around 5 P.M. I showed up in Gearan's office with a new, offbeat execution for our next day's *Hotline* entry. Most were rejected[9] or edited into blandness, but the process of negotiation was nonetheless a highlight of both of our days, as Gearan delighted in torturing me and I (on some level) delighted in being tortured—at least by someone I liked.

By way of compromise, Gearan allowed my *Hotline* entries to become increasingly cheeky, which alone was enough to make them stand out from the rest.

By Mother's Day, the once-perfunctory *Hotline* entries had degenerated into the unsubstantial and wacky, which I counted as a personal triumph, an unlikely victory in a trivial war of wills.

REPORT FROM THE DUKAKIS CAMPAIGN

MOTHER'S DAY EXCLUSIVE!!
Interview with Euterpe Dukakis

Q: What are the plans for Sunday?
A: Michael usually comes over for breakfast on Mother's Day and brings a rose bush to plant in the front lot. When the roses bloom, I am very happy. This year, because of the busy campaign schedule, Michael and Kitty, and hopefully, some of my grandchildren, will come over in the evening for dinner.

Q: As a child, did the governor finish everything on his plate?
A: He did pretty well. Neither boys were big eaters. Never second helpings. Generally, he liked everything I put in front of him and cleaned his plate. That was the rule in the family: you don't throw food away.

---

9. This chapter might have been significantly funnier had these ideas not been lost to the trash bin of history that sat at the foot of Gearan's desk. Register complaints at *mgearan1217@hotmail.com*. Suggested sample e-mail: Hey Gearan. This chapter wasn't the least bit funny and I blame you. Sincerely, [your name here].

Q: Does he still ask you for money?
A: No. He never did. He never even asked for allowance.

Q: Did he ever chop down a cherry tree as a child?
A: No, but we did have a cherry tree that the boys loved very much. They climbed on it and tried to collect the cherries before the birds got to them.
        Contact Mark Gearan (1–800 USA-MIKE)

By the late spring, the Dukakis campaign had fulfilled its early promise, and our candidate was making good on the Joe Klein piece that had emboldened me to move to Boston and work my ass off for a nonpaying job in the first place. Mike Dukakis and his campaign had the discipline, dollars and stamina to outlast the others and keep latecomers from getting in. Having survived a well-spun "bronze medal" (third place) showing in Iowa behind Gephardt and Simon, Dukakis won New Hampshire, only to endure a mixed Super Tuesday outcome, losing Michigan to Jesse Jackson but recouping in Wisconsin later that week. An April showdown in the New York primary versus Jackson and Gore sent Gore back to D.C., and the rest of the way was a slow, tortured dance with Jackson, who was never going to win but was not going away, either. All the while, the political pundits and side-lined sore losers continued to entertain a fantasy convention saved by one of the consensus heavyweights—Mario Cuomo, Bill Bradley or Sam Nunn. But with each warmer week the nomination seemed more secure, and no one could ever blame humorous campaign *Hotline* entries for denying us our date with destiny.

By June, the only other campaign that merited our real attention was the Bush campaign, and that too was the answer to a collective prayer. All spring long, the conventional wisdom around the third-floor copy machine was that Dole was the stronger general election opponent and Bush was the pale placeholder of a presidency in rapid decline. In late June, when Reagan issued a long-overdue endorsement of his own vice president, I had my first opportunity to take aim at our real rivals. Gearan approved an entry that even in 1988 was already a done-to-death rip-off: the Letterman Top Ten List.

WHY REAGAN ENDORSED GEORGE BUSH OVER MIKE DUKAKIS

- Because B comes before D.
- Because Aquarii (Reagan) get along better with Geminis (Bush) than Scorpios (Dukakis).
- Because that's what it said on the TelePrompTer.
- Because Dukakis's name never appeared in Ollie North's diary.
- Because Dukakis forgot to send the Ayatollah a birthday cake this year—or even a card.[10]

Of course, the fact that Gearan was signing off on more humor did not mean that he had signed away his right to torment me. Upon returning from an extended campaign swing through western states, Gearan came directly to my desk before he even bothered to put down his luggage.

"Katz, do you know what I heard from reporters on the plane for four straight days?" he asked.

"No, what?" I asked, hoping for positive feedback on my now-daily comedy output.

"They say, 'Oh Mark, your campaign *Hotline* entries are *absolutely hysterical*! I turn to them right away even before I read anything else!'"

---

10. There were innumerable howlingly funny reasons I wrote that day that Gearan mercilessly killed, none of which I can remember now. Again, that address is *mgearan1217@hotmail.com*.

A big smile came to my face. Gearan went on.

"And do you know what I say to these reporters each and every time they say that to me?"

I didn't know what he was going to say next, but from the glee on his face I had a feeling that it was about to crush me.

"I say, 'Thank you!'" he exclaimed, through a smile even bigger than the one I'd just lost.

I dropped my head and released the sad laugh of defeat into my tie. That sinking feeling was my formal initiation into the bittersweet world of ghostwriting, where even the best-case scenario leaves you with the sensation of a sizable hole in your chest. I am capable of no greater selfless act than to allow another person to bask in my laughs—and I know this because it is the single hardest thing I've ever been called upon to do.

With the nomination in sight, I knew that my gambit had paid off—that I had the good fortune to have nested in the one campaign out of seven that was going to be in business until Election Day and, God willing, the next four to eight years after that. Even in the tentative world of electoral politics, I felt I had somehow arrived upon something that felt like the germ of a career.

By the time the inhabitants of Chauncey Street packed up and left for the convention in Atlanta, the term "President Dukakis" no longer felt like the impossible thought it once had been. In fact, it felt more likely than not. I would have gladly set my alarm a full hour earlier to do the clips had I known the specific joys of being on the campaign that wins its party's nomination. The 1988 Democratic Convention was the most exciting, joyous, electrifying, gratifying, deafening event I'd ever attended that didn't feature Bruce Springsteen. Only Atlanta's oppressive heat distinguished this real-life wonderland from a fantastic dream. Even an exceedingly long speech by a little-known Arkansas governor in praise of our candidate could not dampen a thrill-a-minute week that got better by the day. Each night, the treasured pass around my neck granted access to the floor—a boisterous sea of red, white and blue and rhythmic chanting of the name I had been snipping from newspapers and typing into press releases for nearly nine months. Suddenly, the proper noun that even a semi-assimilated Yiddish immigrant found too silly for words was on the tip of the world's tongue; the sturdy man who made it famous was well positioned to take on the Republican party's undaunting second banana. At one glorious moment in time—the bubble between the end of the Democratic Convention and the beginning of the Republicans'—one well-remembered poll registered Dukakis 53 percent, Bush 39 percent.

Not too many days after the last balloon hit the convention floor in Atlanta, my Grampa Max, nursing a summer cold that had settled in his chest, told my Uncle Stanley that he was going to lie down for a bit. It was a nap from which he would never wake up. But as he removed his glasses and put his bald head on the pillow for the very last time, he was fully confident that his grandson was working for the next president of the United States. And still suspicious that the man was Jewish.

CHAPTER FIVE

The Guy Who Made Mike Dukakis So Funny

THE GROWN-UP WHO HAD AMBLED INTO THE OPEN WORKSPACE OF the press office looked out of place among the many twenty-somethings, like a principal in a school cafeteria. "Which one is Katz?" he asked the first kid he saw.

Pointed in my direction, the recently appointed campaign hon-cho headed right for me. Kirk O'Donnell arrived at the corner of the bridge table that I called my desk and introduced himself by name, which I already knew. Three weeks earlier, at the beginning of July, I had written the press release announcing his arrival, so I knew the bullet points of his résumé as well: former top aide/campaign manager for Boston mayor Kevin White, former chief counsel to House Speaker Tip O'Neill and, most recently, the director of a well-regarded Washington think tank, the Center for National Policy. His title on the campaign was "Senior Advisor," and he looked the part. Wearing the paisley tie and clean white button-down shirt of a professional pol, he was six feet tall and had a Babe Ruth face tinted Irish red. His comb-over hair, slightly hunched posture and fashion-backward eyeglasses gave him the look of a man in his fifties. (I was surprised to learn later that he was just forty-two.)

"Are you the Katz who writes the jokes?" he asked.

I thought I might be in trouble.[1]

"Uh, yes."

"Andy Savitz told me your joke, something about Martin van Buren's wife being Jewish?"

Despite the confused description, I knew exactly what he was talking about. A few weeks earlier, Andy Savitz, who was Kitty Dukakis's press secretary at the time, heard that I kept a private stash of jokes and had shown up at my desk in search of jokes he might give to Kitty. As it happened, later that week, Savitz was informed of something pretty unfunny: Kitty had found someone else to do his job.[2] Cut loose to fend for himself, Savitz met with Kirk to discuss serving as a deputy on the communications staff. In the course of their meeting, Kirk mentioned the need to add some humor to the campaign's message and Savitz pitched him a line that had stuck in his head. "*Not only will Mike Dukakis be the first Greek president, but Kitty Dukakis will be the first Jewish first lady since Shayndel-Leah Van Buren.*"

I thanked him for the compliment, even though I couldn't believe he'd set out to find me just to tell me he liked one of my jokes. When I mentioned that there was more where that came from, he seemed eager to hear the rest. I led Kirk to the press office PC that I shared with nine other people and searched through the C-drive for the folder with my name on it. Even before the document opened, my mind raced ahead to edit it. The stash, such as it was, really wasn't much more than a running list of Gearan's line-item vetoes from *Hotline* entries I had brought to his desk, maintained mostly for my own amuse-

---

1. "How's Aunt Clara?"
2. An ironic consequence of being on the campaign that wins the nomination is that you automatically become a candidate to be replaced in the general election by a "pro" imported from Washington or a high-ranking refugee from the staff of a vanquished candidate. This happens mostly to people ranked captain and up, not press office foot soldiers who do the menial tasks at subsistence wages.

ment. There was plenty of material on the list that merited rejection, and I knew that I would have to exercise on-the-fly judgment as to which jokes to pitch and which might earn the same grimace I got from Gearan. Kirk waited patiently in those long moments, and once the document was open, I started reading down the list:

"If Jesse Jackson wants to be my running mate," I said, loading each clause in my brain before turning my head back over my shoulder, "I challenge him to find a word that rhymes with 'Dukakis.'"[3]

Kirk's laugh brought the press office to a halt, and for a moment I did not know whether to be thrilled or embarrassed. He laughed the way Swiss people yodel—a distinctive, explosive, joyful noise that brings people rushing in from surrounding rooms to find out what's so funny. As his laugh concluded, he got out the words "That's terr-ific, that's terr-ific" with the last few beats. Not surprisingly, I tried another:

"Hi, I'm Mike Dukakis. And these are my eyebrows."

Another score set off another cackle, not a decibel lower. Others might be self-conscious about having a laugh that loud, but Kirk made no effort to contain it and I made no effort to disguise the fact that I was bathing in its approval. I kept going.

"You are looking at a guy who likes to begin his sentences with the expression 'You are looking at a guy.'

". . . George Bush's idea of getting tough on drug kingpins is to stop returning their phone calls."[4]

As Kirk continued to laugh with each new line I fed him, I looked over my shoulder, hoping that the ruckus would bring Gearan out of his office. (Damn, where was he?)

---

3. Uh-oh. Maracas.
4. A Noriega joke.

". . . George Bush cares about the second homeless—those Americans without vacation homes.

". . . I love balancing budgets. On weekends, I balance budgets from other states. By the way, if you are the governor of Oregon— or know how to reach him—please call me right away."

That one died. Instead of eliciting another cackle, it provided the pause for Kirk to dry his eyes from his prolonged outburst. I had gone one joke too far, as I usually do, but his response taught me something I needed to know: Kirk's oversized laugh did not mean he was an easy laugh. He had a good ear for what worked and what didn't—and the jokes that did were registered with a roar.

"Come with me," he said.

I followed him back to his third-floor office in the campaign's executive suite like a puppy at his heels. Once in his office, he summoned Gearan (back from wherever he was) and, as I sat there, discussed the terms of my release from the press office to the communications staff. Gearan, either happy for me or personally relieved, did not put up any kind of a fight. The next time I returned to my workspace, it was to collect my stuff and begin a new assignment as a member of the Rapid Response Team. This was big-time.

The Dukakis Campaign Rapid Response Team, captained by Savitz under Kirk's command, was tasked with responding to rhetorical assaults with speed and wit and the full force of facts. My new job was to bring my skills to bear on the wit part of that equation; as a unit, we hoped to generate the kind of trenchant sound bites that are the hand grenades of modern political warfare. Kirk was the rare breed of policy wonk with a good ear for that kind of thing,[5] and setting up such a squad was on his to-do list from the

---

5. Working as one of Tip O'Neill's top trusted aides, Kirk had authored many memorable battle cries of 1980s-era Democrats:

- "Social Security is the third rail of American politics. You touch it and you die."
- The Speaker to the president: "I don't need batting tips from the Babe Ruth of deficits."

day he arrived. I went to the small second-floor office where Savitz had set up shop, and he welcomed me with this: "Katz, you know those clocks that keep running track of the federal deficit?"

"Yeah."

"From now on, you should assume they are calculating the size of the debt you owe me from now until the day you die."

If I was a comic writer by nature, Savitz was a natural-born comic performer. God had given Savitz a dose of the gift He had given Buddy Hackett: things were funnier just because he said them. The more Savitz came to know me, the more he realized that he could break me up with just about anything he said—and as a result, he poured it on a little thicker for my benefit.

"By the way," he continued, "I am not talking about a debt of gratitude. I am talking about actual cash. In fact, why don't you start by giving me what you've got in your wallet right now?"

As anyone who has ever met him could tell you, Andy Savitz was once a Rhodes scholar—something he mentioned many times a day, despite the fact that he was now in his mid-thirties. It was an important element of his cultivated comic persona, an unedited and unpolished lawyer unafraid of letting you know he was smarter than you, which out of every hundred people he met was true ninety-nine times. (In the Harvard think tank that was the Dukakis campaign, that ratio might have been reduced to nine out of ten.) In addition to being Rhodes scholar–smart, he had also served as a former senior policy aide on Capitol Hill and, more recently, as a loyal Dukakis staffer brought into the campaign in its earliest days by his friend and poker buddy, John Sasso. With Sasso gone and Kitty done with him, Savitz had done well to land on his feet for the general election, as he was just one bad break away from being named Euterpe Dukakis's press secretary.

The ten-by-eight-foot office, built for one, had three desks in it, and I put my things down on the remaining empty one, the smallest and farthest from the exterior window. Just that week, the desk next to Savitz's had been assigned to another new staffer recruited from Washington, a twenty-seven-year-old prodigy with moppish hair and angular features who held the distinction of being the youngest top aide to a congressman on Capitol Hill. Although he was already in the process of making a name for himself, very few people could spell it correctly at the time: Stephanopoulos.

George had joined the campaign for the general election for reasons that were a mix of career adventurism and Hellenistic duty. George was also a former Rhodes, a fact I learned from Savitz as he introduced me to him—just a segue to remind me once more that Savitz was a Rhodes and that I was not. The job George signed on to do was opposition press, which would require him to stay in close contact with the reporters following Bush and work our version of the facts into their stories. But in the aftermath of the Biden/Sasso/Kim tape incident earlier in the campaign, "opposition press" had become a sensitive subject on the Dukakis campaign. Some thought it wise to keep a low profile on such activities, even though they were standard operating procedure on most campaigns. As a result, George's job description around the office was somewhat sanitized, and his placement in Savitz's office initially served as something of a cover. His on-the-record job description was that he was working with Kirk as a deputy to Savitz. But what began as merely plausible soon became fact, as George, if only for reasons of proximity, soon grafted onto our squad as a full-fledged member.

With the addition of an intern our team was complete, and I was pleased to have someone around more junior than me. Michael Peterson, just nineteen years old, sat right outside our office during what should have been the first semester of his sophomore year at Brown. For an intern, he was better connected than most congressmen. His father was a powerful Wall Street dealmaker who had served in Nixon's cabinet as commerce secretary. Schooled at Dalton and Andover and raised on the tony blocks of the Upper East Side, Peterson had a background that would have better predicted an internship on the Bush campaign, if not Pierre duPont's. For the first few weeks in our office, he learned to answer to the nickname "Mole."

Together, we were "Kirk's Boys," and we spent our days executing routine communications tasks and acting upon his orders. Each day, Kirk would arrive at the office having already marked up the front pages of the *New York Times*, the *Washington Post* and the *Wall Street Journal,* circling headlines, bracketing paragraphs and, with various notes and scrawls, turning the margins into a playbook that would take him through noon. These items and others were discussed at the early-morning communications meeting in the third-floor conference room, where ten or twelve high-level aides hammered out the communications objectives of the day. The people assembled in this room—Susan Estrich, Leslie Dach, Jack Corrigan, Mark Gearan, Christopher Edley, John Podesta, Vicki Radd, Robert Shapiro, Susan Brophy, Steven Akey, among others—were the same large cheeses to whom I had delivered clips and *Hotlines* for six months. When I took a seat at the table for the first time, it was hard to gauge who was more startled—them or me.

One person at this table gave me an extra-long fish-eyed look, which scared me more than anything else in that room could have. From the first day I arrived, Deputy Campaign Manager Jack Corrigan had scared the hell out of me. His was the cultivated look of heartless, tough-guy determination. Tiptoeing into his office to drop off the morning clips earned not a "Thank you" but a sideways glance that said, "What the fuck do you want? Can't you see that I'm busy?" I never thought he was a bad guy, just a guy with zero tolerance for nonsense—which threatened me for all the obvious reasons. As Corrigan continued to wonder what the hell I was doing in this meeting, I inched my seat closer to Savitz, so I could be that much closer to Kirk, on Savitz's other side.

A little more than three months remained until Election Day, and the next hundred days would begin with these meetings. After they broke up, our squad's first task was to write up a page of bulleted "Talking Points"—an internal-use-only propaganda sheet designed to put spokespeople in HQ and across the country all on the same page. As the day progressed, we churned out various official campaign statements—the equivalent of press releases, designed to be quoted in wire stories and picked up from there—usually under the name of Kirk O'Donnell or our campaign manager, Susan Estrich. But, most important, we were always on call to respond to the four-alarm fire drill of incoming attacks from Bush and his surrogates. One of the first came not from our opponent but from the president of the United States.

On August 7, the *Washington Times*—a newspaper ridiculed among Democrats for being the house organ of right-wing Republicans[6]—ran a page-one story that put into print something that Republicans had recently been whispering as a rumor, that Dukakis had once been treated for depression. Asked to comment on the report at a White House press conference that morning, President Reagan pretended to beg off, delivering a mean jab with his head-cocked twinkled smile: "Look, I'm not going to pick on an invalid."

News of Reagan's comment was delivered to our Chauncey Street headquarters via the AP newswire machine, the Internet of its day, which was kept in a press office closet to suppress the din of its *clickety-click* noise. When a copy of the wire story got to Kirk's desk, his response was an anger that bordered on outrage. The remark not only derided Dukakis in a false, dismissive and insidious way, it was also predicated upon a medieval understanding of mental health. Kirk had as much experience dealing with President Reagan as anyone in the building, and more genuine respect for him than most. As Tip O'Neill's counsel during

---

6. Also for being cult-owned and operated. The newspaper can be found among the holdings of the Reverend Sun Myung Moon's Unification Church, and there is no easier and more irresistible partisan mock Democrats can make than to put *"Washington Times"* and "Moonie" in the same sentence. (See previous sentence.)

Reagan's first term and into his second, Kirk had served on the front lines of the loyal opposition to the Reagan Revolution. (On many occasions during the campaign, we would come to Kirk with some anti-Reagan reference in our draft and he would kill it almost every time, reminding us we were not running against Reagan and that trying to was almost always a mistake.) But on this day, he thought taking the Gipper to task for an outrageous remark was the right play to call. Together, a group of exercised communications staffers assembled in Kirk's office and hammered out a first draft of a strong response that went something like this:

> Mr. President: Nobody wants you to ridicule challenged people with your schoolyard insults. Nor should you help spread untrue rumors about me.

The more we reworked the response the angrier we became, and some debated if we should call upon Reagan to apologize to the mentally and physically handicapped. But two things had happened while we were preparing a response. First, President Reagan took his next opportunity in front of a news camera to characterize his remark as a failed attempt at humor, a retraction that never came close to apology: "A short time ago, I attempted a joke. I was kidding. I was just trying to be funny and it didn't work."

Second, upon hearing the remark, Dukakis responded as he saw fit. He quickly accepted the president's explanation without any hint of anger, going so far as to renounce his interest in an actual apology. "We all misspeak from time to time."

We were half disappointed that our candidate had failed to stand up for himself as strenuously as he might have, but we were also half proud that he had declined to follow another down a lower road. The next day's papers issued the scorecard on the incident: in the course of a single news cycle, the president of the United States had used his bully pulpit to put an untrue rumor on the front page of many a paper,[7] scored points for owning up to a mistake and showcased Dukakis's failure to stand up for himself, depressed people or even invalids, for that matter. What we didn't know—but should have—was that it was just a glimpse of the campaign to come.

August 1988 was the month that these topics entered the American political discourse: the Pledge of Allegiance, flag burning and Willie Horton. By choosing the Pledge of Allegiance as a line of attack, patriotism became the first refuge of the Bush campaign[8] while the flag-burning issue was a Trojan horse to spread another false rumor, that Kitty Dukakis had once torched an American flag.[9] To make these points, Bush traveled to many flag factories to demonstrate his love of Old Glory, where the derision in his voice as he denounced "card-carrying members of the ACLU" made those who guard our civil liberties sound as though they were members of the Politburo itself. Finally, the Willie Horton "issue" pretended to be

---

7. I read through *When Character Was King* looking for details of this incident, but found nothing. I'll go back and check again.

8. As governor, Dukakis had refused to sign a bill mandating the recitation of the Pledge of Allegiance in Massachusetts public schools on First Amendment grounds. Dukakis's ardent defense of the U.S. Constitution did not prevent Bush from questioning his patriotism. Many times over, he assailed Dukakis for "vetoing the Pledge of Allegiance"—a willfully simplistic attack that ignored context in favor of cheap insinuation.

9. On August 24, a U.S. senator, Steve Symms (R-Idaho), told a reporter: "I haven't seen this, but I heard that there are pictures around that will surface before the elections are over of Mrs. Dukakis burning the American flag while she was an antiwar demonstrator during the sixties." After three days of news stories about the remark—including an unconditional denial by Mrs. Dukakis, along with some fresh quotes by Symms repeating the allegation—no photo was found. The senator issued a non-apology on August 27 once the negative had been proved to his satisfaction: "I'm happy to know Mrs. Dukakis has never burned an American flag . . . I think I'll drop the subject."

about crime the way Nixon's "law and order" campaign once pretended to be about law and order.[10] Even more infuriating, this low road was being paved even as Bush's uncharacteristically precious convention speech phrases ("a thousand points of light," "a kinder, gentler nation," "listen to the pitter-patter of my heart" and other out-of-character stylistic prose) were still echoing in the air.[11]

Of course, our campaign was not having a month that we would look back upon proudly in years hence, either. Our candidate was determined to fulfill what he saw as his first responsibility, being governor of his state, and spent a good chunk of the month in western Massachusetts—instead of in any of the other forty-nine states where he might have made inroads. While Bush and his surrogates impugned his patriotism, Dukakis considered the charges absurd, beneath contempt and unworthy of response. To engage them on their level was to cede the moral high ground, he believed.[12] We did, however, manage to cede our lead. On September 1, we were trailing Bush by 5 points.

On the list of falsehoods assigned to Mike Dukakis was a quote attributed to him two years earlier in the pages of a little-known militia-enthusiast magazine. During the campaign, the quote was emblazoned in three-foot-high letters on highway

---

10. Willie Horton, a black man who committed vicious rapes and assaults while on a weekend furlough from a Massachusetts prison, became the highly visible public face of the Bush campaign's attack on the "dangerously liberal" Mike Dukakis.

11. Do I sound bitter to you?

12. In one of his clumsy ventures into rhetorical hardball, Dukakis used an old Greek expression to connect a Reagan administration transgression (Iran-Contra) to Reagan himself: "A fish rots from the head." It seemed artless even as he said it, and for the rest of the campaign Republicans would justify a negative tone as a license acquired by having been victim to the "rotting fish" insult. By the way, do I sound bitter to you?

billboards throughout Texas by a coalition of citizens who really loved guns:

> **"I don't believe in anyone owning guns except the police and the military."**
>
> **—Mike Dukakis**

Soon, George Bush was quoting the "quote" in his stump speech. The issue of how to respond came up one morning in early September at our seven o'clock communications meeting. Once again, we were in the position of refuting something demonstrably false after the damage was done,[13] but the real question on the table was how to counteract the growing perception that Dukakis was a peace-loving conscientious objector to anything that went *BANG!* or *KA-BOOM!* One ill-conceived suggestion was also ill timed, as it was offered at the precise moment that Savitz was bringing the day's third cup of coffee to his lips. Upon hearing the idea—a photo-op of Mike Dukakis at a firing range—Savitz's reflex-ive laugh sent the coffee flying across the table. He knew Dukakis well enough to know that our candidate would sooner put a gun to his own head than take target practice with a Glock. That idea proved to be a nonstarter, but a Bush photo-op we all saw that night on the evening news helped put another idea into play.

In these last weeks of August, George Bush was polishing his WWII war-hero medals by visiting numerous defense plants and

---

13. I recently heard a rumor that a person matching the description of former Senator Steve Symms of Idaho used to spend his teenage summers as a counselor-in-training at a white supremacist militia unit in northern Idaho, tasked with the specific duty of finding kindling for cross burnings. I'll look into it and report back later.

military bases. Bush, a tall and fit former fighter pilot, looked the part—and evidently the boys down in Scheduling thought we could pull it off, too. On September 6, the evening news showcased a photo-op of our candidate behind the very big gun of an MX tank on maneuvers at a training facility in Flint, Michigan. Once the piece had aired, high-ranking campaign officials who shall remain nameless high-fived each other at the in-your-face retort to the Bush initiative military photo-op. That was Tuesday evening. On Friday night, the evening news ran a piece about campaign photo-ops themselves, the centerpiece of which was footage of a helmeted Mike Dukakis running tank maneuvers back and forth and back again before a bank of cameras. This was the report that first likened Dukakis to Snoopy on national television, an image that stuck and lives to this day. The more the shot was replayed, the worse it became, as small details loomed larger and more absurd. The red power tie that poked through the top of Dukakis's khaki jumpsuit failed to connote power. The chinstrap that straddled his lower lip made the protective headgear he wore seem like a full-metal orthodontic appliance. Worst of all, the name "Mike Dukakis" printed across his forehead denied our spinmasters plausible deniability as a last line of defense. Over the course of the next week, what had begun as a photo-op ended as an enshrined national joke. I'd bet money those two campaign honchos never spoke of their high five again.

Of course, my reaction to the tank was unlike most anyone's in the building. As the candidate's designated joke writer, I resented it. By this point I had assembled pages and pages of jokes our candidate might use, but this damn tank was getting our biggest guffaws. This may explain why, as others tried to distance themselves from the set of circumstances that had our candidate crossing the Maginot Line of military photo-op blunders, part of me wished it had been my idea.

*   *   *

Wednesday, September 7, 1988. In the midmorning, the phone rang in our office and I could hear Kirk's voice boom through the handset Savitz had brought to his ear: "Guys, get up here right away!" From the tone of his voice, we knew that whatever it was, it was serious. A short sprint later, the four of us crowded into Kirk's office as he read aloud remarks Bush had made not an hour earlier to 6,000 members of the American Legion, where he was speaking that day to erase any lingering shadow of doubt that after his many recent trips to flag factories, he *truly* cherished the American flag:

"Today, you remember—I wonder how many Americans remember—today is Pearl Harbor Day. Forty-seven years ago to this very day, we were hit and hit hard at Pearl Harbor and we were not ready."

Every American with a junior high school degree knows that Pearl Harbor Day is December 7, not September 7, and news of the vice president's gaffe was arriving quickly at the desks of reporters and politicos.

"This is a big moment for us," said Kirk, in no uncertain terms. "We gotta come back with something. We gotta hit 'em hard with a funny comeback."

Four pairs of eyes landed on me. Wasting no time to let subtext speak for itself, Kirk put me on the spot: "What'ya got, Katz?" This was the moment of my dreams.

In this dream, I deliver the perfect line to raucous laughter and am carried around on the collective shoulders of the giddy townspeople, whom my spontaneous wit has just somehow saved from the jaws of doom. That's how I'd know it was a dream. During my waking hours, I am nearly incapable of reflexive, real-time retorts, because my brain instantly floods with the thought, "Oh, shit, Katz, you'd better come up with something really funny right now," instead of coming up with something really funny. Opening my mouth at that moment was an act of prayer that the Lord would somehow lend me a joke right then and there. But nothing came out.

"Mark, what's the line? We need a line . . ."

My mouth, now open wider, filled the room with a terrible silence. The long moment ended with a group guffaw, triggered by Kirk, at the comic premise of a comic gone mute at the worst possible moment. I had let Kirk down, but the game was not over yet.

"We'll be back in ten minutes," Savitz promised.

Savitz knew something about me that Kirk did not: while I was capable of producing jokes on demand, the process demanded ten minutes, a blank computer screen, and time to rub my eyes, massage my scalp, mumble to myself and bounce words, phrases and stray ideas through the echo chamber of my brain. These are the time-consuming mechanisms that have always negated stand-up comedy as a viable career choice for me, as hecklers don't have that kind of time.

Nine and a half minutes later, Savitz and I were back in Kirk's office with jokes still warm from the printer.

- *No wonder their campaign can't settle on a date for the debates.*
- *We encourage all of the vice president's supporters to go to the polls on Election Day, November 16.*
- *Okay then, just give me the year.*
- *Great. You just moved up Arbor Day to the middle of January.*
- *This from the man who thinks Dan Quayle ought to be our next Education Czar.*
- *It's time for George Bush to come clean on the bombing of Pearl Harbor: what did he know and when did he know it?*

Kirk gave most of the lines a truncated version of his elongated laugh and brought the page into the office of Susan Estrich. Savitz and I listened outside the door as a cluster of senior staffers laughed aloud and claimed different lines as ones they might use in conversations with reporters. Bush's press secretary, Sheila Tate, dismissed the gaffe by saying, "He wasn't thinking," while the president's eldest son, George W. Bush, failed to see the big deal in getting the small details wrong.[14] Two days later, the gaffe had come and gone; polls revealed that not a single American anywhere had changed their vote as a result of one candidate's mistake and the truly hysterical, well-honed jokes of the opposition. But years later, I still marked September 7 as a day that nearly lived in political infamy.

More and more, our little office became the water cooler of the Dukakis campaign, the destination where people on breaks wandered over to, hoping to share a funny thought or be entertained by the process of watching clever-isms being coined. Our most frequent visitors were issues staffers and speechwriters hoping we might help them crystallize their words into a memorable quote, as if our office were an in-and-out sound-bite shop that worked along the same model as a Jiffy Lube. This was where Savitz did some of his best work, translating detailed substance into accessible sound bites. (A time-consuming part of the process was Savitz having to explain to me the specifics of public policy that my mind was not built to fully comprehend—and, very often, it was the teenager Peterson who understood what Savitz was talking about and then explained it to me.)

---

14. The creation of humor often requires the dissection of logic, and this process had me analyzing the remarks more dialectically than most. Follow me here: George Bush did not say Pearl Harbor was September 7 instead of December 7. That is a mistake akin to confusing broccoli with Brussels sprouts. He said, "*Today* is Pearl Harbor Day." Which means one of two things: he thought (a) that Pearl Harbor Day was in fact on September 7 or (b) that he had woken up that morning thinking that the month was December. Both (a) and (b) are troubling in their own way, and each lent itself to a different line of jokes, (a) that he did not know when Pearl Harbor Day was or (b) that he had somehow lost his way along the time/space continuum. Remarkably—and to their credit, I guess—his campaign's explanation got away with (c), which was, "Oops. Did he say 'September'? He meant to say 'December.'" For the next four days, I complained loudly to anyone who would listen about the logical lapse of their spin, until even Peterson was telling me, "Give it up, Katz," It's many years later and I will not give it up: I still demand to know which one was it, (a) or (b)?

Nevertheless, presented with facts that were the arid stuff of issues papers, together we'd spit back a sentence that had the earmarks of a sound bite:

- *Americans are tired of sweating it out on the Reagan/Bush economic treadmill.*
- *George Bush describes the 225,000 workers who lost their jobs in the last quarter as merely victims of "competitive change" who are "statistically irrelevant." Mr. Vice President, they're not numbers. They're our neighbors.*
- *George Bush's tax plan for working American families amounts to forty cents a day. His thousand points of light are really one forty-cent candle and 999 mirrors.*
- *George Bush has performed a perfect flip-flop-flip on abortion.*

As proprietors in the sound-bite business, we measured our results by the number of sentences that left our office and wound up on the evening news or in the next day's papers. Our team scored enough hits for us to make the claim that we were the resident sound-bite artists, but not so many that we couldn't recount each and every one. And with the presidential debates approaching and the campaign already starting to flail, we saw a great opportunity to make up a lot of ground in a hurry.

The network debates are the title fights of presidential politics and a sound-bite artist's shot at immortality. Reagan raised the tactic to an art form, first marginalizing a sitting president, Jimmy Carter, with a well-delivered *"There you go again,"* and then, four years later, defusing the age issue with the comically deft *"I'm not going to exploit for political purposes my opponent's youth and inexperience."* The mystique of the "Killer Sound Bite" may have been fortified forever during the 1984 Democratic primaries when Walter Mondale unleashed a line borrowed from a popular Wendy's commercial to deliver a blow to Gary

Hart, from which the Colorado senator never recovered: *"Where's the beef?"*[15]

We became true believers in the Killer Bite–the compelling, crystallized line that stymies your opponent, electrifies the audience, astounds the pundits and rallies the undecided Reagan Democrats to your candidate's side. More than that, we assumed that such a magic bullet existed and that it was our job to find it. The pressure only intensified with each pre-debate article we read describing the final debate in Los Angeles as our campaign's last, best hope. So determined were we to write the "Where's the Beef" line of 1988, our team left the office with pads, pens and position papers and set up shop for many hours in a nearby Wendy's. There the three of us sat, two Rhodes Scholars and the kid recently promoted from "clips," hepped up on Frosties and Biggie Fries, filling page after page with would-be zingers, hoping each new offering would be the moment we would brag about at job interviews and cocktail parties for the rest of our lives.[16]

Upon our return, Kirk phoned in from the debate site with something else to add to our sound-bite to-do list: a response to the use of Bush's favorite word to describe Dukakis–"liberal." With only hours to go before the debate, George and I pulled up two chairs to the computer, passing the keyboard back and forth and taking turns writing lines.

If you keep calling me a liberal, I am going to raise your taxes. **NO**

If you promise to stop calling me a "liberal," I promise to stop calling you "Mr. Vice Butt-Boy." **NO**

---

15. The year 1984 also saw the first self-inflicted Killer Sound Bite in a debate, when Walter Mondale said of Reagan, "He won't tell you that he will raise your taxes–and I just did."

16. Instead, there is only this sad anecdote relegated to the footnotes of history.

I know you are, but what am I? [REPEAT AS NECESSARY]
NO

*George, enough with the calling me "liberal." Have you heard me
once use the word "wimp"?* **MAYBE**

Stephanopoulos, who generally had less time in his day for frivolity than I did, used his turn at the keyboard to offer this:

*If I had a dime for every time you used the word "liberal," I'd
qualify for one of your tax breaks for the rich.*

My response was "eh," but we put it on a list of recommended
debate one-liners that we faxed to Kirk at debate prep camp in a
Los Angeles hotel suite. However, later that night, upon hearing
the debate's first question put to our candidate, it occurred to us
that we'd somehow failed to prepare a sharp, funny one-liner in
response to a question that began with the phrase: "Governor, if
your wife Kitty Dukakis were raped and murdered . . ."

Three time zones away, in a Boston hotel suite filled with ten
TVs, twenty PCs and three dozen tasteless sandwiches, the fifty or
so people who comprised the post-debate rapid response team
were as alarmed by the question as anyone not named Kitty
Dukakis could possibly be. We watched as Dukakis did not flinch
when CNN's Bernard Shaw said the word "rape," then "murder,"
then "Kitty Dukakis." He did not even blink until the words "capital punishment" near the end of the question. This was either a
good sign or a very bad one. A collective prayer took the form of
fifty people whispering to themselves, *"C'mon, Michael."*

Looking back, there may have been ninety-nine different correct ways to answer that question, many of which included phrases
like *"strangle with my own hands," "kill him until he was dead"* or *"hunt
him down like the subhuman filth that he is and beat him to death with a
shovel."* Any response that registered genuine anger at the premise

of the question rather than mere mild annoyance at the one who asked it would do the trick. The reply Dukakis gave, however, was as clinical as an answer to the Daily Double on *Jeopardy*, if the category were Hemispheric Crime Summits—which, by the way, was the idea he proposed in response to the violation and violent death of his beloved. Perhaps the sentiment of the room was captured best by the issues staffer who screamed the words "HOLY JESUS MOTHER OF FUCK!" to the beat of a fist pounding against a wall. We had just witnessed the birth of a new species of debate sound bites, a variant of the self-inflicted Killer Sound Bite. This was the Anti-Killer Sound Bite: self-sustained damage as the result of filling the space where the right response *should* go with an answer so anemic and unmemorable, only the question that prompted it remains.

An hour into the rest of the debate, when most Americans had changed the channel but a good many C-SPAN junkies were still watching with one eye, Dukakis did in fact grow tired of listening to George Bush dismiss him as a "liberal"—a word he had used liberally.[17]

> *And I think if we get rid of the labels—and I'm not keeping count, but I think Mr. Bush has used the label "liberal" at least ten times. If I had a dollar, George, for every time you used that label, I'd qualify for one of those tax breaks for the rich that you want to give away.*

That line, distended as it was, became the best-known mildly amusing thing that ever started in our office and ended up crossing the candidate's lips.

---

17. Nine times in the first hour, four of them in this sentence: "But I have defined the issues and I am not going to let Governor Dukakis go through this election without explaining some of these very **liberal** positions. He's the one that said 'I am a **liberal**—traditional **liberal**—progressive **liberal** Democrat.'"

* * *

Two days before the vice presidential debates, Sam Buell walked into our office and closed the door behind him. Sam was an issues staffer who had joined the campaign the same week as I did and had been reassigned to Lloyd Bentsen for the general election. The look on his face said something was up.

"We've got Lloyd's one-liner for the debate."

Savitz, our point man, shot back, "Let's have it."

"If he compares himself to Kennedy again, Bentsen is going to say: 'You're not John Kennedy.'"

Savitz's face did not move. He looked to George, then looked to me. More blank faces.

"That's the bite? What's the bite? I didn't hear a bite," Savitz said, using the shorthand of professional sound-bite experts like us.

Buell was crestfallen as he left the room. The prototype of the only sound bite from our campaign that would stand the test of time had been submitted to the Office of Sound Bites, and we had dismissed it out of hand. Two days later, Bentsen used an improved version of that same sentence to cleave Quayle's sternum and present him with his own still-beating heart:

I knew Jack Kennedy. Jack Kennedy was a friend of mine. Senator, you are no Jack Kennedy.

When the hoots and hollers were over, heads turned to us to see if we had authored the nugget. Savitz, straight-faced, replied, "Yup, that line came through our office."

For all of our efforts, making Mike Dukakis funny was a challenge that, for the most part, eluded us. Nearly each time he met with Dukakis, Kirk would pull out a page of jokes that had earned the biggest laughs and pitch them aloud. His effort was met with blank stares followed by persnickety arguments about the specific reasons the jokes were not funny. Kirk would come from those State House meetings and arrive directly in our office, at pains to describe the intense blankness of Dukakis's face in response to material we all considered incapacitatingly hysterical.[18] As usual, Kirk gave it to us straight: the man we were writing jokes for was pathologically unfunny. (He also told us he was a decent man with the capacity to be a great president, so get back to work.)

Once the debates were behind us, there was still one, lesser-known mano-a-mano face-off left, and with the most unlikely format of all—humor. The annual Al Smith Dinner, named for the former New York governor and the first Catholic to run for president, was a white-tie charity fund-raising event held at the Waldorf-Astoria and hosted by the Archdiocese of New York. After the meal, Bush and Dukakis would take their turns at the podium and deliver dueling humorous remarks. Over the course of the week prior, Savitz and I spent our spare moments writing jokes for our guy that had more than a prayer of being used.

Despite working on a campaign behind in the game, our four-man team was churning on all eight cylinders. Given the nature of our campaign and our candidate, the mission of what started out as the "Rapid Response Team" had been reduced over time. By early September the word "Rapid" seemed an overstatement. As October went on, "Response" was no longer our calling card. For the last weeks of the campaign, Savitz, George, Peterson and I were pretty much just a "Team"—but a good one, at least, and maybe the only group of people in the building who were having a good time.[19] Savitz had taken me under his wing in a way that

---

18. Before the campaign was over, our best material was about the conundrum of making Dukakis funny—but none better than one our press secretary, Dayton Duncan, bequeathed to me to use as my own, which I have: "Writing jokes for Mike Dukakis is like being staff photographer of the *Wall Street Journal*." Thanks, DD.

allowed us to work as a tandem, bouncing jokes and sound bites off each other over the course of sixteen-hour days. George was generally not actively involved in the mirth-making process, and the standard answer to the not-uncommon question—"Is  George funny?"—was this: "George is the short, unfunny Greek guy we use to market-test the lines." (A funny line first delivered by George.)

We all had well-defined roles and Savitz-assigned nicknames. Mine was "the Poodle," a reference to my appearance on the Stupid Pet Tricks segment of the *Late Night with David Letterman* show when I was a sophomore in college. During my two minutes of fame, I dangled a piece of liver over the keys of a piano and implored Wally (my family's toy poodle) to "play"—the anthropomorphic term for a small dog banging his paws on the keyboard while simultaneously barking. Add to that visual image fluffy, oversized ears flopping with each bounce, and the result is something too silly and too cute for words. As I sat at the keyboard, Savitz would pretend to dangle a treat for me and instruct me to "play" as I created my too-cute jokes on the screen. The nickname also took the form of a verb (as in, "Give this to Katz and let him *poodle* it up"), as well as an adjective ("Try again. Too *poodly*").

By now, Peterson's nickname had been changed from "Mole" to "Chef." Of his many administrative tasks, Peterson took special delight in fetching us meals and late-afternoon snacks—which pleased me most of all, because if he had not been there to do it,

---

19. Oh, by the way, as it turns out, there is no conclusive proof that former Senator Steve Symms once collected kindling to burn crosses at a white supremacist summer camp in Idaho—despite matching the (admittedly vague) description I heard by way of rumor (the suspect was believed to be white and male). Besides, the former senator has maintained his commitment to public service by serving as a congressional lobbyist for the chemical industry. So I think I will drop the subject.

it surely would have been added to my job description. At first the three of us would give him specific lunch orders of what kind of sandwich we wanted on what kind of bread. After a while, we learned that given the authority to decide on his own, he would scour the neighborhood and come back with sandwiches more tasty than we might have specified, flavored with Dijon condiments and appropriate garnishes. Also, rather than return to us the change from our ten-dollar bills, Chef would come back with pastries or cookies or delicious delicacies that caught his eye. Peterson worked as many hours as any one of us, often adding helpful comments to whatever we were working on. And as Savitz, George and I hunkered down in the foxhole of the front lines, Michael "Chef" Peterson never forgot that an army travels on its stomach—and added to the axiom that it can flourish on its palate.

George also had taken on a Savitz-assigned nickname, "the Twins"—earned in part because even on a campaign populated with the overambitious, his work habits gave him the output of any two people. George gave off a natural intensity that reminded me a lot of my younger brother, and his nickname echoed the moniker I had long ago assigned to Robert—"one-man gang." This may be why working with George felt familiar to me from the very first day.

"The Twins" also had another meaning, a separate inside joke about the duality in the very nature of his job(s) on the campaign. Each day, George quietly went about his opposition press duties and, in that capacity, kept close tabs on any number of stories making their way through news organizations that had the capacity to embarrass if not derail our opponents, including many lurid rumors we desperately hoped were true.

George had been whispering quietly and listening intently on the phone for quite some time as Savitz and I were busy writing jokes for the Al Smith Dinner. At one point, he hung up the phone, got up and closed the door to our office. That got our attention.

"Guys, it's over," he announced.

For a second we didn't know if that was good or bad, as his face had yet to break into a 1,000-watt smile. When it did, George went on to explain that the next day's edition of the *Washington Post* was going with a story that would close up the Bush campaign before the weekend was out.[20] We jumped up and down and hugged in joy. On a campaign that was failing to make the case with the American people on its own merits, these whispers felt like our last, best hope. We may not have preferred it to a well-earned victory, but to a man, we preferred it to losing. Later that night we left the office eager to return early the next day.

The lead story in the next day's *Washington Post* was not what we expected—"3 Americans' Particle Research Wins Nobel"—and the only apology George could offer was chagrin. The *Post* had held the story, but the rumor of it had been unleashed, and later that day the stock market took a dive as Wall Street calculated the cost of losing a Republican White House. The stocks came back up when investors were assured that no such story would run, and it never did.[21]

Even more shocking was what happened the following evening. Word got back to us through Kirk that Dukakis had taken a liking to the material Savitz and I submitted, with the help of any number of funny people who had pitched ideas in our office or over the phone. We tuned in to C-SPAN that night to watch our guy generate laughter sans helmet.

It's a great pleasure to be here, in this beautiful ballroom, before this magnificent assembly, on an evening when all thought of politics is banished and I can concentrate on what I do best—humor.

---

20. My self-righteous temper tantrum earlier in this chapter regarding the practice of spreading unproven rumors by way of referencing previously published reports prevents me from providing you with details. Damn.

21. Later that day, a high-ranking Dukakis staffer, Donna Brazile, frustrated that the rumor had not taken hold, gave our campaign a black eye by repeating it and demanding the vice president "fess up"—but in the end only succeeded in bringing about her own resignation. It was not a proud day for our team.

. . . What's so funny about that?

Tonight, the rest of America is watching the fifth game of the World Series. Only we Red Sox and Mets fans made other plans.

Now, I've been told that I lack passion, but that doesn't bother me one way or the other.

Some people say I am arrogant, but I know better.

And there are even those who say I am a technocrat, but it's less than 15 percent.

Mr. Vice President, I'm glad to see you here tonight. You've said that you want to give America back to the little guy. Mr. Vice President, I am that man.

No one was happy to see November arrive, with our campaign officially in the ninth inning and down by a healthy rally's worth of runs. The debates behind us, the polls immune to significant change, the only hope we had was the prospect of the greatest political comeback in American history. Every time George hung up from one of his whispered phone conversations, one of us would ask hopefully, "Is it over?" As the days dwindled down, Dukakis headquarters had turned from hotbed to hospice, and each day there was less and less to do. All we had left was waiting it out and spinning ourselves.[22]

---

22. Sample Delusional Talking Point Entries from Inside the Bunker:

- MOVEMENT: Just as voters take a second look at the candidates, they are listening to MSD fighting for their economic interests and rejecting Bush's campaign of cynicism and lies. Last night's ABC/*Washington Post* poll shows only 8 points between MSD and Bush.
- TAKING A SECOND LOOK: Dukakis's free media campaign is working: the ratings for Koppel and the recent PBS special on the history of the candidates were very high, showing voters are still trying to make up their minds.
- SURGING: Reagan Democrats are coming home. MSD is moving in all the key states he needs to win.

Kirk, our usual connection to information and insight, was not in the building but on "the plane"—shorthand for the road show that flew to events from state to state—calling in to us whenever he needed a line or a laugh. The last three days before Election Day had been turned into round-the-clock traveling from key state to key state. Thanks to the modern science of polling, it was accepted fact that we were going to lose, and the only thing that hung in the balance was how much we could energize our own base and thus reduce the gap. This process was hopefully called "The Surge."

I was asleep in my apartment in Boston when the campaign had dwindled down to T minus 50 hours, but Kirk was on the plane flying north off the coast of Oregon. So deep was my sleep that when the phone rang, I did not recognize it as the sound of a phone until the fourth ring, and, upon picking it up, did not recognize Kirk's distinctive voice until the second sentence.

"Mark," he shouted over the roar of jet engines, "we are landing in Seattle in fifteen minutes for a tarmac rally and we need a line for Dukakis to say. I'll call you back in ten minutes."

Okay, now I was awake.

In those frantic minutes, I wrote eight jokes on the back of a bank statement. Five were non sequiturs, two were cogent and one was funny. When Kirk called back, I read him the funny one, premised on an earlier squabble between the Dukakis and Bush campaigns over the number and format of the candidate debates, which the Bushies were eager to duck.

You know the Bush campaign's original proposal called for a single debate on November third at two in the morning on the tarmac of the Seattle International Airport. Well, here I am! Where is George?

Kirk's thunderous response—"That's great! That's terrific!"— made me feel like I had single-handedly preserved The Surge. The next day and a half would determine if my joke was funny enough to make up 8 points in the national polls, within a margin of error of +/–3 percent.

When Election Day finally came to Chauncey Street, it was greeted like dawn on death row. Our squad huddled around the keyboard for what we thought would be our final Election Day Talking Points and could not come up with anything more heartening than this: "If there was ever going to be a great political comeback, this is exactly what it would feel like on the morning of." What we didn't write was that the "it" was the urge to flush your head in a toilet.

Our Last Supper came at lunchtime, as a large group of staffers spent a good portion of what would be their last paycheck on a blowout feast at Legal Seafood, as though we could harden our shells for the next twelve hours by ingesting crustaceans. On the way back to Chauncey Street, I stopped into a deli-mart and purchased a Mass Millions lottery ticket, thinking that even a faint hope for the future might help me make it through the night ahead. It was right around then that I progressed to the next stage of loss, bargaining with God.

The long walk back from lunch was even longer because I took a route that would avoid passing the lobby of 98 Chauncey Street; my old nemesis Tex would have relished an encounter with me on this difficult day. I entered the lobby of 105 Chauncey Street and rode the elevator two flights up. I was not prepared for what happened next.

I stepped out of the elevator to find the second floor abuzz with excitement. The first person I asked told me something that made no sense: "You're not going to believe this. We are still in this thing!"

What?

I ran back to the communications office to see what was up. ABC had shared early reports of their own internal polling, and it had us doing better than we had any right to hope.

Although we had known for at least a week that we were not

going to win, a far-fetched winning scenario was still an abstract possibility: if Dukakis won every state where he was within 5 points of Bush, we could get to 270 electoral votes—the equivalent of running the table. ABC's numbers had us tantalizingly close to that very scenario. The campaign was already forty minutes into a desperate last-minute effort, scrambling to book satellite interviews of Dukakis on afternoon newscasts in key states and coordinating an organized telephone campaign urging likely Democrats in key states to go to the polls before they closed. Chauncey Street was suddenly buzzing like it was Super Tuesday.

The only person in the building who had not jumped headfirst into the pool was sitting at the desk perpendicular to mine. George had come back early from lunch to check in with the networks, and was in fact the person who had brought the ABC numbers to the campaign's attention. But he did not believe them. In the time since, he had continued working the phones, calling his contacts at the network polling units. CBS, NBC and CNN all had Bush ahead comfortably and laughed at the idea that the ABC numbers were accurate. In fact, it was an open joke in those circles that ABC's polling numbers were always wrong.

"Guys, it's over," he said, consciously echoing the phrase from a few days earlier that had the four of us hugging each other in glee. Undeterred, Savitz and I accumulated some spin from the powers that be and pumped out one last issue of Talking Points, obviously written by two people who had been sucking too hard on the pipe of false hope:

Talking Points, 6:00 P.M. EST

- MSD is on the verge of a historic upset. America will not know who its next president will be until very late tonight.

- Americans are fed up with the Bush campaign of lies and distortions. Bush's negative campaign simply ran out of steam.
- Dukakis's message—that he and Lloyd Bentsen are on the side of working families—has obviously gotten through to the voters. When it came time for America's working families to enter the voting booth they decided that Michael Dukakis was on their side.
- Dukakis did an hour of live television this evening to some of the key battleground states. This reflects the fact that the election is very close and that millions of Democrats and working Americans have yet to vote.
- States like Montana, Colorado, South Dakota could make all the difference. The large states are too close to call. We are surging.

Then, on the bottom of the page, in large handwritten block letters, was the final, desperate, hopeful call to action:

GET OUT THE VOTE!!!

We printed it out and handed it to Peterson, who dashed to the fax machine as if each second mattered. Savitz and I were pumped and ready to do more, whatever was required. We grabbed a call sheet of likely voters in western states and began working our way down the lists; in the next forty minutes, I personally spoke to more people from South Dakota than I had previously or have since, reminding them to get to the polls before they closed at eight.

On that day, I chose willful disbelief over the reasoned voice of a smart, dispassionate Greek guy, and I will always be glad that I did. After thirteen months of workdays that started at dawn and ended at midnight, having reason to believe that we might actually win on Election Day was its own reward—let the aftermath be damned.

The aftermath began not ten seconds after 7 P.M. sharp, when a large group of reenergized staffers gathered around the press office televisions to watch the network evening news. Dan Rather intoned that CBS was projecting a comfortable Bush victory. Throughout the fall, Rather had become a crowd favorite to those of us who congregated around the bank of televisions for the evening news, as it was our opinion that he could barely disguise his antipathy for Bush. Tonight's news, as bad as it was, was better for having been delivered by someone we considered a friend. Nevertheless, the heartbroken staffers soon dispersed, not bothering to wait for a Peter Jennings rebuttal on ABC that would never come.

Now it was over.

The open bar at the Election Night "party" at the Parker House Hotel was more open than most, and I soon found myself holding my own bottle of gin. Back in the day of fraternity keg parties, I was well known among the fratschmucks for my ability to nurse a beer, but on this night, the alcohol was tending to me. I was standing there quietly brooding, next to Savitz, Stephanopoulos and Peterson, when a roving band of well-known political scribes joined our cluster. (One of them was Joe Klein, if memory serves, but my brain was pretty pickled at the time.)

Someone made the mistake of asking how I was doing. By this point, my blood alcohol level had risen to the point where my vestigial Brooklyn accent became more pronounced, and I responded to his innocuous question with a long soliloquy of hard-edged humor. Some of my material was probably good enough to be worth remembering for future use, but I was in no condition to operate a writing utensil. In fact, for all I remember, the words coming out of my mouth a mile a minute might not have been funny at all, but the overall picture of a drunk, angry campaign joke writer spewing forth like Mussolini on the balcony seemed to generate some amusement. Of my few specific memories of that night, I vividly recall George standing three feet away with an amazed smile on his face that indicated he was enjoying the show I was putting on. A moment later, his fraternal instincts kicked in and he interrupted me for my own good to say something to the reporters, who were now hanging on every word of my discursive comedy diatribe.

"Guys, everything Katz says tonight is off the record, understood?"

They agreed, if only out of compassion for someone so painfully drunk and defeated. A minute later, my audience had scattered. I continued to drink and spew my comic venom to no one in particular, and before the long night was over, I would also spew the remnants of my $60 oysters/chowder/lobster *fra diavalo* lunch.

The day after losing a presidential election is its own level of hell—and not improved upon with a bottom-shelf gin hangover. To make matters worse, I did not win the lottery. I was one of many staffers who headed into Chauncey Street in the early afternoon because, quite honestly, many of us had nowhere else to go. Upon arrival, I was startled to see the degree to which long-entrenched offices and cubicles had already been disassembled. I was the first one in the sound-bite shop that day. If I was still working my way through denial, I wasn't the only one. Some poor press office schmuck with my old job had come in that morning to do the clips, which were sitting on my desk and filled with news articles that read like obituaries. The second person who walked into our office was not Sav, or George or Peterson. It was Jack Corrigan. I reflexively snapped to attention, unable to process the fact that there was nothing a hard-boiled deputy campaign commandant could do to me now. But even if I had, I would have been wrong.

"Hey Katz, you did good work here."

"Thanks, Jack," was my startled response.

"Especially the work in the general when you were a deputy communications director."

"I wasn't a deputy communications director," I said. I was

confused. I didn't know what my title was, but that wasn't it. I had yet to realize I had just been promoted after the fact.

"Yes you were. That's what you should put on your résumé."

"I can do that?"

"Yeah, you can do that," he said with barely a hint of a smile. "If anyone has anything to say about it, you have them call me."

I was as surprised by the new title as I was by the warmth of our conversation. If it was meant to make me feel better, it worked. As Corrigan turned to leave the room, probably on his way to the ninth floor to anoint a new deputy Midwest field director, I pushed the limits of a newfound friendship.

"Hey Jack, is there a retroactive raise involved?"

He took me in one last time. "You don't know how to quit when you're ahead, do you?"

The healing process continued when the others showed up and we decided to put out the final issue of the campaign talking points, the familiar morning ritual for as many mornings as I could remember. But on this day, there was nothing left to spin but spin itself.

Daily Talking Point, Wednesday November 9, 1988

• Mike Dukakis only lost the presidential election once. Adlai Stevenson lost twice!

We printed it out, posting the first copy on the door to our office, and then set off with the second copy to deliver to Kirk, on the hunch that he could use a laugh and that we could stand to hear it.

The four of us had come to the office that day wearing the T-shirts and sweatpants of defeat; Kirk may have been the only person in the building still wearing a shirt and tie. Upon seeing us standing outside his office, Kirk finished up a phone call and waved us in for one last meeting. "Come in here, you guys, I want to talk to you."

Like all the memorable meetings of the last few months, this one began with the closing of the door, sealing off a temporary cocoon. Kirk's mood was upbeat. The deep loss the rest of us were still processing, he had already clarified.

"I want you to understand what happened here. We lost to a pretty weak candidate playing a very strong hand. Reagan is still very popular, and so is peace and prosperity. And the only way we were ever going to win this thing was to run a damn-near perfect campaign and *then* catch a break," he said, starting to laugh. "And—as you guys know—that did not happen."

Kirk went on to point out that our own unofficial campaign slogan—*The best America is yet to come*—practically conceded the point: in 1988, most people thought they already had a pretty good America, and had voted to give Ronald Reagan's third term to George Bush when Mike Dukakis failed to create a mandate for change.

Then, in the same serious tone of a hundred meetings when we thought the future election could be won or lost, he had one more important thing to say: "Listen to me. This is not over between us." At his prompt, we huddled. In fact, we hugged. As the rest of Chauncey Street was being packed away in boxes, Kirk wanted us to know that our team had created something more lasting, that he was proud of the work we'd done together and that we should be too. Sav, George, Peterson and I left his office with our heads high, while Kirk packed up his things to fly back to Washington later that day.

A half hour later, my head still pounding from the night before, I set out to the elevator to find some kind of over-the-counter remedy. The elevator door opened and Kirk was in front of me, suit bag in hand on his way to the airport. Maybe it was slightly awkward to see him again, so soon after our male equivalent of a poignant farewell embrace. But in the minutes in between, I had thought up a joke I had yet to try out.

"Hey Kirk, I got Dukakis's sound bite for tomorrow's papers."

"Yeah? Let's hear it."

"*I have not yet begun to fight.*"

Pay dirt. Kirk's roaring laughter simultaneously warmed my heart and rattled my hangover, and with the last few raucous beats, he rolled out the words, "That's terr-ific! That's terr-ific!"

CHAPTER SIX

A Different Kind
of Campaign

"THERE ARE NO RULES IN ADVERTISING."

These were the words that the short man in Dockers pants printed across the chalkboard as the class began. Twenty people in various stages of career crisis dutifully wrote them down. Seated in the back of the classroom (old habit had taken me there), I smiled to myself. This sentence spoke directly to my inner anarchist in a way that reinforced my recent decision to pursue a career as an advertising copywriter.

This was February of 1989, three months since I had left Boston and returned to the suburbs of New York to reclaim the bedroom I grew up in. For the first six weeks of campaign detox, I engaged in an intense regimen of sleeping until noon, watching television until midnight and, at least once a day, heating up a Stouffer's French bread pizza. My twenty-fifth birthday had come and gone, and I had yet to figure out what I was going to do next. But these lost weeks were more productive than even I knew. The more hours of TV that I watched, the more I found myself paying attention to the commercials. As my subconscious pondered my future, I arrived at the same thought that has dawned on almost every person who has ever sat down in front of a television set: "Hey! I can write stuff as good as this crap!"

The impulse was reinforced each Tuesday at 10 P.M. Having resisted an *L.A. Law*–induced legal career earlier in the decade, my weakened conditioned left me vulnerable to another well-watched career/lifestyle showcase, a show called *thirtysomething*. Michael and Elliot, a creative team in an advertising agency, dressed as they pleased, engaged in witty banter, espoused trite liberal bullshit, experienced generational angst and played Nerf basketball throughout the course of their eventful days–and then drove their Saabs back to their nice homes and gorgeous wives. Now these were the role models I needed! Perhaps it was one of the actual commercials that punctuated the show, thirty seconds of wind and rustling leaves that purported to be about an Infiniti sedan, that helped me to finalize the decision.

The more I thought about it, the more sense it made. Advertising was the perfect way to continue to develop my recently discovered snappy writing skills in a way that did not require 270 electoral votes. What I did not know was that I was not yet qualified even to be *rejected* for a job in advertising.

Ad agencies, it turned out, required would-be copywriters to present a portfolio of make-believe ads, fifteen or twenty hand-sketches for products, real or imagined. This portfolio was the only résumé anyone cared to see, analyzed by those who might hire you as though they were X-rays of your innate ability to think and write. Generating sample ads for such a portfolio was the purpose of this class I had signed up for, a night course in advertising copywriting. And the rule written on the board, "There are no rules in advertising," was the industry's attempt to indoctrinate the next generation with its favorite maxim about itself–that each new ad has the obligation to break through the collective clutter of every other ad, and that those who write them have the license to create something unlike anything they've ever seen before.[1]

Upon entering the lobby of the School for Visual Arts, I came across a sign that identified the building on East Twenty-third Street as the former home of the NYU Dental School, my father's alma mater. I stopped and stared, identifying the moment as a milepost on a crooked career path that had taken its first sharp left turn when, at age fourteen, I declined to pick up the torch of suburban orthodontics.

The first assignment for this class was to produce a print that advertised yourself. After all, these classes were designed to help you get your first job in advertising, and the product you were selling to agencies was yourself. That was the week I wrote my first ad and, simultaneously, sold out the very man I had spent the previous year promoting.[2]

This would be my next eight months: living at my parents' house, working on my portfolio by day and driving into Manhattan to take classes at night. Each class brought assignments for new products (Zippo lighters, BMW motorcycles, Dial liquid soap,

---

1. Yet somehow, each new day, another product proudly asserts that it is "improving [something], one [whatever] at a time."

2. Abandoning your principles is compulsory for admission to the advertising business.

Timex watches). Each retail item I encountered in the course of my day was catalogued as an assignment I might give myself (Panasonic TVs, Casio digital diaries, Trident gum, Stouffer's French bread pizzas).[3] Each ad I saw or read was studied and rewritten in my head; the creation of my portfolio had turned me into a full-time unemployed copywriter. I transformed my bedroom into a studio filled with sketch pads, Magic Markers, various epoxies and glues, advertising trade publications and print ads ripped from magazines. Eventually, I had amassed enough spec ads to meet the threshold of a portfolio, and I began the process of shopping it around to New York's many ad agencies, learning the streets of Manhattan as I never had before.

Not very long after that, I could hardly believe my ears when I heard my mother hollering from the bottom of the stairs: "Mark, there is a Richard Kirshenbaum on the phone for you . . ."

My mother probably assumed that Richard Kirshenbaum was just another Jewish kid I knew from school or summer camp, but he was, in fact, one of the hottest names in advertising. His agency, Kirshenbaum & Bond, was all that people in advertising (and those on its outskirts) were talking about that month. Three weeks earlier, *New York* magazine had run a four-page spread about their smart and smart-alecky ad campaigns for Kenneth Cole, among others. Suddenly, everyone in my advertising classes was eager to work there, including myself. The day that I dropped off my recently completed portfolio at their downtown offices, I placed it on a pile that was already four feet high before the clock had even struck noon.

"Hi Mark, this is Richard Kirshenbaum from Kirshenbaum & Bond."

"Hello!"

---

3. It was during this learning-curve period that I wrote what might be the worst advertising headline ever put to paper. The product: Elan Frozen Yogurt. The headline: *All the flavor that Häagen-Dazs, Takes out the fat that Häagen-Dazn't.*

"I looked at your portfolio and saw some stuff that I liked. I wonder if you would be available to come in and work on a free-lance assignment for us this week."

This was better than I had hoped. Richard Kirshenbaum of Kirshenbaum & Bond was calling me not just for an interview, but for an actual job! He seemed pleased, though not surprised, when I blurted out "Yes!" But this wasn't good enough for me, and I pressed him further.

"By the way, which ads in my portfolio did you like?"

This may be my signature character flaw as a writer: no one loves positive feedback more than I do. Any person who has ever said a remotely kind thing about something I've written immediately becomes a focus group of one, prodded for more specific and flattering responses. My query changed the tone of his voice.

"I don't remember. I looked at it yesterday. We get a lot of portfolios in here, you know."

I backed off the question, asked him what time he wanted me there and got off the phone without having my very first advertising job offer rescinded. The next call I made was to my brother Bruce, asking if I could stay on the couch in his apartment for the remainder of the week. Bruce was thirty years old, a young attorney living in a small, one-bedroom apartment on the Upper East Side. He had recently broken off his engagement to a loud and unpleasant woman, so he was especially happy to have the company. That night, my father drove me into Manhattan and dropped me off at my brother's apartment.

I arrived at the downtown offices of Kirshenbaum & Bond at 10 A.M. the next day, determined to do my best work and make my best impression. As it turned out, I was one of eight or nine fledgling freelancers who had been called in for various assignments. In the aftermath of the *New York* magazine article, the agency had been asked to pitch more business than it could handle, so they were rounding up migrant copywriters and putting them to work for $100 a week.[4] Before long, I was in my very first creative brief, a meeting where an associate creative director told us about this week's assignment, El Presidente brandy. Everyone around the table got to know one another a little better as we each took a swig of the product out of plastic cups and then took turns describing its taste. (My favorite: "NyQuil-gone-bad.")

Looking around the room, I noticed that I was the only person not wearing black. In fact, every person I'd seen since walking off the elevator was dressed practically the same way, not just in black shirts but in black pants as well. I was wearing pressed khaki pants and a knit royal blue sweater with a red polo shirt underneath it; on my feet were brown, sans-style Top-Siders. No wonder I stood out: I was an un-updated, primary-colored collegiate dresser in a downtown, black-on-black Prada world.

The next morning, I got out of the shower after Bruce had left and scavenged through his closet looking for anything darker than green. Reaching my arm deep into a pile of clothes, I pulled out a black wool sweater with a single oversized argyle of beige and gray. Instead of khakis, I put on Bruce's darkest denim jeans. Then, thanks to a pair of ultra-thin socks, I squeezed my feet into Bruce's silver-buckled black boots—a full size too small—and set off for the subway.

During my second day in advertising, I began to experience the euphoria of my first real advertising job. This day began not with anxious moments in a waiting room but rather with reporting to a desk that had been assigned to me. I knew my way around the agency, I was dressed like those around me—and, after many months of hard work, I was finally part of the process of generating ideas with professional colleagues at the white-hot epicenter of New York's advertising scene. That feeling lasted all the way until noon. Passing the waiting area outside the elevators while on my way to a 12:15 meeting in the glass-walled conference room, I saw some-

---

4. Seriously.

thing that stopped me in my tracks: Stacey, my brother's ex-fiancée. It was as strange an encounter as any disconnected plot point that might occur in the deep stages of REM. The situation was (slightly) more confusing than awkward, and both of us struggled to understand what the other was doing there. I explained that I had been hired for a freelance assignment. Stacey told me she had stopped by for lunch with her good friend from college, Richard Kirshenbaum.

This was not good.

Not surprisingly, the break-off of Bruce and Stacey's engagement had unleashed ill will from all sides and generated a number of predictable aftershocks. Still to be resolved was the situation involving an unreturned engagement ring held as collateral against the nonrefundable bookings of a caterer and a band. In the months afterward, the hardball tactics of hostile lawyers, Bruce among them, had ratcheted the situation up. I made my way to the conference room behind glass walls, where we were assembling to present initial ideas for El Presidente, but I was distracted by the encounter I had just had and how it might affect my career as a copywriter at Kirshenbaum & Bond.

A moment later, Richard Kirshenbaum, dressed in black and off-black, arrived at the waiting room to greet his dear old friend and lunch date. I watched Stacey's lips as she mouthed my name and then my brother's. Richard's mouth dropped open and then formed the words "That's Bruce's *brother*!" in an *oh-my-God!* manner that suggested he was well informed of the situation. He shifted his body to take me in through his peripheral vision, caught my eye and looked away. I watched each beat of their incredulous pantomime as the conversation progressed. Then the talking stopped. Richard walked resolutely into the conference room, suspending the meeting in midsentence, and addressed me directly.

"You are wearing Stacey's sweater."

No one around the conference table knew what he was talking about, including me. But a full-body neurological hiccup prevented me from responding.

"That's Stacey's sweater," he repeated.

"It is?" I asked.

"She wants her sweater back."

The look on his face told me he wasn't kidding. My eyes glazed over; my brainwaves downshifted to stupor.

"She'd like it back right now."

I stood up and pulled the sweater over my head, exposing the better part of an unsculpted belly and leaving me red-faced and hair-mussed in a not-black, not-clean Nike T-shirt with pronounced, freshly dampened armpit circles.[5] I believe that this was the lasting impression I made, and at the end of the week, for whatever reason, I was not invited back.

Updated with my unused spec ads for an off-brand brandy—*El Presidente. Get drunk with power!*—my portfolio returned to the market. I continued taking classes, creating new material and circulating my portfolio to Manhattan agencies that I knew were good or might be hiring. The more my portfolio improved, the more encouraging responses and informational interviews I got—but still, no offer for a job. Then, on a lark, and with an upcoming family trip in mind, I sent one of my portfolios to a very good agency 3,000 miles away that had gotten a lot of headlines after landing a huge new account. The trip was to San Francisco to attend the surprise fiftieth birthday party my Aunt Doris was throwing for my Uncle Stanley; the agency was the well-regarded Hal Riney & Partners; and the account was the most sought-after assignment that had come along in a decade, the launch of a new car company called Saturn.

Hal Riney & Partners had won the account on the strength of its warm, feel-good-Americana ads for clients like Bartles & Jaymes,

---

5. Let's not forget to add to the list of indignities that I was wearing a woman's sweater. I seem to recall thinking that morning that Anne Klein was probably a Calvin Klein knockoff.

Alamo cars and Gallo wines. The agency had been built on the shoulders of its namesake, Hal Riney, a living legend whose name had been transformed into an industry adjective—"Rineyesque"— to describe the lump-in-your-throat commercials that were his trademark. His soothing heartland voice, which narrated many of the agency's ads, made the commercials all the more compelling and distinctive. Not knowing any better, I sent my portfolio to Hal Riney himself—a bit like calling up and asking to speak to J. Walter Thompson. But a week or so later, my mother was yelling up another name from the bottom of the stairs:

"Mark, there is a Curvin O'Rielly on the phone for you . . ."[6]

Curvin O'Rielly, I was about to learn, was the recently named creative director of the Saturn account. He called to tell me that he had seen my portfolio and liked it, and he invited me to stop by when I came out to San Francisco. I did, and at the end of the meeting he offered me a job. It was just that easy. As it turned out, I had spent the better part of a year looking for a job in the wrong city.

There's a chance I may have walked away from the Dukakis debacle and the long period of unemployment that followed having learned the wrong lesson. At this particular moment in my life, I was nearly certain that I was a genius. On the heels of my ascent from volunteer news clipper to "deputy communications director," I had, in a relatively short amount of time, assembled a portfolio that got my foot in the door at one of the best ad agencies in the country and then walked away with a prized job. I went home to New York to pack up my stuff and made it back out to San Francisco in less than two weeks. I came back to the West Coast with every expectation that my recent past would be prologue—and that, in the course of my experience there, I would continue this brisk pace along the fast track to produce brilliant material and lay the groundwork for a fabulous career. By the time I showed up for my first day of work as a

6. I really needed to get my own phone line.

junior copywriter on the Saturn account, I was a person who might be described as a confident young man. You could also make a convincing case that I was an insufferably cocky punk.[7]

I arrived outside Curvin's office in the midst of an early-in-the-day crisis. The agency had won the Saturn account four months earlier with a campaign that would be centered around this tagline: *A different kind of company. A different kind of car.* But that morning, news had broken that an ad campaign from another car company threatened to steal some of the line's thunder: Ford Taurus was about to run ads with a tag something like, *A car of a different kind.* This sent shock waves through the agency, and a call went out for possible replacement taglines.

Curvin cut his welcome speech short and instructed me to write as many taglines as I could and come back to him in an hour. The assignment released a flood of adrenaline and prompted a vivid flashback to my days on the Rapid Response Team, with Curvin O'Rielly as Kirk O'Donnell. Even I knew that coining a tagline for a major account was the stuff careers were made of, and at that moment it was within the realm of possibility that I might make mine in my first hour on the job. Curvin's assistant, Marcia, showed me to the cubicle that had been set aside for me. I pulled out the chair, fired up the state-of-the-art Mac Plus computer on the desk, and wrote out the tagline that I had to find a way to re-express: *Saturn. A different kind of company. A different kind of car.* I typed out the word "Saturn" and then plunked down a period.

Okay. Now it was time to fill in the blank.

Having spent nearly every day of the past two years trawling my brain for killer sound bites, headlines and taglines, I had developed a set of mental exercises that amounted to a personal technique. My routine begins with the assumption that the

---

7. How else would you describe someone who had arrived for his first full-time job in advertising but had already selected the adjective that would one day be applied to his body of work? ("Katzian")

crafted-by-God-silver-bullet perfect line already exists, floating in the far reaches of the universe and waiting for me to track it down. As I set out to find it, I consider myself more a detective than a writer, and the deductive process leads me to extract what clues I can. I imagine I've just heard IT (God's crack at this thing), and I try to experience the visceral response it elicits. Am I smiling? Laughing? Nodding my head in concurrence? Feeling tingly up and down my spine? Do I like the person or company who said it? Yes/No? Why/Why not? My body becomes a tuning fork in search of the tone that makes me resonate. And, of course, I do all of this with my head buried deep in the palms of my hands, rocking myself gently as I mumble stray words to myself. What appears to others as a breakdown or a one-man séance is actually my way of generating work-product. It was the making of this elaborate Zen-bullshit methodology over time (which, by the way, does actually help me come up with stuff) that reinforced my self-image as a truly gifted prodigy.

In the course of this exercise, my head popped up to tap out notes on the keyboard. Most were just free-association reformulations of all the standard-issue clichés that tried too hard to resonate: *Saturn. The New American Car . . . Saturn. Reinventing the wheels . . . Saturn. Built new from the ground up . . . Saturn. New ideas on wheels . . . Saturn. Still has that new car company smell.*

In the process of writing dozens of lines no more inspired than these, I found a few others written mostly for my own amusement.[8] But before the hour was out, I arrived at the burning-bush moment that I had sought, receiving a gift from the oracle, and beheld its brilliance:

Saturn. *Neo automotive americanus.*

---

8. Saturn. Hand-built by Hillbillies.
   Saturn. GM? What's GM?
   Saturn. It's not your father's Chevette.
   Saturn. Remember Pearl Harbor.

To me, it expressed everything I had been struggling to com-municate—that this car was a new, more highly evolved species of the American vehicle—and what better way to announce it than with the language of taxonomy itself! Staring into the screen and taking in the tagline's magnificence, I honestly believed that before lunch on my first day in advertising I had just written the new tagline for the Saturn account. I am not kidding.

I printed out the list and made my way to Curvin's office. I placed the sheet on his desk and, apologizing for the first twenty attempts, directed his attention to the last entry, which I had printed in bold italics for added emphasis.

"What's this? I don't get it."

I didn't understand what he didn't get, so I read it aloud. *"Neo automotive americanus."*

"What's that? Latin?"

"Yes, it's the classification of genus and species," I offered matter-of-factly. I refrained from mentioning the name of Carl Linnaeus, the father of modern taxonomy, whose system of binomial nomenclature was one of the few things I remembered from A.P. Biology. (Also, the Krebs cycle.) But I was quietly very pleased that these many years later I could recall the name "Carl Linnaeus," as well as the term "binomial nomenclature."

Curvin gave me a long look through his thick glasses, which made moon-pies of his eyeballs: "Katz, this is your first day, so I am going to fill you in on something: we write our ads here in English. This isn't going to be a problem for you, is it?"

Maybe there were some rules in advertising I needed to learn after all.

The fact was, I did pretty well in my first few months in both a new city and a new career. I had found a great studio apartment in my favorite section of the city, North Beach, which was the best approximation of my native New York: dirty, loud, congested and brimming with authentic Italian and Chinese food. My Aunt

Doris introduced me to a lovely young woman, the daughter of family friends, and soon I had a girlfriend who could show me around. But more to the point, I was accomplishing what I had set out to do, to get my advertising career off to a promising start. While the account's senior creatives (the agency's real *thirtysomethings*) were all busy writing, pitching and shooting the first round of sixty-second spots to launch the car and the company—the advertising equivalent of a feature film—I cut my teeth writing print ads that fell through the cracks. Many were small ads that ran in trade publications and local dealership circulars.

On slow days, I would find myself sitting across from Curvin's desk, talking about advertising. Curvin liked to lecture, and I liked to listen. Before too long, I had been handed a plum assignment, to write one in a series of national print ads that would introduce the car to the American buying public. Six weeks after that, I autographed copies of ads I had written that were featured in *Time* and *Newsweek* and sent them to my parents as evidence that I was finally a professional copywriter. I hoped that this subtle hint might discourage them from forwarding the law school brochures that were still showing up in the mail.

I was following the Dukakis Plan, working as hard as I could, doing the best work that I was capable of and waiting for my big break to come. One Monday morning, I arrived at my cubicle to learn that things were about to change. Curvin had been fired. This was an important lesson for a greenhorn like me: unceremonious firings are a very common management tool in the high-pressure, highly subjective atmosphere of advertising, and the only thing that had prepared me for these kinds of tenuous employment conditions was growing up as a fan of George Steinbrenner's Yankees. Curvin had cleaned out his office and headed out of town before I even got a chance to thank him for hiring me.

Later that week, we were introduced to our new creative director. Ken was maybe forty and had a thin build and a thick beard. He was soft-spoken but sharp, and he had a reputation as a first-rate writer. Like everyone else in the group who now worked under him, I was eager to show him that I was a talent, too.

From the day he arrived, Ken clearly had a lot on his plate. He had taken the reins of a $100 million account that would make front-page headlines in the trades, whether the work was terrific or terrible. It made perfect sense that he would have little time to take an interest in a junior copywriter at the bottom of his roster. This truth, however, did not stop me from regularly knocking on his door.

Maybe I had just gotten too accustomed to my own good fortune in recent years, working for people older and wiser who saw a spark of talent and took an interest in me. Maybe that's why I looked at Ken and saw my next mentor. Anyone who was smart and talented would be able to see that I was, too. But with each desperate attempt of mine to dazzle Ken with my work, I walked away sensing that I had only confirmed his impression that I had a very high opinion of myself.

This was the beginning of a very bad dynamic. Word had gotten back to me that Ken thought I was arrogant, and I could tell that depending on his mood, he found me either mildly entertaining or genuinely annoying. This only made me try harder, which only made him less inclined to be impressed. Soon, I was demonstrating my passion for advertising by arguing strenuously for the ideas I held dear, and I made my case in an assertive New York style that made me stand out from my "whatever, dude" California colleagues. Eventually, word got back to me that Ken thought I was a pain in the ass. No matter how desperately I wanted Ken to take me under his wing, I was in the process of finding out that he was not the nurturing kind. My luck had run out. Ken was the anti-Kirk.

I may have been the only person in the building who missed Curvin O'Rielly. It had taken me six months to realize how unlikely it was that I had ever arrived there in the first place, and the fact that Curvin had hired me brought me greater insight into the reasons he might have been fired. As a workplace, Riney was fundamentally northern Californian, vaguely Presbyterian and distinctly Republican, none of the adjectives a person would use to describe me. Hal himself was well-known as a rock-ribbed Republican, and so too was his cadre of lieutenants. In fact, some of his most memorable work had been for President Ronald Reagan. Hal Riney was both the author and the voice of the "It's morning again in America" ads that are still regarded as some of the finest political advertising ever produced. And as time went on, it made less and less sense that a wiseass Jewish Democrat from New York had ever been assigned a cubicle in his agency.

There was more to Hal Riney's agency than met the eye. Starting late in the afternoon, at around 5 P.M. on most days, senior-level people could be seen taking a walk in the direction of a well-stocked liquor cabinet in the executive suite lounge and returning to their office, drink in hand. Twenty minutes later, many of them would retrace their steps. By 6 or 6:30, a small crowd of people would have assembled—the older men who ran the place and some of the young, attractive women who were in-house producers or personal assistants—and by nightfall the fourth floor would have taken on the furtive atmosphere and boozy aroma of a swanky hotel bar.[9]

But there was also a contingent of nonsocial drinkers, those who quietly mixed their drinks and returned to their offices to put in late hours. This was Ken's category. Slowly but surely, Ken's habits began to redefine the workday of everyone in the group. The later we worked, the later we'd come in the next day. Eventually, people were getting in around noon and doing some work in the afternoon only to watch it redone, reassigned or killed altogether in the hours leading up to midnight, one or two. This environment was all foreign to me, because I came from a family of eaters, not drinkers, and had always been something of a morning person. But when

---

9. I may have been more aware of these workplace conditions because I was taping the Clarence Thomas–Anita Hill hearings and watching them on weekends.

Ken stayed late, as he almost always did, it was hard to know which option was safer: to stick around or to call it a day. Usually I stayed. Never in my life had I put in such long hours to accomplish so little—and I had worked on the Dukakis campaign.

What began as an impossibly exciting venture to a wonderful city to work on a great account had surely and sadly degenerated. The worst days lasted for a few months, as I spent the better part of my afternoons competing with colleagues for the highest Tetris score in the building and waiting in dread for the night shift to begin.

Maybe it was 8 or 9 P.M. one evening in the early fall of '91 when I knocked on Ken's door to present some work. I had tried to get in to see him earlier in the day, but he kept telling me to come back later. In my hand were pages of proposed ideas that fit within an existing campaign for some regional TV spots for local Saturn dealers. Many weeks had passed since an idea of mine had lived through one of these meetings; over time, I argued for my favorite ideas less and less strenuously, as these instincts had yet to serve me well.

The room was completely dark but for the desk lamp that hovered low on the desk, its glare bouncing off the white pages and lighting Ken dramatically from underneath. An arm's reach away, a thick beveled glass was half full with equal parts scotch and ice. I sat in the chair on the other side of his desk and watched as he put his pen to paper and systematically killed everything on the page. But perhaps for the first time, I did not whimper even a word of defense. Maybe I was only projecting my own self-pity, but when he looked up, I thought I saw sympathy in his eyes. And as he handed me back my rejected pages, he offered this in consolation:

"Let me tell you something, Katz—there are no rules in advertising. Only arbitrary decisions made by assholes. Now don't you wish there were rules?"

Ken, the mentor who would not "ment," had just given me the only lesson in advertising I ever needed to learn.

CHAPTER SEVEN

Road Trip to Little Rock

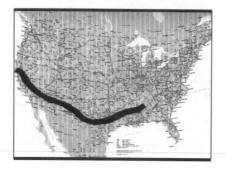

I WAS STRUGGLING TO PENETRATE THE MENTAL FOG BETWEEN SLEEP and consciousness and remember where I was. In the past six days I'd woken up in six different places, and each new morning was a little more disorienting than the last. The first light of this day again had me seeking clues, and it was not until I heard the sound of somebody already in the shower that my whereabouts dawned on me: I was 95 percent certain that I was in Little Rock, Arkansas, sleeping on George Stephanopoulos's sofa.

The weeklong road trip that had started in northern California may have contributed to the blurring of what was real and what was not. Those many days of eight-hour drives in a rented Buick LeSabre were just vivid flashbacks now, like quick-cut scenes set to a grooving soundtrack. The long gorgeous drive down the Pacific Coast Highway with the windows open and the radio blasting. The endless expanse of interior California where lush groves yield the figs, avocados and Brussels sprouts I routinely walk past in the supermarket produce aisle. My self-consciously mystic, predawn excursion to the southern rim of the Grand Canyon to watch the sunrise on Thanksgiving Day. The moonscape desert roads of

New Mexico, where 360 degrees of unobstructed horizon can really freak New Yorkers out. But most of all, the night I spent in Van Horn, Texas, which was the real-life nightmare from which I could not wake up.

Just starting to tire after a full day of driving, I pulled into a border patrol stop a few miles outside of El Paso about an hour after dark. I asked the unsmiling officer whose dog was sniffing the backseat of my car where I might stop for the night if I wanted to drive another hour or so. A town called Van Horn, he told me, and then he waved me back onto Interstate 10 heading east.

An hour later, around 9 P.M., I was pleased to come to the exit sign for Van Horn, as this was my tenth hour on the road. I hit my blinker and pulled off the interstate that had taken me all the way from Phoenix. But at the end of the exit ramp, there were no more visual cues to be had. I'd arrived at an unlit, unmarked road that only paved the way further into the darkness. Assuming that something would present itself soon, I drove down the road, but with each billboard or sign I did not pass I became more confused. "A border patrol guy a hundred miles back sent me *here?*" I asked out loud. For each hundred yards barren of clues, I asked myself that question again—each time with greater incredulity, anger and fear. Eventually I saw some lights and came upon something that was less of a town than a junction. On one corner was a closed diner and on the other, a lit sign that read MOTEL. I pulled into the gravel parking lot and turned off the engine. This, I guessed, had been my destination all along.

I saw a light in an office. I rang a buzzer and a human appeared in the window.

"Excuse me, am I in Van Horn?" I asked the man.

"Sure are."

"And this is a hotel?"

"Motel."

"Motel, right. Okay. Do you have any rooms available?"

That was more of a courtesy than a question; there was only a beat-up Datsun on cinder blocks in the parking lot.

"How much money do you want to spend?"

I did not know what he meant by the question.

"Just the usual amount," I answered, not knowing what that meant, either.

"Do you want a sink and a shower?" he asked.

Oh my God. Where was I?

"It's eight dollars for a room with a shower and five for one without."

I handed the man eight one-dollar bills. He handed me back a piece of paper.

"No thank you, I don't need a receipt," I told him.

"It's not a receipt. You're in number three."

He had handed me a sequence of numbers, the combination to a padlock. Room #3 was one in a series of windowless sheds that were the rooms of this motel, this one in the row of executive suites with heating and plumbing. I tried to remain calm, so as not to give away my fear to anyone who might be watching, but it took my trembling hands numerous attempts to spin the numbers of the padlock to the right combination. On the other side of the door was all the ambience eight dollars got you: garage sale furniture, dingy quilts, a thin mattress, a hot plate and, as advertised, a sink and a shower fit for a campsite. My accommodations looked like a crime scene waiting to happen, and I would have gladly fled if I'd had half an idea of where to go. The only place that came to mind was 100 miles back at the border patrol stop outside El Paso, where I might find the guy with the badge and the dog and ask him: *"Hey—you sent me* here *?!?"*

Seeing no choice but to stay, I settled in for the night—but not before I retrieved the tire iron from the trunk of my car, anticipating that I might need to defend myself in some not-too-hard-to-imagine worst-case scenario. By the bed there was a clock radio—which seemed like the height of luxury—and I turned it on for the comfort of a human voice. Dialing it to the strongest signal I could find, I reached the fire-and-brimstone sermon of a radio-vangelist and took some comfort in the scriptures of God, even one who was not my own. I got beneath the blanket fully clothed and couldn't decide if it was better to keep the light on or turn it off, not knowing which offered the safety I sought. (As I peered out over the covers, I finally made sense of the wall hanging by the door—but to be fair, I had never seen a gun rack before.) Eventually, I found the courage to close my eyes, which only brought on visual images of me sobbing while being forced to dig my own grave by the serial murderer who spent the off-season in room #7. I also imagined that before the night was through I might get to see my old friend Tex. Around 2 A.M., the radio station played the national anthem and went off the air. Even God had left me now, that anti-Semite bastard. In the hour after that, I listened to my own breath while remembering loved ones and revisiting cherished childhood memories. Any sleep I got that night was exceedingly shallow, interrupted by noises real and imagined.

Sometime around 4:30 A.M., I heard the unmistakable sound of a vehicle pulling into the parking lot, its wheels slowly crunching the gravel below. I leapt from the bed, pressed my ear against the door and spent the longest two minutes of my life listening for the cock of a rifle, the buzz of a chainsaw or the sinister laugh of a remorseless killer who'd realized that the driver of a late-model Buick with California plates lost in west Texas was just on the other side of a plywood wall. But the silence alone was terrifying, and after enough of it had passed I grabbed my duffel bag, unlocked the door and raced to the car, swinging a tire iron at anyone who might get in my way. I was still alive, dammit, and it was not too late to get out of Van Horn, Texas, unhacked to death.

I peeled out of that parking lot and found my way back to the exit in the scarce light of the coming day, exhausted by fear and fatigue and buzzing on an emergency packet of No-Doz I kept in the glove compartment. Now my plan was to do the eight-hour drive to Dallas on my personal reserve-tank fuel.

I had been back on the highway for three or four minutes when I came to the road sign announcing the *second* exit to Van Horn, followed by billboards for the colony of Ramadas, Comfort Inns and Motel 6's therein. That's when I realized—and screamed it out loud—*"Wait a minute—a border patrol guy a hundred miles back sent me here!"* I imagine it all might have been quite funny if anyone in the car were in any mood to laugh. Too wired to stop and with a schedule to keep, the scariest night of my life was followed by the most boring day I'd ever lived. Only the choking stench of live-stock penetrated the mind-numbing hours of eyesore flatness between there and Dallas.

George Stephanopoulos was the first familiar face I'd seen in 1,800 miles, and the rented couch in his rented condo was as comfort-able as anything I'd slept on since I had packed my futon and the rest of my belongings and shipped them back to New York. It was the first day of December 1991, ten days since I'd left Riney and a month before I was set to start a new copywriting job back in New York. These weeks in between were a vacation back to my old line of work.

George emerged from the bathroom wrapped in a robe. He bid me good morning with something like this: "I'm outta here in ten minutes if you want to catch a ride with me—or I can write down the directions and you can come in later." Unwilling to get back behind the wheel of an automobile or take the chance of getting lost, I took one of the quickest showers of my life, put on clothes that could pass for clean, and set off with him to do what I'd come all this way for: to spend two weeks working in the head-quarters of the Clinton for President campaign.

The fact that I was now on board with Clinton had more to do with connections than conviction. If George had signed on with

Senator Bob Kerrey,[1] I'd have been just as likely to have road-tripped to Nebraska. A pact we had brokered in the aftermath of the Dukakis campaign was working out well for us both.

In January 1989, I had lunch with George during his brief stop as the top aide to the director of the New York Public Library. I explained to him that because I was preparing my résumé to highlight the (laughable) fact that I wrote jokes for Dukakis, I needed ownership of just one line for an example someone might have heard of. George proposed a deal: he would transfer authorship of that line to me and I would remain available to him for a lifetime of phone consultations on any occasion he or his boss needed a funny line until the day one of us died. Desperate as I was, I took it.[2]

Having traded away the rights to one line for a lifetime's supply, George had snookered me pretty good and called every now and again with a request for a joke on this topic or that. I was actually lucky, though, to be permanently indentured to a guy whose career was in orbit. Soon after the Dukakis Rapid Response Team disbanded, George had graduated from prodigy to player, and the trajectory of his career was a marvel even then. He was all of twenty-eight when he became the top aide to House Majority Leader Richard Gephardt. A profile of him in *Rolling Stone* magazine not only described him as one of the most powerful nonelected people on Capitol Hill but also featured a rock-star-treatment photograph that made him appear tall. In October 1991 he had signed on for a new job even more heady than his last. And when I called him during his first week there to suggest

---

1. He almost did. George Stephanopoulos, *All Too Human* (Boston: Little Brown and Company, 1999), 26.
2. If this anecdote sounds familiar to you, that may be because it can be found on page 263 of a best-selling political memoir. Now that George has reclaimed ownership of that line, I hereby declare myself released from an indentured servitude agreed to under duress.

that I might have the time to come and help out, he did not hang up–a response I found so encouraging that I rented a car and drove for six days straight.

Yet even as I walked through the front door of Clinton's head-quarters with the newly named deputy campaign manager, I did not have strong feelings about Bill Clinton, positive or negative. I had heard the same rumors that everyone else had about his past private life–a "zipper problem" was the delicate phrase that I heard most–and assumed they were neither fabricated from scratch nor a disqualification.[3] But I had also heard him described by people whose opinion I respected–Kirk O'Donnell, Mark Gearan and George as well–as "the real deal." This, more than anything, had brought me all this way.

The aftereffect of the Dukakis campaign had left Democrats like me less principled and more pragmatic. Over the past three years, each time I encountered President George Bush on television I'd mumble under my breath the painful-but-priceless line that made me laugh through my tears when I heard it on a *Saturday Night Live* sketch of the '88 debates: *"I can't believe I'm losing to this guy!"* Even as George Bush skillfully waged a popular war, presided over the fall of communism and registered a 91 percent approval rating, I couldn't forget that back at Chauncey Street we'd once salivated at the prospect of running against him. But the ignominy of the campaign we went on to run followed me everywhere, and I bris-tled at the badge of dishonor that it had become. "The Dukakis campaign" was now pop-culture shorthand for inept campaigning on behalf of an inadequate candidate, and the "Dukakis Cam-paign Rapid Response Team" on my résumé had become a stand-alone punch line. At social functions over the previous few years, I had come to learn that any chitchat in which I mentioned my

---

3. In fact, I had arrived in the week following the first in what would become a series of "bimbo eruptions"–as they came to be known within the campaign–but the allegations by a woman known as "Sweet Connie" were barely a bump in the road.

unlikely credential as that campaign's joke writer would earn me some version of this: *Oh yeah? Are you the guy who put Mike Dukakis in the tank?* For me and for Democrats everywhere, the Dukakis campaign was the curse that kept on giving.

This was the mindset of many as 1992 approached. Even as the economy was sinking, unemployment was rising and deficits were expanding, the most salient statistic for most Democrats was that our team had lost five out of six of the last presidential elections. Among the candidates other than Clinton who were deemed to be "serious," Tom Harkin and Paul Tsongas were smart, principled and good Democrats—but both of their names seemed to fit too neatly into the blank at the end of Humphrey, McGovern, Mondale, Dukakis, _____. In recent years, the term "New Democrat" had entered the lexicon of partisans and pundits as a code word: "new" meant "electable." Clinton was the archetype of this new species, determined to stake out the middle ground. He was southern,[4] pro-death penalty,[5] supported the Gulf War,[6] liked to preach about personal responsibility[7] within the context of welfare and not above advocating a middle-class tax cut[8] despite a large federal deficit, which was seen by some as a tacit concession to trickle-down Reaganomics. New Democrats, as best I could tell, began with the principle that suburban whites and Reagan Democrats (a.k.a. "the forgotten middle class") decided presidential elections and arrived at appealing new policies through the process of deduction.

Not that I was above compromising my principles, either. The fact that Clinton was in favor of the death penalty might once

---

4. Not liberal.
5. Not liberal.
6. Not liberal. (A footnote to the footnote: Actually, he had hedged his bets in a way that would come to be known as "Clintonesque": he "would have voted for the resolution to invade Kuwait" but was "sympathetic" to the arguments made by those who opposed it.)
7. Not liberal.
8. Not liberal.

have been a disqualifying factor for me,[9] but somewhere along the way (probably Texas) I had arrived at the conclusion that I'd prefer to see serial murderers get the chair than Democratic presidential nominees become toast yet again. As 1992 approached, I was one of the millions of registered Democrats who, through the process of humiliation and exasperation, had arrived at this idea: *Let's try to nominate someone who could actually win one of these things and see how that works out.* Just like the poor schmucks who'd bought K-cars and Chevy Novas and were eager for Saturn's "new kind of car," I was open to the idea of a new kind of Democrat. More specifically, I was interested in the kind that could win. And as best I could tell, Clinton was that guy.

It was 7:30 on a Monday morning, and the office was already alive with early risers. The headquarters, once the home of the state teachers' union, was a low-slung brown brick building that could pass for a local library. George grabbed a stack of newspapers and his messages and had me follow him back to his office. He said that he had two assignments set aside for me during my stay. First was a new brochure that needed to be written, a necessary hand tool in the retail politics of the New Hampshire primary. The second was to prepare sound bites for a nationally televised debate two weeks away. He found me an empty desk, and throughout the course of the day he introduced me around as the campaign's visiting "sound-bite artist" or "joke writer." (Of the two, I preferred the first. Even joke writers like to be taken seriously.)

Before I could be of any use at all, I had to get up to speed. I spent my first two days taking notes on Clinton's speeches, position papers and the recent wave of mostly positive press that had pushed Clinton to the top tier of Democratic candidates. Surprisingly, I found that most of the articles devoted more space to speculation about the one candidate who refused to say whether he would run than to the other five who had already declared.

---

9. Liberal.

Mario Cuomo was the name next to the first lever I ever pushed in a voting booth, and his career-making speech to the 1984 Democratic Convention was the first time I'd whooped in delight at a televised political event since the Watergate hearings. His opposition to the death penalty seemed to me a genuine act of political courage, and the impassioned reasons he gave helped me to understand why capital punishment troubled me so much. In 1988, Cuomo toyed for months with the idea of running for president (and with many Democrats' hearts as well), but as 1992 approached, my strong feelings about him were the political equivalent of love-gone-sour. Now he was just really, really annoying.

Even as the week progressed and I worked on my first assignment, I could not get the sound of Mario Cuomo's voice out of my head. That was because the person I shared an office with, an issues staffer named Joel Berg, was sitting in front of a TV/VCR cart and reviewing the governor's recent appearance on *Meet the Press*, taking careful notes. I watched with increasing anger as Cuomo again refused to commit to running but was eager to make the case that we should only be so lucky. He took a few potshots at Clinton's national service proposal (the future AmeriCorps) and never missed an opportunity to diminish the entire roster of candidates he cagily refused to join. Most of his comments regarding the other candidates sounded something like this:

None of these guys have a plan.

Where's the plan?

If you are going to run for president, you need to have a plan!

The American people want to know that you have a plan.

I'll ask again, where is their plan?

By the end of the interview, I could barely hear him over the grinding of my teeth. Not only could this guy not make up his own mind, he seemed actively interested in disrupting the decision-making process of others. A moment later, I punched out a headline for the brochure on the keyboard of the PC on my desk, printed it out and showed it to Joel.

"I love it!" he said.

Encouraged, I headed straight for George's office.

"Hey George, did you see Cuomo on *Meet the Press?*" It was a dumb question, to be sure.

"Yeah."

"How's this for a headline for the brochure?" I placed the page in front of him. It read:

Somebody <u>does</u> have a plan!

"Yes!" he said, slamming his fist down on the desk. Clearly his reaction to the Cuomo interview was similar to mine. We exchanged high fives, probably the first celebration we'd shared since *"Senator, I knew Jack Kennedy . . ."*

"You just earned your keep," he said.

I took it as the positive feedback that it was, although I was startled to learn that his continued hospitality was conditional.

On his second look, George suggested that the first word of the headline ought to be changed from "Some*body*" to "Some*one*," and we spent two or three minutes debating which version had the right cadence and resonance. (See visual aid to learn who won.[10]) That very afternoon, the brochure made its way to union shop printers,

---

10. I also lost the debate about the quotation marks. "And I still don't understand who is being quoted."

where it was run off by the thousands and shipped to storefront Clinton offices all over New Hampshire.

How's that for swift and purposeful decision making, Mario?

With the brochure off my desk, I turned my attention to my second assignment, generating a memo on sound bites for the NBC debate. The debate was predictably turning into a showcase event for the man who would not be there. The rumors that Cuomo was serious about getting into the race were getting louder each day, and as the debate approached, the pundits framed it as a playoff among the many non-Marios to see who might emerge as his prime opponent. George read through a memo I prepared of suggested sound bites, checked off a few that he thought were useful and told me there was a debate prep meeting the next day with Governor Clinton and that I should be there.

On a Saturday afternoon, a dozen aides congregated in the basement of the governor's mansion, just a romp room filled with tables and chairs, a TV, VCR and desktop podium. Making the cut for a debate prep session was a threshold I had long wanted to cross; on the Dukakis campaign I had never once been in the room with our candidate for anything more strategic than a staff party. The room was filled with the rest of Clinton's senior staff—David Wilhelm, James Carville, Paul Begala, Bruce Reed, Bruce Lindsey, Richard Mintz, Betsey Wright—as well as his media advisor Frank Greer. In the minutes before Clinton arrived, I tried to be as unobtrusive as possible so nobody would question whether I needed to be there. When Clinton entered the room he gave a casual hello to his high command, and everyone returned the greeting—campaign staffers addressing him as "Governor" and the Arkansas faithful just calling him "Bill."[11] When the moment was right, George introduced Clinton to the one unfamiliar face in the room.

---

11. Frank Greer was the only non-local to call him "Bill," and the eye-rolling of the Arkansans registered their opinion of that. A few months later, I read in the paper Greer had been replaced. These guys were strict!

"Governor, this is Mark Katz. He was the official joke writer of the Dukakis campaign and is down here working on sound bites and one-liners for the debate."

Clinton's eyes lit up. He knew a good setup line when he heard it.

"Are you the one who put Dukakis in the tank?"

I repressed the impulse to sigh and instead surrendered a hearty, unheartfelt laugh. Before I could think of something to say, Clinton had already turned to make his way to the snack table to grab a cold-cut sandwich before the prep session began.

For the next hour and a half, many aides asked him questions and listened to his responses, offering alternate answers and strategic notes. I stayed in the back, kept my mouth shut and watched like the fortunate spectator that I was. Every once in a while I'd write down a suggested sound bite on a pad and hand it to George, but I don't recall that he sparked to any of them. I was not the only staffer in the room who was pitching without success, however. Clinton would listen to the feedback of the room, but he rarely—if ever—took a phrase he had heard and incorporated it wholesale into his next attempt. Instead, he came out with a variation of his previous attempt, expressed differently and usually better. He clearly chafed at being scripted and could think on his feet. Maybe this guy was the real deal after all.

Clinton did not use any of the material I had submitted, but miraculously he did just fine without it. The debate was a success, in that he did not stumble in any way or give anyone else an opening. Besides, the audience was largely limited to the hardest-core C-SPAN watchers: on at the same time that Sunday night was a well-hyped, late-season matchup of the Washington Redskins and their archrival, the New York Giants. (If I had not been watching the debate with a huddle of campaign staffers, even I would have spent the ninety minutes flipping back and forth.)

My assignments were done, and the next day I went into

George's office to thank him for the opportunity and the couch—
and also to bid him farewell and good luck. Then he said what I'd
hoped to hear:

"You know there's a job for you here if you want to stay."

His words were all the more amazing since I had been his
houseguest for more than two weeks. And having actively hoped
to hear them, I already knew the answer. Like the governor of my
state, I desperately wanted to be wanted but did not have it in me
to say yes. George had offered me an exciting prospect that made
no sense. I had spent the last three years laying the groundwork
for a post-political career and could not forgo advertising to join
an upstart campaign that could be over by Lincoln's birthday.
George agreed, having already calculated that it was not my best
move even before he asked me. I told him I'd call with my new
phone and fax numbers when I got back to New York, and he jokingly assured me that he would continue to exact the dividends
of the all-you-can-eat-sound-bites-for-life plan. The shorthand of
our shared experience from the last war was still intact as he prepared to fight the new one. That day I went back home to New
York for the New Year and a new job.

I got my first assignment during my first week at work at McCann-
Erickson, and I'd be lying if I didn't admit to feeling a letdown. I
had gone from working on a presidential campaign to working on
a new instant cappuccino. I reminded myself that I'd spent the last
three years getting into advertising, and this was my opportunity
to write my first television campaign—even if it was for a product
that was the coffee-based equivalent of Tang.

On the very day I was preparing to pitch my idea to our client,
Bill, the art director who was my partner, shared a terrible premo-
nition about the ultimate fate of the cappuccino campaign we
had written. The theme was "Stir it up," and that tagline served as
the payoff for a series of humorous scenarios in which various people decide against their everyday drink and instead prepare a deli-

ciously frothy and hot instant coffee-based beverage. (The scripts were no more clever than your average Bud Light commercial, but I considered them breakthrough at the time.) As I typed out "Stir it up" for the fiftieth time, Bill predicted the ultimate version of this campaign: nothing but close-up beauty shots of the product set against the soundtrack of the old Bob Marley tune "Stir It Up." This, of course, would be the most expensive and dumbed-down version of what we proposed, and I shook my head at the imagined horror as I continued typing.

The client meeting went as well as I had hoped, and the "Stir it up!" campaign won out over the three or four executions presented. As the dozen people left the conference room, my creative director, a guy named Irwin, put his arm around me and exclaimed, "That's my boy!" Two weeks later, I was in a meeting with the agency producers who were helping to select a director to shoot the scripts when I heard the distant sound of an eerily familiar reggae tune. I followed it around the corner and toward Irwin's office. His art director/partner, Matt, saw me coming, shut the door and turned off the music.

Oh no.

The next day, I learned that the client had had "a change of heart"[12] and had bought a new campaign authored by Irwin and Matt. The rights to the music had already been purchased for a small fortune, and close-up cappuccino beauty shots were already in the works.

My memory gets hazy after that but I seem to recall that from behind closed doors, a mild temper tantrum was thrown. Complicating the situation were thin walls and unusually good hallway acoustics that delivered vivid and specific assessments of character to the ears of those described. The next thing I remember, I was reassigned to a new creative group with different accounts. As I felt myself vanishing further and further into the labyrinth of a

---

12. Clients with hearts? It was an obvious lie.

large, soul-deadening advertising agency, I could not help but revisit the decision I had made not to stay in Little Rock, incurring a few self-administered forehead hematomas in the process. The campaign was taking off and I was going nowhere.

I used my considerable downtime at my desk to fax in lines, both solicited and unsolicited, to the Clinton campaign, which by the late spring had expanded to include many old Dukakis friends who'd occasionally call or, at the very least, return my messages: Dee Dee Myers, Bob Boorstin, John Podesta, Gene Sperling, Mark Gearan, Steve Silverman, Wendy Smith, Susan Brophy, Dave Leavy. Mostly, I used my many contacts and banked goodwill to weasel my way into the frequent campaign stops in New York—fund-raisers, rallies and celebrity-hosted private parties that were all schmoozing, boozing and personal politicking set against an endless loop of tracks from *Clapton Unplugged*. In the three months since I'd left Little Rock, Clinton had sewn up the nomination and, just as amazing to me, my friend George had attained the newfound status of a generational icon.

The only break I caught was that the 1992 Democratic Convention was being held two subway stops from my midtown office and three from my apartment on the Upper West Side. Conventions provide all the fun and excitement there is to be had in the world, a Mardi Gras for political junkies, and I couldn't stand the thought of missing a minute of it. Over the past three and a half years, many a Dukaki had called to ask if I could write them a joke or two, and I suddenly realized what to do with all the chits I had accrued. I hit up as many of them as I could for invites to every reception, fund-raiser, soiree and after-hours party that was being held over the course of that third week of July.

On the Sunday night before the convention began, I attended the *Rock the Vote* MTV party at Webster Hall. I was busy bumping into familiar faces from the campaign trail when I recognized someone I knew from even further back in my past. Caren had been a year behind me at Cornell. She had big blue eyes and long wavy

brown hair, and during my junior year I had asked her to a fraternity formal—but she begged off because of a term paper due the
next day. Seven years later, she looked even better than she had the
day she dissed me. We spent the next few minutes exchanging
explanations about why we were there. She was in law school down
in Maryland, volunteering on the campaign in her free time, and
she had come to New York to spend the week at the margins of the
hoopla, hoping to get into the convention. I explained my connection to the campaign, and when I mentioned offhandedly the two
weeks I had spent on George Stephanopoulos's sofa, her eyes lit up.

"You know George Stephanopoulos?!" she let out, in a tone
just shy of a squeal.

I could see that this was an avenue worth pursuing.

"Oh yeah. We shared an office together back in '88. He calls
me all the time." (For the past six months, it had been his assistant,
Heather Beckel, who had been calling me, requesting occasional
jokes per George's instructions and explaining that he did not
have time to talk.) Caren wanted to know everything I could tell
her about George, and with my own agenda in mind I quickly
offered that I also knew his girlfriend well and they were *very* serious. I, however, happened to be available, and I offered to do
what I could to get her convention passes. We had a great conversation, although I wasn't certain if her enthusiasm was just the
spillover of the George Effect. Not that it mattered. Clearly, hor-
mones had been released, and I was the best-looking politico in
her immediate field of vision promising to get her onto the floor
of Madison Square Garden.

There was only one slight complication to these ambitious
plans and full social calendar. Technically speaking, I still had a
job. Each morning of that week, I'd go into McCann-Erickson to
make sure I was seen by all of the people who might be asked if
they'd seen me, then go out to lunch and never come back. The
afternoons were spent a few blocks away at the InterContinental
Hotel, Clinton campaign central, as a hanger-on hitting up old

friends for not one, but *two* floor passes. Instead of cashing in old favors I was racking up new debts, but life is long and jokes come relatively easily. All I knew was that I had a lot riding on getting a pair of passes.

I was working it pretty hard in the lobby of the hotel when I heard the rumor that Ross Perot had pulled out of the race. I weaseled my way upstairs and watched Perot's speech with a roomful of high-fiving staffers, as this was widely seen as a tactical checkmate against Bush's electoral strategy. The campaign was fluid and exciting, and so much was at stake that I longed to be helpful in ways other than by attending every party I could. By the second night of the convention, the unfolding drama surrounded defeated candidate Jerry Brown and whether he would be awarded the prize of a prime-time speech. *"Let Jerry Speak!" "Let Jerry Speak!"* was the incessant chant of his faithful, eccentric minions—many of whom looked confused enough to think that "Jerry" was Jerry Garcia. But for a lifelong wiseass, that name conjured another Jerry altogether—and suddenly, I knew how I might pitch in for my team. Deigning to return to my office, I found a picture of Jerry Lewis in a book on my shelf and begged an art director to help me with an important project, a two-sided placard of the now-famous chant. By seven o'clock that night, I was ready for the evening ahead.

That was a great night, and so was the night after that. Political conventions are designed to build momentum as they go along, and Thursday night was the grand finale, the showcase of Clinton's acceptance speech. Since the day I left Little Rock I had watched Clinton from afar, but what I saw largely reinforced the reasons that had once brought me there. In the weeks before New Hampshire, the Gennifer Flowers fiasco had made him look like Chuck Wepner on the ropes against George Foreman, but the night I watched him fighting back on the eleven o'clock news conjured the image of Rocky Balboa instead. His voice hoarse but his spirit intact, he jutted his jaw, steeled his eyes and punched his fist in the air: "The hits I've taken are nothing compared to the hits being taken by the American people." His stamina and audacity stunned me. I never would have thought to segue from allegations of personal indiscretion to the economic conditions of working Americans, but I couldn't help but marvel with something akin to admiration at a man who would. He was a candidate unlike any I'd previously imagined, a force of nature in a suit and tie. Throughout the campaign, he impressed me time and time again, up close and from afar, confirming my image of him as the guy who could smash the myth of a Republican "electoral lock."

On the convention's crescendo night, I was standing among the throngs, contributing to the deafening drumbeat of his name, alternating between *CLINT-ON! CLINT-ON!* and *WE WANT BILL*! Suddenly, the lights dimmed and a screen descended. The next segment of the evening was not another speech but an audiovisual presentation that was met with the kind of relief schoolchildren feel when the teacher announces a filmstrip. We were about to learn more about this man from Hope.

The music was stirring, the visuals were beautiful and the film was a compelling, if propagandist, biography done far better than most. Then came the moment no one was prepared for, featuring footage recently unearthed and saved for this day: the teenaged Bill Clinton deferentially shaking hands with President John F. Kennedy, a few precious frames from someone's Super 8 camera that had been slowed down to augment the dramatic effect. We had just seen with our own eyes the archival evidence of the torch being passed to a new generation of Americans, and the crowd's gasp could not have been louder if Clinton had come center stage and pulled Excalibur from a freaking rock.

At that moment, I was glad the house lights were down because I was crying. There I was—political operative, professional wordsmith and advertising huckster—and the goddamn message was manipulating me! I was embarrassed but helpless. No longer was Bill Clinton just the horse I thought Democrats could ride all the way to the White House, he was the man I desperately wanted to be my president. As of that moment, I was a true believer.

Caren handed me a tissue and tried to assuage my embarrassment by telling me she thought my tears were sweet. I dried my eyes and lent my loudest yell to the roar of the crowd. By now he was on a giant screen, striding heroically, with his family in tow, from the streets of the city through the passageways of the convention hall and onto the world's stage. As he came to the podium to deliver his acceptance speech, I was overcome with deafening noise and a full-body tingle.

CLINT-ON! CLINT-ON! WE WANT BILL!

Then he gave a speech about the kind of America I always wanted to live in and allowed me to feel both patriotic and Democratic at the same time. It set off all the screaming, balloon-dropping, goose-pimply euphoria there is to be had in an arena full of zealots. And when he finished with "I still believe in a place called Hope," I did not fight back my tears—if only to showcase my sweet sensitivity once more to anyone who might be watching.

Over the course of the half-dozen parties I attended that night, I hugged and kissed and high-fived friends from this campaign trail and the last. Nights like this are as good as it gets, and it was all the better for having a pretty girl on my arm. Spotting an old friend at the center of a horde, I wormed our way in to make a special introduction. The closer we got, the tighter Caren's hand got in mine. Upon reaching the epicenter, I gave George a hug of heartfelt congratulations and whispered in his ear:

"Listen to me carefully: I am going to introduce you to someone and I need you to talk me up." God bless him, he was right there with me.

"George, I'd like you to meet my friend Caren."

"Hi Caren, it's so nice to meet you. A friend of Mark's is a friend of mine."

"Oh my God, it's nice to meet you! And congratulations!" she screamed, to make sure she was heard.

"You know, I begged Mark to stay in Little Rock but he's got this unbelievable advertising career going now and we just couldn't compete with that."

"Oh my God." She was impressed.

"Clinton keeps asking about you," he said, turning to me. "He says he thinks he could have won New Hampshire if you had stayed on and nearly fired me for letting you leave." He said it with a nearly straight face, his arm wrapped around me as if we were long-lost brothers.

George was very good at his job, and at that moment he was working hard for me. The conversation went on for another minute or two, and we caught up as best we could under these manic conditions. I was glad to feel connected to him again, because the more celebrated he had become, the more tenuous I imagined our friendship to be. I suppose it was a natural response to watching someone you know ascend as he had. The George I knew from the Dukakis campaign was like the Elvis who drove trucks. But this conversation made him familiar all over again, and after he finished talking me up, he pulled me aside and quietly informed me that should he ever have children, they would be entitled to limitless jokes for their lifetimes as well. At that moment, it seemed a small price to pay.

That was one of many highlights of an evening and a week I would never forget. Before the night was over, I would go on to two more parties—one at a blues club where B. B. King pumped out an infectious tune that would replay in my head for the rest of that fall: *"PUSH-BUSH-OUT-THE-DOOR!-PUSH-BUSH-OUT-THE-DOOR!"* I stayed out until I thought my legs would collapse from exhaustion and my cheeks might fall off from a nine-hour ain't-this-great grin. After that, I got naked with a gorgeous girl. Life was good and I was back. Cappuccino Boy was stirring it up!

Returning to my job as a copywriter that Monday morning was another in a series of crushing letdowns. The circus had left town and I was back in my office, writing ads for creative directors who did not know my name. By now, I had bounced from account to account—from AT&T to USAir and, most recently, to Coca-Cola. The modus operandi of this agency was known as "gang bang"—a free-for-all process involving as many people as possible working on the same assignment, which was demoralizing even for the winners. The whispers around the office were that the agency was in danger of losing the Coca-Cola account, but the campaign I was most interested in was Clinton versus Bush. I was at my desk one morning reading the *New York Times* when I came across an article that informed me that I was closer to the front lines of the presidential election than I'd realized. The article was about the advertising team for the Bush campaign, one of whom was a top exec at McCann-Erickson, Gordon Bowen.

I'd never met Gordon Bowen, but I knew he kept his office cattycorner from the creative director of my group. And as I sat at my desk just two flights up, I couldn't help but wonder about the treasure trove of confidential Bush campaign memos, storyboards and scripts that might be sitting on his desk. Each time I passed his office, I found myself peering in to see if he was there, or listening intently on the off chance I might overhear a phrase or a comment that offered a clue. Soon I was daydreaming about scenarios that would make me a hero to my friends back in Little Rock, generating high fives and hugs and shouts of "It's over!" by those who could put sensitive strategic information to good use.

These delicious self-aggrandizing daydreams seemed to percolate particularly well in the ethics-free zone of a soulless advertising agency. But whether or not I was actually casing the joint was inconsequential, as I was nearly certain I could never sink to the depths of the Watergate burglars I once reviled. And even if I could, I knew I lacked the raw courage required for breaking and entering.

This was all just harmless, private musing until the day I was working late to complete an assignment. It was maybe seven-thirty or eight when I went down to my creative director's office to leave some revised material on his secretary's desk. Almost everyone was gone and the floor was now the province of the cleaning person, who was vacuuming Gordon Bowen's office, with her well-stocked cart parked right outside. I went back to the elevator to return to my office on the nineteenth floor. But before I pushed the button, I stopped in my tracks and stood for a minute, thinking. The vacuum cleaner was off now. I made my way around the corner once again, as if I had forgotten something on my first trip. The cart was now one office down the line and the door to Bowen's office was locked up tight. But another detail caught my eye: the large olive-green bag of garbage that was hanging off the cleaning cart, containing the collective refuse of the seventeenth floor—including what had been, until a moment ago, the contents of Gordon Bowen's trash can. And who's to say what was in there?

This circumstance presented a new ethical question I had yet to consider: was I willing to steal garbage? The longer I stood there, the more obvious it became that the answer was maybe.

I needed to get a better look at the cart to more seriously consider what I was seriously considering. Right about then, the vacuum cleaner went on and I quickly recognized it as the cover I needed. The now-or-never moment had arrived, and I headed straight for the cart, the drone of the vacuum masking the sound as I snatched the bag without any trouble at all—not that surprising, when you consider cleaning carts are not designed with security in mind. Garbage in hand, I moved briskly toward the stairwell that was already in sight.

By now my mind was racing ahead to think about all the things I had previously failed to consider. For example, what if someone saw me walking down the hall with a big lawn bag of garbage? What possible answer could I give? (*I lost my retainer?*) I held the bag low to the ground, planning to drop it without breaking stride if I spotted anyone coming my way. Then I could be just as confused as anyone else about the mysterious bag, should the topic arise: *Yeah, what is that garbage doing there? Why would someone leave a big bag of garbage in the middle of the hall? Who me? Are you accusing me of stealing garbage? Why would I steal garbage?*

This was the imaginary conversation I had as I climbed the back staircase up to the nineteenth floor. I poked my head out of the stairwell door to survey the landscape of the last twenty-five feet back to my office and then completed the final cautious steps of my furtive mission down a darkened hall. As I closed the door behind me, I felt neither proud nor ashamed, just relieved. Only after I began picking through garbage did the shame start to kick in.

Piece by piece, I pulled out the pages that were my prize. Hoping each new sheet might alter history, I uncrumpled client time sheets, internal memos, routing envelopes, junk mail, real mail, many versions of the same damn (non-Bush) scripts, many editions of that day's *Daily News* and a storyboard for what hoped to be the new campaign for Ritz Bitz crackers—*Bitz are better by a lot!*—but seemed worthy of the garbage. I had gotten to the bottom of the bag and all that was left were moist tissues, orange peels, coffee cups and oil-stained brown paper bags.

Disappointed, I still knew there was one task left to complete:

discarding the garbage. I filled up my garbage pail with stolen garbage and swapped it with an empty one somewhere on the floor, a process I repeated a dozen times. That took the better part of an hour, but it was well worth the time. If Watergate had failed to teach me a moral lesson, at least I remembered its most practical application: don't let the cover-up be worse than the crime.

On November 3, 1992, Bill Clinton was elected the forty-second president of the United States of America. I was excited about America's future and happy for my many friends who worked on the campaign, but it was all tinged slightly with the regret that I was once on the ground level of a juggernaut and got off on the first floor. This terrible choice was made all the worse exactly two weeks after Election Day, when Coca-Cola announced it was leaving McCann-Erickson and McCann-Erickson announced it was laying off forty people. As a journeyman copywriter with a reputation for taking very long lunches, I'm sure my name was at or near the top of the list. On the Tuesday before Thanksgiving— exactly a year since I was behind the wheel of a rent-a-car on my way to Little Rock—my creative director asked to see me. I had a pretty strong feeling that I was not about to get a raise. As soon as I heard the word "sorry" in his first somber sentence, my own internal monologue slowly drowned out his rehearsed but heartfelt spiel that many others would hear that day. I was not thinking about the road not taken, the Clinton campaign that had gone on to realize a dream of mine without me. The past was the past, and I was thinking about the future. The immediate future. I was thinking about the Friday of that week, the day of my ten-year high school reunion. And as this person was explaining to me that I no longer worked there, all I could think was *Goddamn it! Now I have to show up at my high school reunion as a goddamned unemployed person.*

It just wasn't fair that I would have to revisit my past as some schmuck who was "between jobs." In the ten years since high school, so many exciting things had happened to me—Cornell, Stupid Pet Tricks, Moynihan, Dukakis, advertising, Saturn, San Francisco, Clinton, instant cappuccino commercials—yet I was going to show up at my reunion as one of those guys who, within two sentences of "What are you doing these days?," you can tell are obviously peddling a pile of crap and probably living at home with their parents.

I had prepared an answer for the unavoidable question and tried my hardest to say it with confidence. "I am a freelance writer," I said to many people that night with look-'em-in-the-eye conviction. But when follow-up questions came about the nature of my projects, I quickly changed the subject or waved over their shoulder to say hello to someone who wasn't there and excused myself to talk to "Steve." For a guy who'd been trained in politics and advertising, you'd think I'd be a more convincing liar. But then again, I was no longer employed in either line of work.

CHAPTER EIGHT

White House Operator Calling

ON MONDAY, MAY 3, 1993, SOMETIME BEFORE NOON, I WAS STILL damp from a late-morning shower when the telephone rang.

"Hello?"

"White House operator calling for Mark Katz."

"This is Mark Katz."

"Please hold for the president of the United States . . ."

Fisher.

It had to be Fisher.

My certainty that this was Fisher was reinforced by the fact that I could not be completely certain that it was Fisher. Borderline plausibility was the signature element of his telephone mind games. And on this particular morning, the thought that President Bill Clinton might be calling me was actually borderline plausible, as I had written a speech he had delivered not forty-eight hours earlier. And the slight margin between unlikely and not-impossible was all the room that Fisher needed to pick up the phone and tele-torment me as he had done so many times before. The truth was, I had come to live in dread of my friend Fisher.

Like so many of life's enduring problems, Fisher showed up when I was fourteen years old. He was in my ninth-grade English class, the skinny kid with stringy hair who came to my attention as a rival source of back-row humor. The day Mrs. Evansburg revealed to us that the furious rhythmic gyrations described in D. H. Lawrence's "The Rocking Horse Winner" symbolized sexual intercourse, Fisher raised his hand and asked if she approved of premarital horseback riding. I knew right then that this kid was good. Later in the school year, Fisher and I agreed to coauthor a book report on *A Tale of Two Cities* and exchanged phone numbers so we could contact each other after school. How could I have known that giving Fisher my phone number that afternoon would haunt me for the rest of my days?

As I soon learned, the classroom was not even Fisher's best forum. Mere interjections from the back of the room did not take full advantage of his true gift. Fisher's brain was built for calculated telephone hoaxes the way Lex Luthor's was hardwired for global chaos. Armed only with a phone and a tidbit of information, he could wield his talent for pitch-perfect impersonation and inventive deception to instill panic on the other end of the line. The phony phone calls that started in high school continued through college and beyond. In the years I have known him, I have picked up the phone to be subjected to this:

- A phone call from an administrator at the Educational Testing Service the day after the SATs, citing an unusually low score and inquiring if I had mistakenly used something other than a #2 pencil.
- A call from the stern-sounding father of Debby Sandler, my well-built date to the junior prom, informing me that his only daughter would be dusted for my fingerprints upon her return home by midnight—or else.
- A call from the New York State DMV informing me that I had done so well in my written exam, my road test had been

waived and I should drive over to pick up my license at my convenience.

- A call from an associate dean of admissions from the University of Pennsylvania to conduct a supplementary interview on my wait-listed application. I didn't realize it was Fisher until the fifth question: "What are you wearing?"
- A call from the dental office of Dr. Brettner, on the heels of a checkup, informing me I had tested positive for chronic halitosis.
- A call on my first day of work at Kirshenbaum & Bond advertising agency, an abrupt command from a deep, muffled voice: "Mark, come into my office right away." Click.

Sometimes he got me and sometimes he didn't. The degree to which Fisher could reel me in was the degree to which I was mocked. Not only by him, but also by our core group of developmentally stunted high school friends that has remained intact since then. Over time, Fisher expanded his repertoire to take advantage of unfolding technologies. With the advent of conference calling came confused conversations between two Fisher victims struggling to determine the identity of the other. Then came the argument over who called who. All the while, Fisher held his hand over a receiver and laughed his ass off. With speed dialing came Fisher's covert reprogramming, putting you a touch of a button away from old girlfriends, suicide hotlines and, on one occasion, a clinic whose ad in the *Village Voice* ran under the headline "Penile Enlargement."

Perhaps Fisher's most inspired work occurred the day he patched together Famous Ray's Pizza with Original Ray's Pizza. According to legend, it went like this:

Famous Ray: Hello, Famous Ray's . . . Hello . . . Hello?
Original Ray: Hello. Ray's Pizza.
Famous Ray: Hello.

Original Ray: Hello.
Famous Ray: Famous Ray's, can I help you?
Original Ray: This is Ray's Pizza. Would you like to place an order?
Famous Ray: Who is this?
Original Ray: Ray's Pizza.
Famous Ray: Yes, this is Ray's.
Original Ray: This is Ray's Pizza. Who is this?
Famous Ray: Yes, this is Famous Ray's Pizza. Do you want to place an order?
Original Ray: What?
Famous Ray: This is Famous Ray's.
Original Ray: You mean Original Ray's.
Famous Ray: No, Famous Ray's is the original Ray's.
Original Ray: No, this is Ray's, the original Ray's.
Famous Ray: This is the original Ray's. Famous Ray's.
Original Ray: This is the *original* famous Ray's. Do you want to order something?
Famous Ray: Am I going to order something???
Original Ray: Hey asshole, are you going to order something or not?
Famous Ray: Yeah, where are you located, Original Ray? 'Cause I'm gonna come there and kick your original ass.
Original Ray: I'd like to see you try, motherfucker.
Famous Ray: Go to hell!
Original Ray: Fuck you!
Famous Ray: Fuck you!!
Click.
Click.

For all of these reasons, as I stood there in my bath towel I was not predisposed to believe that I was actually holding for the president. I pressed the phone to my ear and prepared to analyze the voice that would greet me after my stay on hold. My brain was on high alert.

"Hello, Mark?"

BRAIN: Fisher *or the* president? Fisher *or the* president? *Not enough syllables to make a conclusive identification.* **Proceed with EXTREME caution!!!**

"Hello."

"Mark, you did great work helping out on the jokes for the White House Correspondents' Dinner. You did a terrific job and I just wanted to call and thank you again."

BRAIN: Holy shit! If this is Fisher, it's his best work yet—even better than his near-flawless impersonation of Vice Principal Speranza. Permission granted to engage voice in conversation. WARNING: the next words you say may be used to mock you for the rest of your life.

"You bet, sir."

I was determined to maintain my reticence until I achieved a higher degree of certainty. My silence compelled the caller to move the conversation forward.

"I really loved that William Henry Harrison joke. That one still cracks me up. '. . . already been dead for sixty-eight days!' Ha!"

BRAIN: **Identity confirmed!** *This is the third time the president has mentioned that he loved the William Henry Harrison joke.* **YOU ARE TALKING TO THE PRESIDENT! REPEAT: YOU ARE TALKING TO THE PRESIDENT!**

Now I was excited.

"You got a great laugh on that one, Mr. President." It was the first time in the conversation I dared address him with that, but there were plenty more to come. This, I would learn, is a common phenomenon among people who find themselves in a conversation with a president. They interject the words "Mr. President" into nearly every sentence, as if afflicted with a very proper strain of Tourette's syndrome. There is just something about talking to the president that makes you punctuate your sentences with the words "Mr. President." Not because he wants to hear it—he knows very well who he is—but because you just love to hear yourself say it. After all, when is the next time you'll get to say "Mr. President" in a sentence? A co-op board meeting? More than that, interjecting those words adds import to any sentence you might say. Compare these sentences:

A. Cheese sandwiches are very tasty.
B. Cheese sandwiches are very tasty, Mr. President.

This condition is only made worse by the fact that speaking to the president can also make you talkative to the point of babbling. This happens for much the same reason: you are not really talking to the president, you are listening to yourself talking to the president. Your brain, so absorbed in listening to the conversation, becomes a cognitive bystander engaged in an internal monologue that goes something like this:

I am talking to the president.

I am talking to the president.

I just said something to the president.

The president is responding to something I just said.

For the rest of my life, I will be able to preface what I just said to the president with the words "As I once said to the president . . ."

Does anyone here remember what I said to the president? I'm gonna need it for when I tell people this story.

The president stopped talking. It is my turn to say something. Now I am going to listen to what I am about to say to the president. I wonder what it will be?

As it turned out, here's what I said to the president next: "You know what Mel Brooks says, Mr. President: 'Comedy equals tragedy plus time.'"

He had no response to that. Very few people quote Mel Brooks to the president. I explained further.

"What I mean, Mr. President, is that joke probably would not have gone over too well if Millard Fillmore said it."

"Millard Fillmore completed the term of Zachary Taylor," he said. "John Tyler succeeded William Henry Harrison. But I think I know what you mean . . ."

He'd given me more credit for my wrong reference than I deserved. I didn't know that Millard Fillmore had completed the term of anyone—I had just pulled out the name of a funny-sounding, obscure, mid-nineteenth-century president. At this point, the president must have remembered that he had called to thank me, not to administer a pop quiz.

"Anyway, I just loved that William Henry Harrison joke."

The president's tone let me know that this conversation was winding down. He encouraged me to fax him jokes if ever I had an idea for something funny he might say. A few seconds later, he was saying good-bye. Before it was over, I got to hear myself say it one last time: "Thank you for calling, Mr. President."

The president hung up the secure phone on the oak desk in the Oval Office and went back to his job as the head of the executive branch of the U.S. government. I dropped my cordless phone back onto the laundry pile on my bed and resumed my duties as a "freelance writer," which on that morning had me getting dressed and dropping off two suits, a tuxedo and a bunch of shirts at the dry cleaner. Plus I had to call Fisher and tell him his fifteen years of sustained mental torment now had me tormenting myself without even taking time out of his day.

A few weeks after the inauguration of President Bill Clinton, I had received a phone call from Mark Gearan, once my boss on the Dukakis campaign and now a high-ranking White House official. Madeleine Albright, a fellow Dukakis alum who had become America's ambassador to the United Nations, had been invited to deliver a humor speech to the Gridiron Club, and Mark was calling to ask for my help. I confided in Mark that while I had been calling myself a freelance writer for three months now, that description was still more hopeful than accurate. My interest and availability were both very high.

This very first assignment of my self-employed life took me from the lonesome ignominy of occupational displacement to the heightened reality of one of Washington's most exclusive events. On Saturday, March 27, the night of the 108th annual dinner of the Gridiron Club, I was dressed in the full rented regalia of white tie and tails and breathing in the rarefied air of an inner-sanctum ballroom. The room was filled with the venerable publishers, editors, columnists and reporters who were the Gridiron Club members, as well as the cabinet members, committee chairmen, generals, senators and power brokers who were their guests. (When I checked my overcoat earlier in the evening, I was the only one in line who wasn't James Baker or Henry Kissinger.)

Five hundred other people were wearing the same uniform as I was, yet I could not have felt any more out of place had I been dressed as the San Diego Chicken. I was a full thirty years below the room's median age and perhaps the only one there who had never appeared on *Nightline*. From a seat at the far end of the room, I watched with amazement as Washington's wise men—and just a handful of women—were entertained all evening by songs and skits performed by two dozen costumed Gridiron members with more verve than talent (think dinner theater in Pensacola, Florida). The political vaudeville was mercifully interspersed with a trio of humor speeches from our highest national leaders. In addition to Albright, the Gridiron Club was entertained that evening with the comic stylings of President Bill Clinton and Senate Majority Leader Bob Dole.

In the two weeks I'd spent preparing Albright's speech, I'd learned more than I'd ever known about Washington culture. Specifically, I learned that an invitation to speak at the Gridiron Club was a very big deal. Except for the president, who spoke every year, the invitation is usually a once-in-a-lifetime honor, a coming-out party for big-time Beltway players who have ascended to the top tier of the Washington Establishment. (Dole, well-known as a Washington wit, was also an exception to this unofficial Gridiron rule.) Albright had been a familiar face in Georgetown circles for a long time, but these last months were her first in high office.

The theme of her speech was post-Dukakis redemption. Albright presented herself as the archetypal long-suffering party loyalist who had been waiting around for decades to serve in a Democratic administration:

> *I've been working in politics at a pretty high level since Ed Muskie was an up-and-comer. I was a foreign policy advisor to Democratic presidential candidates when Russia was known as the Soviet Union and George Stephanopoulos was better known as "George Stuffin'envelopes."*

> *In the spirit of full disclosure, I must confess this: I was in the room when the decision was made to put Michael Dukakis in that tank. But I can assure you our party will never make that mistake again. By 1996, if we have our way, there won't be any tanks.*

> *However, I do have a note of caution for those who might underestimate me: Korbel, my middle name, is Czech for "Rodham."*

Albright's well-received speech represented my debut as well. After the entertainment had concluded and while dessert was being served, I was introduced to the president as the person who had worked with Albright. Clinton praised the speech and congratulated me for my part in it. He told me he especially liked the Bob Dole jokes and had scribbled them down, hoping to borrow them himself:

> *Bob Dole has drawn blood so many times that Liddy had to go work at the Red Cross.*

> *Bob keeps saying how much he wants the president's programs to succeed. C'mon, Bob. Nobody believed you when you said that about George Bush!*

> *Anyone who knows Bob well knows that behind that sarcastic grin is a man of sincerity and caring—and behind that, another sarcastic grin.*

Before we were done, the president asked if I would work on his next funny speech.

"Well, how much money are we talking about?" I replied. It was a stupid, easy joke, but he laughed at it, thank God.

Six weeks later, on the Monday morning of the last week of April, the phone rang in my studio apartment. It was Dee Dee Myers, another Dukaki done good, calling me from the White House.

Her request was simple. The White House Correspondents' Dinner was that Saturday night, and she wanted to know if I would fax down a few pages of jokes that the president might use later in the week. In fact, the request was so simple, it was downright disappointing. When the president had asked me to help on his next speech, I imagined that he and I might spend a day together, pitching jokes back and forth in the Oval Office or on a lazy Sunday out at Camp David. Hey, if need be, I would've found the time to meet with him on *Air Force One* on his way to a summit or something. Writing jokes in my bathrobe from the Ikea couch in my studio apartment on West Ninety-seventh Street and faxing down pages to the press office was less than I had in mind.

"It's funny you should call me today," I told her. "It just so happens that I am on my way to D.C."

It just so happens that I was lying. The previous week, I'd received an invitation to attend the Washington premiere of the movie *Dave*—a comedy set in the White House, of all places—sent by its screenwriter, Gary Ross. I'd met Gary five years earlier during the Dukakis campaign. We traded jokes Dukakis might say (but never did) almost every day by phone and fax and had stayed in touch since. I had already regretfully declined the invitation for the Tuesday evening event, but as of this moment, my plans suddenly changed.

"Since I am going to be in D.C. this week anyway, why don't I plan to stay over an extra few days and come by the White House and see if I can help out in person."

My response caught her off-guard. "Huh. I guess we could . . . Okay then. Well, sure."

With that, I had invited myself to the White House, something most world leaders cannot pull off so easily. This was an audacious move, but a dangerous one as well. I am the world's worst liar—a liability that has hampered my professional career and personal relationships at every turn. I felt bad about lying to Dee Dee, but the rationalization was easy enough: it had been a lie when I said it, but within minutes it was true. I retrieved the *Dave* invite from the trash and called the RSVP line to un-regret.

Emboldened by my own on-the-fly gumption, I continued working the phone to arrange this impromptu trip, making train reservations, canceling newspaper deliveries and—not aware at the time of the relaxed policies regarding the use of the Lincoln Bedroom—securing the living room sleep-sofa of a reliably generous friend. I went to my closet, reached past the sharp copywriter blazers I had collected in recent years, and pulled my pragmatic political wardrobe out of retirement. I filled a garment bag with two dark suits and a collection of blue and white shirts and red and blue ties. The last thing I squeezed into the bag was my tuxedo—purchased months earlier for Fisher's wedding—despite the fact that I hadn't a clue about how I was getting into the black-tie White House Correspondents' Dinner.

I was twenty minutes away from heading out the door when the phone rang again, another call that further compounded the chaos. It was a good friend of mine who answers almost exclusively to the name "Helmet Head," or "Helmet" for short. Eager to hear myself recount it out loud, I told Helmet Head about my conversation with Dee Dee Myers. By the time I had finished, his excitement surpassed mine.

"Let's go," he said. "I can be at your place in an hour."

"What?"

"Let's go. I'm driving," he said. "I have some people I want to see in D.C. this week and maybe I'll stick around for the dinner. If we leave by four, we can be in D.C. for a late supper."

I should have anticipated this response. Helmet Head was some kind of entrepreneurial and/or business consultant with a schedule and lifestyle even more untethered than mine. I had known him since college and, in fact, was in the room when his nickname was assigned. Concerned about my friend's high-octane personality, which caused him to bounce off the walls and ceilings, one of my apartment-mates suggested that some sort of protective headgear might help to ward off concussions.

For some reason—probably fiscal—I let Helmet talk me into his plan. Two hours later, I was seated in the crushed-velour passenger seat of his climate-controlled, full-sized Cadillac heading south on the New Jersey Turnpike.

Late-model Cadillacs have always been Helmet's chariot of choice, and his wardrobe also reflected the preferences of an old Jewish man. His clothing consisted of two basic categories, business suits and cruise wear, and on this day his outfit combined the two: dark slacks, a shiny shirt, a tennis jacket and wingtip loafers. A short haircut and (unfashionably) unfashionable eye-glasses completed his look. Behind the wheel, Helmet was weaving in and out of lanes, hoping to break his personal best time to D.C. When the car in front of him refused to cede the fast lane, he opened the window and screamed at him, "Hey jerko! I got Bill Clinton's joke writer in here! Don't make me get out of the car and slap you!"

Somewhere around Trenton, I asked him, "Explain to me again your plan?" For as long as I have known him, about every third question I've asked Helmet begins with the inquiry "Explain to me again . . ." Questions like:

Explain to me again what you do?

Explain to me again where you do it?

Explain to me again when you sleep?

"I have some people I want to see while I'm in D.C. for a project I am working on." He couldn't to be any more specific than that.

Long before, I had winnowed my speculation about his true occupation to eccentric trust-fund baby or rogue operative of an international intelligence organization. On another day, I might have questioned him more vigorously, but experience had taught me this would only result in mental exhaustion. In these hours, I needed to give my full attention to the stack of *Time* and *Newsweek* I'd brought with me, necessary topical research for my impending assignment. I arrived in D.C. around 8:00 P.M., impressed that this bold, makeshift plan had already taken me three hundred miles, and amazed where it would take me next.

White House Week

At nine o'clock on Tuesday morning, I was being waved through the West Wing gate, a mysterious process that involved date of birth, Social Security number, proper identification and FBI and Interpol databases. A Secret Service officer on the other side of a bulletproof window handed me a visitor's badge to wear around my neck, a hefty laminated object bearing a large letter "A"—which, if it stood for anything, might well have been for "Awestruck." He pointed me down a paved path that put the vision of the White House in my left eye and the West Wing in my right. This angle of the White House was a view familiar to anyone who had ever watched Wolf Blitzer reporting live on CNN, and as I continued down the path, I felt as if I were entering a movie. I could hear my footsteps but could not feel my feet as the West Wing continued to grow larger.

As I reached the entrance, a large marine with impossible posture opened the door smartly, making no distinction between cabinet member and itinerant wiseass. I quietly traced the very different paths that had brought us both to this spot and, for a moment, contemplated my own truncated military career, which had been cut short by a run-in with a very mean Cub Scout troop leader.

After being escorted through a series of oak doors and narrow halls, I arrived at Dee Dee's office, where she welcomed me with a warm hug. There we were, together with countless Dukakis refugees in offices nearby. To me, it felt like we had all been happily reunited in the Heaven of Political Afterlife. (Is Fritz Mondale here? Was that Hubert Humphrey I saw in the hall?) Joining us was David Dreyer, a deputy communications director and another familiar face from the campaign trail. Inside of fifteen minutes, the two of them had briefed me on the details of the speech, almost all of which were news to me. (When Dreyer parenthetically mentioned that the dinner was held at the Washington Hilton, I tried not to betray the fact that up until that moment, I had assumed the dinner took place in the White House itself. I held my tongue, so as not to alarm them with the naïveté of the person who had volunteered to write the speech.) We went over the topics to concentrate on, such as Clinton's First Hundred Days in office, and others to avoid: gays in the military, the recent Waco raids and a $200 haircut on the LAX tarmac topped the list.

Afterward, Dreyer walked me next door to the Old Executive Office Building, better known as the OEOB,[1] an enormous wedding cake of a building that dwarfs the West Wing in every aspect but prestige. He showed me to an empty desk in the communications offices on the first floor and left me there as I unpacked the contents of my shoulder bag.

Any writer will tell you that the scariest part of writing—even joke writing—is sitting down to start. (A famous quote by Truman Capote in response to a critic encapsulates just about everything there is to be said about writing: "Where were you when the page was blank?") I suffer from an acute case of this occupational affliction, and in order to illustrate the anxiety I was experiencing at that moment I'd be forced to admit the courage that I once had to summon back in the days of the "Stir it up" campaign. Over time, I've learned to stare down the empty page by starting with material I know I could never use, relieving me of the onus of having to produce anything worthwhile. Just as I began my instant cappuccino assignment with the words *"None of that authentic cappuccino taste—but without the wait!,"* so too I began this process by tapping out jokes on the topics Dee Dee and Dreyer specifically told me to avoid—as well as others they didn't need to.

- When I finally got to the White House, I vowed never to forget that famous sign hanging above the copy machine at my campaign headquarters in Little Rock: *It's gays in the military, stupid!*
- I know a $200 haircut sounds like a lot of money to pay, but—if I may say in my own defense—that included a $40 tip for the person who shampooed my hair.

---

1. *Oh-Ee-Oh-Bee.*

- Contrary to published reports, my haircut did not cause a single plane to be delayed for a single minute. All those delays were a result of the aromatherapy. And dammit, I want a retraction!
- The Health Care Task Force would have been here tonight but the first lady refused to disclose the names of people who would be seated at their table.
- I'd like to thank the plurality of the White House Correspondents who voted for me to be your speaker tonight.[2]
- *More like that but even less funny.*

With those out of the way, I started with a few jokes that would not get me escorted from the building. With each day of that week, the list got longer. I faxed them to funny friends, who sent them back with edits and jokes to add. On the door of the office, I posted a handwritten sign, COMEDY WAR ROOM, and whoever stuck their head in to satisfy their curiosity was more often than not subjected to focus-group testing of material. Every few hours, I checked in with David Dreyer. At every stage of the draft he gave me edits, encouragement, direction—and, as nicely as he could, killed the jokes that crossed a line. Many jokes went into his office and never came out:

- I'd like to thank the president of the White House Correspondents' Association for inviting me—and apologize for eating off his plate.
- You know, Jimmy Carter was the last Democratic president to speak at this dinner. It would have been unwise to hold your breath waiting for the next one, but I, for one, have not inhaled since then.
- Let me make a special mention of the audience at home

---

2. Clinton's 43 percent presidential victory was one of the hushed topics in this White House.

watching this White House Correspondents' Dinner televised live on C-SPAN. [looks to camera] Hello . . . Hello . . .
Hello . . .
      . . . There, I think that's everyone.
• I know all about these sophisticated political dinners from
  when I was governor of Arkansas. By the way, where are we
  gonna roast the possum?

Over the course of the next few days, I holed myself up in
that vacant office in the OEOB engaged in a full-throttled joke
cram. Cramming, a technique I mastered in college, has
remained the modus operandi of my professional life for the
unfortunate reason that it works for me. (A 3.5 GPA!) It operates
like a one-man war room, turning any objective (i.e., a term
paper, a speech or instant cappuccino commercials) into a
lifestyle that requires all of your attention for all of the waking
hours that a deadline allows. In this case, joke cramming
entailed long days of reading large stacks of newspaper clips as if
I were studying for some kind of final exam in the short history
of the Clinton administration. Each sentence in every article
entered my brain as an impulse stimulus, a potential setup line
that dared my gray matter to spit back a punch line. Each half-
baked notion was registered on a notepad or word processing
document as part of a labor-intensive process that gave rise to
my long-standing motto/work ethic: *a joke a minute, a laugh an hour.*
The joke cram is all about finding enough hours. The true sickness
of cramming is that in its most severe cases, you come to regard
sleep and other distractions (i.e., meals and trips to the bathroom)
as your enemy, in that they are time away from the mirth-making
process. It was about eleven at night when I came across the article about the Hundred Day accomplishments of previous presidents, wherein it was mentioned parenthetically that America's
ninth president, William Henry Harrison, died on his thirty-second

day in office. With a little subtraction, and the addition of context, a joke was born.[3]

After experiencing a moment of joy at a strong and funny joke, I was stricken with panic: *What if I had left an hour ago and had never come across the fact that spawned this idea? Would it ever have come to me, or would it have been lost forever?* This is the sick psychology that fuels the process that has produced every page of humor I've ever compiled, and that kept me at that OEOB desk from eight in the morning to twelve at night for four days straight. Except for Tuesday night, when I went to the *Dave* premiere and occasionally scribbled down jokes when my mind wandered. Seated next to me at the premiere was my guest, Helmet Head, wearing a double-breasted suit and power tie. He had scheduled some meetings for his vague business ventures and had been keeping himself busy all week. But one item near the top of his to-do list was proving to be more elusive than he'd anticipated.

"Any chance the White House can score me a ticket to the dinner?" he asked.

"I can ask, but I was only half promised one ticket for me."

Honestly, two seemed out of the question. A good number of White House underlings were still scrambling for a ticket, and I couldn't imagine how I could get my hands on a spare one. Helmet continued to rack his Franklin Day Runner in the days ahead in search of someone who might know someone who might get him in.

"By the way, you didn't tell me this was a black-tie dinner!" he added.

---

3. The actual origin of this premise, which I would have sworn was all my own, was pointed out to me recently by a friend—that great punch line, "When Mozart was my age, he was dead for eight years." More evidence to the assertion that there is no such thing as a new joke, which is a maxim that is depressing and liberating at the same time, allowing you to mine joke books and quote books to resurrect funny lines that were already stolen in the first place.

Oops.

"Well," I said, "the good news is, you don't have a ticket so it won't be a problem." I was issuing him a challenge and he knew it. I also told him that renting a tuxedo was a small price to pay for attending the White House Correspondents' Dinner. He scoffed at that idea. On Thursday morning, he set out on an errand, a road trip back and forth to Florham Park, New Jersey, to retrieve the proper attire for an event he didn't even have a ticket for. For Helmet Head, seven hours back and forth in his car is like a trip to the video store for you and me.

By Thursday night, Helmet had returned to D.C. and I was closing in on a completed draft of the speech. The themes were well established, and the list of jokes beneath them had been improved through collective effort and editing. By Friday night, the document was ready to be submitted to the president through the official routing of the staff secretary. Dreyer wrote a cover note for the president's benefit as well as mine:

> Mark Katz, who wrote Ambassador Albright's remarks for the Gridiron Dinner, has prepared *excellent* material for your use during tomorrow night's dinner. It is attached for your review this evening. After the radio address on Saturday, we might get you together with Mark briefly to react to the material he submitted.

Oval Office Meeting

The next day at around 10 A.M., I was one of fifty or so people filing into the Oval Office for the president's weekly Saturday radio address, each of us giddy with our own good fortune in landing this White House equivalent of a backstage pass. Our unit was filled with the close relatives of senior White House staff, Arkansas travelers and, most notably on this day, Hollywood honchos in town for the *Dave* premiere and that evening's White

House Correspondents' Dinner. Beaming faces more famous than mine included Penny Marshall, Kevin Kline, Phoebe Cates and Michael Douglas.

But unlike the others, I was not there as a mere celebrity, lucky tourist or hanger-on. I was a highly skilled humor specialist, there to assist the president in his hour of comic need. This was the moment for which I had spent my entire life unknowingly preparing. More than that, it was the fulfillment of a fantasy shared by every good citizen and/or egomaniac: that at a critical moment in our national life, your unique skills would be brought to the attention of the president, and he would summon you to his side. It happened to Samuel Morse and Thomas Edison, Einstein and Oppenheimer. And today, it was my turn. On this day, I had been summoned to the Oval Office as the president's Senior Advisor for Mirth and Jocularity—my self-imagined, non-cabinet-ranking title.

The president entered his office to our applause and sat down to deliver a short speech into a microphone on his desk. His attire was Saturday casual (a striped polo shirt under a blue blazer) and his mood was relaxed. The topic that morning was his proposed National Service Program, and the small crowd in the room applauded heartily at the speech's conclusion. Afterward, everyone had their picture taken with the president before being politely escorted from the room. Worried about being confused with a mere Oval Office sightseer, I remained within close range of George Stephanopoulos, who gestured to the gatekeepers that I was okay to stay behind.

When the room had been cleared, George and David Dreyer approached the president, reminding him of that evening's event and handing him a fresh draft of the speech. I quietly moved myself to the outer perimeter of the conversation, but the president had yet to make eye contact with me. Instead, he leafed through the draft, his face unlit with unenthusiasm.

"Yeah, I read it last night," the president said. "It's not so great."

Did he know that the author of the material was standing right there? George made sure that he did.

"Mr. President," George said, "you remember Mark Katz. He's the one who wrote the Albright Gridiron speech and he put this draft together."

Clinton lifted his eyes from the page and made quick contact with mine. "Hi," he said, as he reached into his blazer pocket for his half-frame reading glasses.

"Hello, Mr. President."

So far, with the disparaging comment and a halfhearted hello, this was not the hero's welcome I had imagined. It was certainly less effusive than FDR's greeting to Einstein or Nixon's to Elvis. I could not tell if he remembered meeting me before or not. Perhaps the real compliment was *not* to be fawned over as a guest, but to be matter-of-factly accepted in the room with the unspoken assumption that I belonged there in the first place. Surely he doesn't high-five Al Gore or Leon Panetta every time they come to see him, I told myself—which made me feel better for a fleeting moment. He returned his attention to the page and leafed through the rest of the draft. The three of us watched him, waiting for a pronouncement of some kind.

"Albright's speech was funnier than this," he said, giving me the worst compliment I'd ever received.

I couldn't imagine what to say in response, and even if I could have there was no way I could possibly have brought myself to say it. That was probably for the best, as it prevented me from saying something defensive, or worse yet, making a joke that could have fallen flat. This was a critical moment, and the author of an allegedly unfunny speech who then made an unfunny joke would have sealed his own fate.

The good news was that George was on hand. Those dark days on the Dukakis campaign had taught him the expression on my face that registered deep psychic scarring. After a quick look in my direction, George jumped in and tried to put the conversation back on course.

"There is a lot of funny material here, sir. A lot of us have read it and think it's very funny."

You tell him, George! He'll listen to you.

"Did you get to the part about the advice you've received from the White House press corps? They're gonna eat that up."

"Yeah, there may be some stuff in here that we can save," was the president's response.

I could feel my chest constricting.

Dreyer, taking the cue from George, also tried to steer the conversation away from the rocks. "There's also a lot of funny stuff about your First Hundred Days." He pointed his finger to some material on the second page.

The president read on. Then, thank God, he broke up laughing.

"Oh, this one I like!" He finished a full second laugh before he could say it out loud: *"I don't think I'm doing that badly. After his First Hundred Days in office, William Henry Harrison had already been dead for sixty-eight days!"*

On his third laugh, I laughed along with him but a bit too loudly—only because it might have been the first breath I'd taken in over a minute. This is a known defect of my central nervous system: whenever placed in a high-stress situation, I forget to exhale. This broken mechanism of my fight-or-flight response is particularly detrimental because it denies my brain oxygenated blood just when it needs it most. (The condition was brought to my attention by college classmates. During final exams I would go two to three minutes without breathing, only to crack the room's silence with a sudden expunge of depleted air, followed by a full-throated thoracic gasp. Once a guy asked the proctor for a new seat assignment, dubbing my technique "the Lamaze method of test-taking.")

George and Dreyer, who had been inhaling and exhaling at regular intervals all along, also joined the chorus of chuckles, more in relief than amusement. Finally, there was laughter emanating from our comedy meeting.

"The speech needs some more jokes like that, like the William Henry Harrison joke." I did not take him to mean he wanted more jokes premised in the tragedy of previous administrations. The president was asking for some jokes that were funny.

"Are there any jokes we can use from the Albright speech?" the president asked me directly. "Anything that got cut?" The Albright speech, once a feather in my cap, was now my burden to bear.

"It depends," I replied. "Did you grow up as a young girl in war-torn Czechoslovakia?" This joke, a high-risk maneuver given my emotional state and questionable real-time comedy skills, paid off. It elicited the second laugh of the conversation, but unfortunately, not one that corresponded to a joke on the page. Suddenly, I was funnier in person than I was in print, and this unsettled me. Now more than ever, I needed my handiwork on the page to generate the laughter. When this laugh was over, the president returned his attention to the draft he regarded as dubious.

"The Larry King joke—why is that funny?" he asked. In the years that followed, I learned that this question was a near-perfect pre-dictor of a joke that would die. I saw it as a lose-lose situation; being required to explain a joke is the same as performing its autopsy. In this case, the joke he was asking about was premised on a panel assembled on *Larry King Live* that week, with the major network White House correspondents engaged in a roundtable discussion of Clinton's First Hundred Days in office. During the '92 campaign, Clinton had appeared on *Larry King* and on soft news shows like *Donahue, Arsenio* and the like, as a way of circumventing the harder-hitting journalists of the evening news. It was a successful strategy that the political press corps openly lamented. Hence this:

I was watching CNN the other night and I couldn't believe what I saw: Andrea Mitchell, Susan Spencer, Brit Hume and Wolf Blitzer— all on Larry King Live. *Imagine that: the media going around the president to take their message directly to the American people!*

With a quick explanation of the irony, George saved this joke from the trash heap of history.

"Oh, I like that," the president said, as his face lit up in response to hypocrisy exposed. In fact, the joke seemed to change both his mood and focus.

"Enough jokes on me—we need to do more jokes on all of them," meaning the media. "I thought this was a press dinner where I get to make fun of the press."

With that, we arrived at a fundamental dividing line. It is a well-known, practically written rule that the endgame of these ritual humor dinners is to ingratiate oneself to the audience—in this case, the press—and that the speaker is his own primary target. But self-deprecating humor is almost exclusively instinctive only to the most skillful public practitioners of power and your average Jew. From what I could tell, this did not come naturally to Bill Clinton. I had the feeling that he couldn't understand why we had handed him pages of self-deprecating jokes to tell to the people who depre-cate him for a living. It's easy to understand: for starters, in only a relatively short span of his national public life, he had endured as contentious a relationship with the press as anyone since Richard Nixon, and he had been subjected to more invasive personal scrutiny than Gary Hart. To him, it must have seemed like appeas-ing Torquemada by placing yourself on the rack until you confess.

This was also another symptom of the political culture shock of going from Little Rock to Washington. Clinton was raised in a polit-ical culture where gentle, self-effacing humor was all but unheard of, and political humor dinners featured a much meaner brand of funny. In Arkansas, I was told by people who'd know, humor is a stick that you beat other people up with. Clinton kept in his head a running list of the personal hypocrisies, professional double standards, specific unfair shots and falsehoods uttered against him. He wanted to recite them all, and if they were expressed in the form of a joke, well, that was fine too. But left to his own devices, the defining tone of his speech to the Washington press corps would be *"Katy, bar the door!"*

There were a half-dozen jokes about specific White House correspondents, but he wanted more and he wanted them to be harder hitting. In the margins of my draft, I had been marking with x's and ✓'s the jokes he responded to and his specific requests for changes to be made in the final draft. So far, I had written down:

- Not as funny as Albright
- More jokes that are *funny* i.e., WmHH
- Meaner jokes on press

These were not the minutes of a successful meeting. Nor were they the plaudits of praise that I'd hoped to hear as I entered the room. They were terse instructions to a staffer whose job was to give the president what he had asked for. The sense of wonder and self-congratulation I had quietly conjured had been all but depleted. In fact, I couldn't wait for this moment that I had waited for all my life to be over, so that I could go someplace and put my head down on a desk. But before we were through, he added one more item to the list.

"You know what else? We need some jokes on my National Service Proposal."

Huh?

He was ordering up a joke the way someone might order up a sandwich, but it was unclear to anyone what was or what might be funny about his National Service Proposal. I knew something about it, as I had just listened to him deliver a radio address to the nation pleading its virtues. It was a noble, even exciting plan in the true "Ask not what your country can do for you" JFK tradition. He had sent the legislation to Capitol Hill, where a couple of Republican senators led by Bob Dole had given it a cool reception and consigned it to the back burner. Perhaps they disagreed with it on the merits: harnessing youthful idealism into vital public service is an inherently divisive issue and one in need of careful scrutiny. Or maybe they were doing it only to annoy Clinton by denying him his pet project for no other reason than that they could.

And if their intent was to annoy, they were doing a very good job of it. He was pissed, and it occurred to him that this might be an opportunity to toss a joke grenade in their general direction. All that being true, he did not *need* a joke on his National Service Proposal. Under no circumstance would any person leave the room that night and say these words: "That was a very funny speech—but where were the jokes on the National Service Proposal?" Clinton was not just asking too much of a humor writer, he was asking too much of humor itself.

Very quickly, here is all the response from an audience a good joke can hope to accomplish: *You know what? I kinda like this guy.* Here is a response no joke can ever hope to accomplish: *You know what? Thanks to that joke, I can see myself as I really am for the very first time: a shameless, partisan hypocrite who is abusing power to stand in the way of what's right for America. I am going to change my ways starting now!*

But even I knew that this was not the moment to engage the president in a humor dialectic. He had given me a specific and direct order to write some jokes on this topic, and I knew I had to come back to him with something. At this point, I was eager to leave the room before he added NAFTA and auto emissions standards to my comedy to-do list. After we reached the last page of the draft and our meeting wound down, he thanked me for my effort and I left the room. George and Dreyer remained behind to discuss something of real importance.

From deep inside the West Wing, I stumbled back to my makeshift workspace in the OEOB to complete an assignment that felt like a punishment—as though the president had instructed me to write "This speech was not as funny as Madeleine Albright's" a hundred times across a blackboard. I was sitting at my desk with my head bowed, my palms cupping my eyes and my mind mining the comic possibilities of "National Service Proposal" when I heard the door open. It was George.

"Listen, you've got to believe me," he said. "That was a very good meeting."

George had come all this way to make an extraordinarily nice gesture. Having a high-ranking White House official lie for your benefit is usually an honor reserved for the president himself.

"George, I was there."

"I know you think that meeting was a train wreck. What you don't know is, that was the first speechwriting meeting in a month where he didn't rip up the draft and ask for a new one."

I still didn't believe him, but I was now flattered that he was taking time out of his day to spin me.

"I'm totally serious. He's hated every speech we've brought in to him. You don't want to know what happened when *[name withheld as a professional courtesy]* came to him with a draft of the *[name of specific speech withheld as a professional courtesy]* speech two weeks ago."

I did, actually, but I didn't have time. The potential disaster associated with my name was only a few hours away. I still had jokes to write and revisions to make. We talked for a few minutes about the National Service Proposal and arrived at a premise that eventually became a functional joke:

> *The Senate Republicans are concerned that my National Service Proposal will just create more useless federal make-work activity. This from people who filibuster for a living.*

For the next few hours of that sunny Saturday afternoon, I sat in that office and wrote the next draft. I brought it to Dreyer's desk, where we added his edits to produce a third. The revisions included the National Service joke, a line borrowed from the Albright speech rewritten to work for the president and a few press jokes at the expense of Morton Kondracke and George Will—not bad work for a guy teetering on emotional exhaustion. By five o'clock, I left the OEOB with just enough time to go back to my friend's apartment for a shower and a tuxedo makeover.

White House Correspondents' Dinner

Having never been to an event anything like this, I set out that night without tangible expectations. Even so, I was taken aback when the evening of the seventieth annual White House Correspondents' Dinner began with an unflinchingly gay cocktail party where hors d'oeuvres were served by shirtless, muscular men with studded dog collars around their necks.

The invitation-only soirée took place at the apartment of Mark Robertson and was co-hosted by Mark Miller, two well-known Washington political media types whom I am nearly certain I have not just outed. Although my name was not on the guest list, my posse of senior White House aides vouched for my good standing to the leather-clad gentleman at the door. A few steps in, I encountered the first of several strapping waiters with trays of finger food. Momentarily flummoxed, I failed to thank him for the crudités. Honestly, despite having lived in both New York and San Francisco, I'd never attended a man-on-man sadomasochism-themed party. I only knew that at that moment I had no desire to hurt anyone or to be hurt myself. But this was clearly *more* than a party, it was a statement. And that statement was: "We're not in the Bush administration anymore."[4]

I was not uncomfortable with any of this, except that I desper-

---

4. To his credit, this was exactly the kind of party that Jesse Helms predicted would happen if Bill Clinton was elected president of the United States.

ately did not want to appear uncomfortable. This is a problem for me, because the same attribute that ranks me among the world's worst liars[5] also makes me a painfully bad actor. And at this moment, I looked like a guy who was trying to look like a guy who was so very cool with all of this. Which, of course, I was.

As I ventured further inside the living room, I saw a few people I knew and many people I recognized: Andrea Mitchell and Alan Greenspan, Kay Graham, Ben Bradlee and Sally Quinn, Arianna Huffington, Maureen Dowd and Frank Sesno, to name a few. But everyone in the room, no matter how boldface their name, was angling to meet the party's guest of honor, Sarah Jessica Parker. (Even Alan Greenspan seemed uncharacteristically exhuberant during their exchange.)

About ten minutes into the party I found myself in a small circle of people listening to James Carville dispense a cocktail-party version of his tirade in defense of Bill Clinton on a subject I can't remember. (Actually, you don't listen to Carville speak, any more than you *listen* to Mick Jagger sing. You watch in open-mouth, low-grade hypnosis.) When he concluded—or was it an intermission?—George introduced me to Carville. I had anticipated James's response and he did not disappoint, giving me a quick nod and a "Nice to meet ya" before turning his attention elsewhere.

It was a familiar exchange. In the past year and a half, I had met James Carville many times at various Clinton events in New York, but none had taken. For whatever reason, I do not register on his radar screen. This phenomenon is not exclusive to him, of course, and is one I've been sensitized to since high school when Suzette Amazon (her real name!), a girl with double-take good looks, acted as though we'd never met for year after formative year—despite the fact that she had lived just one bus stop away since grade school. (The one time she did address me in the halls of high school, she called me "Mike"—and I surrendered my chemistry notes to her

---

5. Okay. Okay. My GPA in college was a 3.3.

anyway.) It is hard to know how to respond to people like this, except to remind yourself that you do exist and you have the paperwork to prove it. Over time, my interactions with James Carville became a game I played for my own amusement: meeting James Carville for the first time, time and time again.[6]

As the hour of the dinner approached, the party depleted cluster by cluster. At around seven o'clock, I arrived at the Washington Hilton for the city's biggest social gala of the year. If Washington is, as Meg Greenfield described it, "high school with higher stakes," then the White House Correspondents' Dinner is the prom with overage drinking. And like high school, it sets off a peer group dynamic akin to showing up with a date deemed to be either hot or not. On that night, status was measured by the prestige of the news organization at whose table you were seated, ranked by informal consensus opinion. An invitation from ABC News was better than the *Washington Post*, which was better than *U.S. News & World Report*, which was better than the Cox Newspaper Service, which was better than *Transportation Weekly*, which was better than nothing. But best of all was a seat at the table of the magazine that most aggressively asserted itself as America's monthly chronicle of power and prestige, *Vanity Fair*. This is where I was sitting.

All week long, Dee Dee Myers had made it her business to procure me a seat at that table. Yes, it was at their second (a.k.a. "B") table, where we could only bask in the overflow glory of the prime face-time table adjacent to ours, at which Hollywood stars Michael Douglas and Dana Delaney flanked editor and host Graydon Carter. But the real value of the seating arrangements on this night was not the table you actually sat at, but rather the table you were able to tell people you sat at. Throughout the night, I was able to

---

6. My patience was rewarded at a party in 1999 when I was introduced to him once more. "Yeah, I think we've met," he said, to which I replied: "No, no. This is the first time. I'm sure of it." My original plan had me addressing him as "Jack" in that exchange, but I chickened out.

make small talk about the speech I had written for the president
and the seat I had at the *Vanity Fair* table.

Sometime during the appetizer, I felt a tap on the shoulder. I
turned around to see Helmet Head, replete with a tuxedo and a
wide grin. I was not terribly surprised that he had infiltrated the
event, but I was definitely curious to learn the specifics. We went
out to the lobby and he told me the story. Having failed to procure
an actual ticket, Helmet Head launched Plan B, the elements of
which included a tux, an air of confidence that neutralizes suspicion and an agile mind that is the handmaiden of good luck.[7] On
this night, fortune came in the form of spotting Dennis Hopper as
he made his way through the lobby trailing an entourage. Helmet
Head got on line behind him and—by gesturing toward the movie
star to the ticket checker—made it past Checkpoint Charlie and
into the fabulous ball.

On the way back to my seat, I took a good long spin around the
room, negotiating the space between tightly packed tables by pretending to have a destination, when in fact my only agenda was
gawking. Starting from the back of the room, I did not see a face I
recognized until about halfway to the stage, when I began noticing
people familiar to me only because I watch too much C-SPAN and
once worked in a campaign press office. As I moved closer to the
front of the room, the people became better-looking and their
names increasingly noteworthy. At tables with journalists who
occasionally show up on a roundtable on CNN's *Inside Politics* were
the White House aides you might see interviewed on *Inside Politics*.
Finally, about twenty feet from the dais, I reached the spot where
the highest echelon of celebrity-journalists entertained celebrity-
politicos and celebrity-celebrities. This was the front-row realm of
Sam Donaldson and Dan Rather, Ted Kennedy and Mack McLarty,

---

7. In his pocket, Helmet Head also had the makings of Plan C: a Xeroxed copy
of a ticket to use as a prop in an elaborate story he had yet to invent that he would
plead to a security guard. Each of his schemes would have made an excellent Men-
tos commercial.

Sigourney Weaver and Richard Dreyfuss. And directly in my path, I could see what had many of these heads turned: Barbra Streisand and Colin Powell fully engaged in conversation.

From the looks of it, the conversation had not just started and was not just an exchange of pleasantries. I dared to walk past them—pretending not to notice the obvious spectacle—while listening carefully to snippets of their dialogue. In the few seconds I was within eavesdropping range, I thought I overheard the words "multilateral," "unconscionable" and "unintended socio-geopolitical consequences"—none of them out of the mouth of the chairman of the Joint Chiefs of Staff.

I returned to my seat as the president of the White House Correspondents' Association began the evening's program. While Clinton was being introduced, the buzz of the room dialed down to a low murmur, then exploded in applause as he assumed the podium.

My respiratory system disengaged as he began to speak. He settled into the room with some jokes that I'd never heard before, drawing only polite laughs. He was off-script already. Instead of the self-effacing jokes at the top of his draft, Clinton skipped ahead to begin with jokes at the expense of his hosts, the White House press corps. The first joke of the night that I recognized was his third joke in—the Larry King joke, introduced with a slightly meaner preamble:

> I want to complain about something—this is my night—you all complain to me all the time. I watched CNN the other night, one of those Hundred Day stories—and I couldn't believe it. There were Andrea Mitchell, Susan Spencer, Brit Hume and Wolf Blitzer on *Larry King Live*. Imagine that: going around the president to take their message directly to the American people. I was really offended!

The joke elicited the first real laugh of the night and my first breath. He continued on, giving the same slightly meaner interpretation to the jokes that followed:

I'll tell you something else. You all never let me get away with hypocrisy. If I do the slightest thing different from what I said in the campaign, I hear about it for months and months. You know Benjamin Franklin once said that our critics are our friends, for they show us our faults. But look at what I've been criticized for. I was criticized for fierce partisanship by Pat Buchanan.

    . . . I was called an effete intellectual by George Will.

    . . . Mean-spirited by Bob Novak.

    . . . Wavering and indecisive by Morton Kondracke.

    . . . I was accused of pursuing failed economic policies on the editorial page of the *Wall Street Journal* . . .

On the heels of the sustained, rolling laughter he had built with that scripted litany, he added this extemporaneous sarcasm to his reference to the *Wall Street Journal,* whose editorial page was his most zealous (mainstream) critic.

    . . . that great bastion of conservatism that took us from a $1 trillion to a $4 trillion debt in only four years.

The jokes on the page on that topic stopped there, but the president ran the red light and kept going. He added this capper and the afterthought that followed.

    . . . And I've been called too fat by Rush Limbaugh.

    . . . Did you like the way Rush took up for Janet Reno the other night on his program? He only did it because she was attacked by a black guy.

The audience responded with swallowed, nervous laughter to the assault on Limbaugh. So did the president.

He's here, isn't he?

The people seated around me looked to me, the speechwriter, for guidance. They had no idea how to respond, and neither did I. Those last few sentences were so terrible for so many different reasons. Here are a few, but I'm sure there are more:

The raid on the Waco compound, which had occurred not even two weeks earlier, was already a hypersensitive issue before anybody introduced racism into it. A week after it was over, Janet Reno had testified before Congress on the raids and come under some sharp criticism from committee chairman John Conyers, described here by the president as a "black guy." It was one of the most tone-deaf jokes I'd ever heard.

But it was so much worse than just that. Not only had the president acknowledged that Rush Limbaugh—a demagogue in the full-time business of fomenting the froth of fellow Clinton-haters—existed, but also that *he listened to his program*. What thought could please Rush more? Here's some more bad: Rush was not there that night, but the president had imagined that he was. What more evidence could you need to conclude that his well-founded antipathy for Rush was descending into paranoia?

There was absolutely nothing good about the president's Lim-baugh remarks,[8] and—probably having figured that out—he quickly moved to his next block of jokes. They were the self-deprecating jokes, arriving not a moment too soon, that had been pushed back in the order in favor of the score-settling media hypocrisy section and the diatribe that validated his worst public enemy. But at least he kept some of them in:

I've been wondering about these grades on a hundred days. You can't imagine how disappointed I am by that—this whole grade thing—because my mother still keeps all those report cards on her refrigerator.

---

8. Limbaugh went on to make hay of this ill-considered accusation of racism on his radio *and* television programs for weeks and weeks later.

. . . And I knew you'd give Hillary higher marks than me. It's just like law school all over again.

I was hoping this sustained laugh might erase the shaky beginning. And for a while it did.

You know, you hold me to impossible standards. One of you wrote a column the other day comparing this to Genesis, saying God got more done in six days than I did in a hundred. I'd just like to point out that his efforts were not preceded by twelve days from another administration.
    . . . *I'm not doing so bad. I mean, at this point in his administration, William Henry Harrison had already been dead for sixty-eight days!*

This biggest laugh of the night was followed up with an expertly timed kicker:

. . . I mean, my stimulus package lived longer than that.

This double hit of self-effacement was the high-water mark of Clinton's humor that evening. Even his most ardent foes were applauding and/or shaking their heads in bemused admiration. It is impossible not to like a person who would make these jokes at his own expense during the moment he makes them—even if you already hate him. The contradiction puts a crack in what was a hardened opinion; this is the real and not insignificant power of humor.

But the high point was short-lived. A few sentences later, the president found another opportunity for an unscripted sidebar sting, directed at Majority Leader Bob Dole, who was nowhere to be seen and mentioned apropos of nothing. Citing a recent article in the *Wall Street Journal* as his source, Clinton launched into a long story about a certain senator who had opposed his economic stimulus package as a wasteful boondoggle—but had called for twenty-three million federal dollars to turn a Kansas senior citizen center into a boathouse. He ended the story with an apology soaked in sarcasm to the majority leader, pretending to cede him the fiscal high ground. It was long, confusing and unfunny.[9]

After he mercifully ended that, Clinton launched into some closing thoughts, on a serious note, that captivated the room:

> I confess that sometimes I get impatient with the pace of change. I've been that way since I was a little boy. But I believe this: I believe we have begun to change this country for the better. People no longer ask whether we're going to reduce the deficit, they ask how much and how fast. People no longer ask whether we are going to do something about health care, they say exactly what and how much will it cost. People no longer ask whether we're going to have a partnership with the government and the private sector, now they say, what will the shape of it be. They no longer even ask whether we're going to try to make government different; they just say, will you do it right, will it matter this time? I think those are important changes . . . And I appreciate my Louisiana mentor—Mr. Carville out there, has a lot of sayings. One of those things that he said to me tonight again that he's said before is, if you never want to stumble, stand still. So you tell them when I stumble, but always tell them I'm not standing still.

Like the soliloquies on Limbaugh and Dole, not a word of this existed on the pages he had brought with him to the podium. But this was Clinton at his best. Standing on his feet, he summoned

---

9. It also wasn't true. There was no federal money involved in the project. Within forty-eight hours of the speech, the White House was forced to issue an apology to the majority leader and incur a number of critical newspaper editorials about Clinton's angry "joke" as a result. But no one knew this at the time.

words that no hired wordsmith could equal—measured, eloquent, generous, thoughtful and even inspiring. They seemed the true realization of his voice, his candor and his gift for self-expression. Enough of the jokes had gotten enough of a laugh to make this humor speech pass muster, but these final thoughts left the evening's deepest impression and made the humor resonate funnier after the fact. He received the response that only true talent can elicit from these, the most cynical people on earth: *Damn, this guy is good.*

Having just saved his own speech, he left the podium to a standing ovation. By this point, I had slipped behind a curtain that brought me backstage. Putting myself in his path at that moment was pleading for a compliment. It was shameless, but not beneath me.

"Great job, sir," I offered first.

"Thank you, Mark. And thanks for all your help." He looked me in the eye, shook my hand with his right hand and squeezed my shoulder with his left. Then he moved on. His thank-you was both sincere and brief. I'd be lying if I told you that this aftermath was all I had imagined (I had in mind a tasteful Truman Balcony reception), but unlike the Oval Office meeting earlier in the day, it didn't dishearten me in any way or subtract from the exhilaration of that moment. It was a lesson in speechwriting itself: a speechwriter can rightly feel pride of ownership in the written document, but the speech, once spoken, belongs to the speaker.

The *Vanity Fair* Party

As I found my way though the dispersing crowd, I was the proud recipient of some very nice compliments. I responded to them all by saying some version of "the president was great"—a technique I had picked up by watching people smarter than I pretending to deflect credit while at the same time informing the flatterer that they have delivered their praise to the exact right person.

In many ways, this night was just beginning, and there was still so much more praise to deflect and humility to feign. But there was really just one place to do it to maximum effect: the after-party hosted by *Vanity Fair*.

I walked across the street, up to a stately Wisconsin Avenue apartment building, and made my way through a considerable crowd outside the entrance. When I got to the front of the line, I told a gentleman holding a clipboard my name. He eyed me suspiciously and checked his list.

"Nice try. Mark Katz already went up."

I told him he hadn't. But for the actual invitation, a picture ID and, more important, a *Vanity Fair* party planner I met at dinner who was in the immediate vicinity, I might have been relegated to the teeming crowd of wannabes.

I had arrived at a party already in progress. The party was at the residence of Christopher Hitchens, the *Vanity Fair* political writer with strident opinions and a spacious book-lined apartment. The room was a concentrated version of the dinner itself, all the highest-profile people of the political media and popular culture mingling among themselves—minus, for the most part, the gallery of gawkers. But most startling of all was the sight of Helmet Head over by the buffet table, holding a full plate of shrimp. I walked up to Helmet and extended my arm. "Excuse me, but is your name Mark Katz?" I asked. I was too impressed with his endless ingenuity to pretend to be angry.

But I had not come to this party to mingle with Helmet Head. Looking around the room, I could see George Stephanopoulos standing in a doorway talking to a tall, strikingly beautiful woman. I recognized the face but couldn't associate the name. At the risk of stepping in on his rap, I walked toward the door, ready to walk past him if he didn't pull me into the conversation. He caught my eye and turned toward me.

"Mark, have you met Vendela?" he asked.

I shot George a look and he began to break up.

"No, oddly enough, I've never met Vendela. Which is weird because we travel in the same circles and have a lot of friends in common."

Vendela, the *Sports Illustrated* supermodel who had graced the cover of the swimsuit issue the previous year, was in on the joke and the three of us shared a laugh. George then introduced me to her in the context of my role in writing the president's speech. She smiled brightly, patted me on the shoulder and said something. I'll be dammed if I remember a word of it, but for as long as I live I will be able to assist a sketch artist in rendering her face to haunting likeness.

A few mingles later I encountered an immediately familiar face, Madeleine Albright. She greeted me with a kiss on the cheek and told me she had heard the rumor of my involvement in the president's speech. She leaned in to whisper, "My speech was funnier."

"You're not the only one who thinks so," I said. I told her about the president's comment, and she gave me a look that expressed sympathy for enduring a tough Oval Office meeting. I had the sense she might have attended some herself.

Throughout the night, Helmet Head checked in, reporting on the conversations he'd had and the people I needed to meet. His ubiquity in the room quadrupled my exposure, as he was effectively acting as my agent. Nearly every conversation I had that night began with someone saying to me, "Oh, you're Mark Katz. I met your friend before."

I was circulating near the balcony when I heard a voice from behind. "She wants to meet you! She wants to meet you!"

My screenwriter friend Gary Ross was pulling at the collar of my tuxedo.

"She wants to meet you!"

"Who wants to meet me?"

"Just come with me!"

Without bothering to excuse myself from the sentence I was in the middle of, I turned and followed Gary through the crowd. I could see that we were approaching a small circle of people ensconced around Barbra Streisand. This was too much. Gary approached and presented me to her.

"You're Mark Katz?" she asked incredulously.

"You're Barbra Streisand," I said in a matter-of-fact manner that belied my stupefaction.

"Oh my God, you're so *young*!!"

She did not say the word "young": she screeched it, raising her pitch and extending it to a full two syllables. And then—just as she finished the second syllable of "young"—Barbra Streisand ran her fingers through my hair.

"Oh, such a nice Jewish boy," she said.

I don't know if it was her fingers, or my conditioner, or the combination of the two, but something felt like butter.

Now that she had stroked my brown locks, we kind of had to talk and get to know each other a little better. We talked about the speech ("a very funny speech—but more than that—an important speech"). She wanted to know the details of the rehearsal and was surprised to learn there really was none ("Uh, what a talent he is! What an absolute talent!"). She told me I should write a speech just like that for the first lady ("Hillary has a wonderful sense of humor and no one knows it!"). She even wanted to know more about me—who I was and how they found me. As I began to tell her of a Gridiron Dinner six weeks earlier, she interrupted:

"Wait—you're not the one who wrote the Albright speech?"

What was I going to do, lie?

Her fevered pitch picked up from there. We stood there speaking for some time, and I remember being embarrassed that the people who were eager to make her acquaintance might think that I was hogging her. Her response to me was so affectionate, if not maternal, that I thought she might adopt me. But then I remembered her recent relationship with Andre Agassi, and I was forced to consider other directions this might take. Now the transformation of my ego was complete: inside of a week I had gone from an unemployed copywriter to someone trying not to get Barbra Streisand's hopes up.

She kept on asking me questions and I kept on answering. She wanted to know where I grew up, and I told her I was from a suburb outside New York. ("New York! Where else?") And for some reason I can only attribute to nerves, I segued from there to a fact about my high school experience I thought might be of interest to her.

"You want to know something funny? I played the second cook in my high school production of *Hello, Dolly!*"

That struck me as something I should say to Barbra Streisand. As if that might foster a bond between us. As if we might both start singing "When the Parade Passes By."

She had no response to that but I was confused by her confused look. I thought she was struggling to remember the part of the second cook. It was, after all, a very small part, albeit a character in a crucial scene where Dolly Levi returns to the Harmonia Gardens restaurant for a fabulous dinner and an ornate dance scene with gleeful waiters so glad to see her, they break out in the title song. So I proceeded to repeat the two lines I'd spoken on a high school stage a dozen years earlier.

"Rudolph, it's true, no? . . . Ach, Rudolph, it's like old times again!"

Again, no response. I was babbling to Babs. Apparently, neither of the two cooks at the Harmonia Gardens restaurant had made lasting impressions. Finally she interrupted:

"Tell me—were there political jokes in the president's speech that got cut or you couldn't use? Or Albright's? Or maybe you could write some political material for me to use."

I pulled out my wallet and handed Barbra Streisand my (sans) business card. On the back of my party invite, I wrote down her fax number in New York and, per her request, promised to transmit a copy of the Albright speech. Shortly after that, she caught the eye of Ron Howard. Before I knew it, I was being introduced to Ron Howard. By Barbra Streisand. The surrealness was coming at me so fast, I secretly wished there was some kind of pause button to hit so that I could experience each new episode without still being dizzy from the last.

At different moments throughout the evening, I think it would have been impossible to distinguish the real events unfolding before me from psychotic episodes I might have been experiencing. There seemed to be no reason why, before this night was over, I wouldn't find myself in conversations with Abraham Lincoln, Julius Caesar and Helen of Troy. Without being completely certain I did not descend to pure madness that evening, I do recall socializing with several other party guests whom I'd previously encountered in the pages of *People* magazine while waiting to have my teeth cleaned.

With the possible exception of Helmet Head, I may have been the last non-busboy to leave the *Vanity Fair* party, so desperate was I not to let the evening end. By 4 A.M., I was back on a sleep-sofa, trying to comprehend all that had happened to me and vowing never to forget the details of a day and a night like none I had ever known. Before I drifted off, one last thought interrupted the euphoric semiconsciousness preceding the REM in eyes that had taken in so much:

"Wait a minute—what happened to the National Service joke?"

CHAPTER NINE

People Who ▇▇▇ People

Author's Note: Portions of the following account have been reviewed by a team of lawyers enforcing a nondisclosure agreement.

December 28, 1993

As I slid my card key into the hotel door lock, the phone inside what-was-not-yet-my-room was already ringing. I assumed it was my mother who had managed to track me down, as she likes to be the first person to wish me a happy birthday and this was the day to do it. I left my luggage in the hallway and raced for the phone.

███

███

██████████████████████ . ███████████████████

███

Happy birthday to me.

Six weeks earlier, on the day I called in to my answering machine to hear ████████ voice, I nearly fell onto the pavement beneath the pay phone. In the aftermath of having written a funny speech for President Bill Clinton, I found that opportunity had been tracking me down more and more, and I had developed the very annoying habit of checking my messages every fifteen to thirty minutes whenever I left my apartment. But this was the best one yet, by far:

"██████████████████████████ . ██████████████

███

███

███

█████████████████████ "

Maybe a week after that, I decided to call a friend from college, Jeff Frankel, a Brooklyn-bred lawyer transplanted to a big-time L.A. law firm, to ask him his advice on handling my very first "gig." Soon we agreed that he would represent me—for a fee so low, it could have gotten him fired. Now I had a lawyer and a gig, both of which I enjoyed saying, especially "gig." "How much money should we ask for?" was the first question I asked my lawyer about my gig.

"Well, let's see: █████████████████████████████

█████████████████████████████ "

I had always liked Frankel's no-bullshit bravado, but now I liked it even more. I hadn't earned too much more than that in the year since the McCann-Erickson checks had stopped coming in and the New York State unemployment insurance expired. Two weeks later, when █████████████████████████████████

"████████████████████████████████████
████████████████████████████████████
███████████████████—and I'm from Canarsie!"

But by now, I was something of an adventure junkie, and this had all the feel of an exciting one. Besides, this way I wouldn't have to make plans for ███████'s Eve. ████████████████
████████████████████████████████████
████████████████████████████████
████████████████████████████████ "

"███? I just read that ████████████████
██████████ and I'm living on corn flakes and macaroni & cheese!"

"Listen, Mark. I already told you: ████████████ ██████ █
████████████████████████████████████ "

████████████████, I agreed to the contract that included an ironclad ████ ████████████████████. ████████████████
████████████████████████████████

This was all my friend Helmet Head needed to hear. After all, Helmet was there the night ████████ ████████████ at the █████
████████ ████████████ █████. He immediately volunteered to accompany me on the trip as my bodyguard/business consultant. I'm not sure which idea appealed to me more, bringing a friend along for laughs or pretending to be such a professional entity that I traveled with my own people.

Before too long, the number of my people doubled with the addition of my friend Cindy Chupack to the roster. In the years since Cindy and I had become fast friends in the back row of advertising classes, she had moved to Los Angeles in pursuit of a TV writing career, gotten married and worked her way onto the staff of a sitcom. More recently, she had separated from her husband, a very nice guy who had discovered later in life that he wanted a husband of his own. From the earliest days of our friendship, Cindy and I demonstrated a special knack for having fun together, and I pitched her a plan to cheer her up:

████████████████████████████████████

(Her humor still intact, Cindy suggested that her soon-to-be ex-husband might be even more excited to attend a ███████).
So few were her options that this sounded like a good idea to her too—provided that if any one of our trio had to be assigned a couch, it would not be her. Done! Cindy booked a flight from L.A. to ███ ███ ███.

With Helmet and Cindy not due to arrive for a few hours,█

██ !!

██

██

███████████████████████████████████████

" ██

██

████████████████████████████████████ " as I ironed the tuxedo shirt I was to wear later that week.

By the time Helmet and Cindy arrived, I was already quite confused about the fact that ████████████████████████████

██

██

██

██

███████

For the next three days, ████████████████████████████

██

███████████████████████████ [1] despite the fact that ███████

███████████████████████ . All the while, ████████████████

██

██████████████████████ ? But what did I know? I was just the joke writer.

---

1. Not to mention Elayne Boosler!

and

but

the

Notwithstanding

and

.

when

then

as if

But then

Whereas ███████████████████████████████████
█████████████████████████████████ and ████████
the ███
████████████████████████████████ but ██████████
██
██
██████████████████████ so ██████████████████████
████████████████████████   ████████████████████
██
██
██
██
██
██
██████████████████████████ if not for ████████████
██
██
██
██
██
██
██
██
Well then, ████████████████████████████████████
██
██ and or
██
██
████████████████ somesuch ████████████████████
██

████ I told him I would have my lawyer Jeff Frankel contact him directly.

Even I knew that. ████

████. In fact, this

They were fun to write, and once I started going I could hardly stop.

- ████
- ████!!!!!
- ████?
- ████ ████
- *More like these*

For all of my effort, Cindy—reading the list I had compiled over my shoulder—managed to top them all: ████ ████ ████! Helmet, Cindy and I spent the next ten minutes laughing at her great line and writing a few more to boot. Even Helmet, not a comedy writer by trade, got into the act, offering this bon mot: ████ ████." And that got added to the list as well.

Sure enough, twenty minutes later

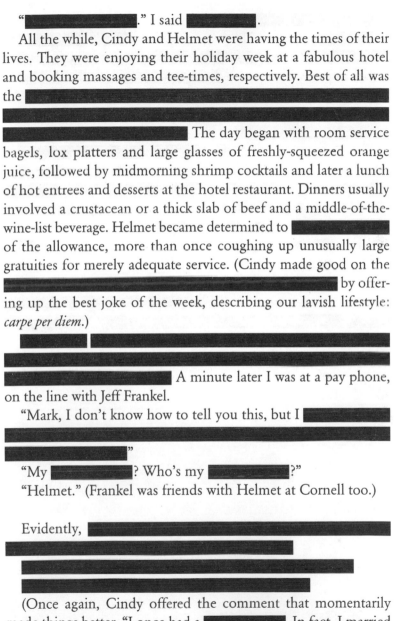

"██████████." I said ██████████.

All the while, Cindy and Helmet were having the times of their lives. They were enjoying their holiday week at a fabulous hotel and booking massages and tee-times, respectively. Best of all was the ██
██
██████████████████████ The day began with room service bagels, lox platters and large glasses of freshly-squeezed orange juice, followed by midmorning shrimp cocktails and later a lunch of hot entrees and desserts at the hotel restaurant. Dinners usually involved a crustacean or a thick slab of beef and a middle-of-the-wine-list beverage. Helmet became determined to ███████████ of the allowance, more than once coughing up unusually large gratuities for merely adequate service. (Cindy made good on the ██ by offering up the best joke of the week, describing our lavish lifestyle: *carpe per diem*.)

████ ████████████████████████████████
████████████████████████████████
██████████████████████ A minute later I was at a pay phone, on the line with Jeff Frankel.

"Mark, I don't know how to tell you this, but I ███████████
██
███████████████████"

"My ██████████? Who's my ██████████?"

"Helmet." (Frankel was friends with Helmet at Cornell too.)

Evidently, ████████████████████████████████████
████████████████████████████████████
██

(Once again, Cindy offered the comment that momentarily made things better. "I once had a ██████████. In fact, I married him!")

███████████████

████████ was right. Not long after that, ████████████

█████████████████████████████████████

Before the week was over ███████████████████████

█████████████████████████████████████

█████████████████████████████████████

██████████████████

On the way home, I realized I ████████████████ ████████ in
return for the rights to write about the time ███████████

█████████████████████████████████████

██████████████████████ as I had come to ████████ ecstatic to
█████████████████████ for a ████████████ extravaganza but
left there █████████████████.
    Oy!

Postscript: Nine weeks later ████████████████████████

█████████████████████████████████████

CHAPTER TEN

Boring-gate

I WAS WATCHING THE *TODAY* SHOW WITH ONE EYE AND PACKING MY bags to catch a morning Amtrak Metroliner to Washington when I heard it:

"Al Gore is so boring, his Secret Service code name is 'Al Gore.'"

Al Hunt, the well-regarded *Wall Street Journal* columnist who was participating in the show's weekly political roundup, barely got the words out of his mouth before he'd cracked up himself. A millisecond later, both Katie and Bryant were crumbling in laughter as well. My immediate response was to scramble for pen and paper before I lost a single syllable of a killer line.

This joke commanded my full attention because it was explosively funny, but also because I was on my way to Washington to write a speech for Al Gore. Weeks earlier, his press secretary—Lorraine Voles, yet another redeemed Dukaki—had called to ask if I could work on his speech to the Gridiron Club, the same rarefied white-tie-and-tails humor event that had been the occasion for the Madeleine Albright speech exactly one year earlier. I eagerly signed on.

By the early spring of 1994, a year and a half since I'd been fired

from McCann-Erickson, calls like that one were slowly distinguishing me from an unemployed person. Being a freelance writer
is not a job as much as a chronic economic condition, and with each
new assignment that came my way the likelihood of having to
return to advertising diminished. In addition to the ███████████
extravaganza,[1] I had recently completed humor speech assignments for House Speaker Tom Foley[2] and the Clinton White
House Republican-in-residence David Gergen.[3] Each successful
project seemed to beget another, and soon I had all but officially
rejoined our economy.

    Although my new circumstance had come at the price of a sig-
nificant pay cut, I found enormous psychic reward in this new line
of work. As a thoroughly humbled former cocky punk, I found
redemption each time I sat across from a high-profile, powerful person who wanted to know what I thought was funny and was willing
to pay me to tell them. I was thirty years old—too late to be a
prodigy, perhaps, but not too late to be a genius. The invoices that
these projects generated were sent out on letterhead for "The Sound
Bite Institute," a "creative think tank" that listed me as its "resident
scholar." The most accurate description of this "institute" could be
seen in those hours that took me from New York City to Washington, D.C.: a guy on a train tapping out jokes on a laptop computer.
The computer was a recent purchase, a hard-won trophy and also a
major investment in my new *have-jokes-will-travel* lifestyle. And the
first sentence I entered that day into this $2,500 sixteen-megahertz
marvel was *"Al Gore is so boring, his secret service code name is 'Al Gore,'"*
which I had to type fast, because my computer's battery was good
for only thirty-five minutes.

---

    1. Okay, who showed this chapter to those fucking lawyers?
    2. "Presidential candidates always make a big deal about where they were born. In
a log cabin. In a place called Hope. I was born in a dark blue suit and wingtip shoes."
    3. "My remarks tonight will be in two parts: first, I'd like to share with you my
honest, most heartfelt opinions accumulated over twenty years of public service.
And then, I'd like to offer a rebuttal."

For the next few minutes, I stared into the screen, studying the joke and trying to understand it as if it were an algebraic equation or a code that needed to be cracked. Not for a moment did I assume that Al Hunt had written this joke. This was clearly the work of a comedy professional, and a good one at that. I knew that somewhere in these sixteen syllables was the comic $e = mc^2$ that had cracked Katie and Bryant up. My job was to figure out how to harness the powerful laughs Al Hunt had just gotten at Al Gore's expense.

When my train arrived at Union Station, I jumped in a cab to drop off my things at my Washington home-away-from-home—my brother Robert's one-bedroom apartment.[4] Upon hailing another cab after that, I got to hear myself say the most self-aggrandizing instructions a person can give to a taxi driver: "To the White House!" Soon I was walking through the Pennsylvania Avenue West Wing gates with 90 percent of the awe I had felt my first time through ten months earlier. Only this time, I was not a tourist who'd shown up on a lark. I was a bargain-priced hired gun and man on a mission. With three to seven years left for the Clinton administration, I knew I had the inside track on the job I'd once daydreamed about while clipping Mike Dukakis's newspapers: writing funny speeches from inside a Democratic White House. What I didn't know was that I was about to meet the man who was every bit as serious about comedy as I was.

When I was introduced to Vice President Al Gore late that afternoon, I was startled when he seemed equally excited to meet me. Lorraine shoehorned in as much of a meeting as his schedule that day would permit—ten stolen minutes in the hallway of the Old Executive Office Building between other events. When she

---

4. After Harvard, my alter-ego brother maintained the altitude of the academic upper echelons: law school at the University of Chicago, a clerkship in Boston for federal appeals court judge Stephen J. Breyer and now a position in the Justice Department in Washington. But I avoided law school altogether, so you tell me who's smarter.

reminded him that I was the person who had worked on the funny speeches for Clinton and Albright, both of which he had attended, he nodded and asked for my thoughts on his Gridiron speech. Having spent the last three hours on the train imagining what this speech might be, my head was swimming with ambitious ideas and I disregarded the standard political practice of reducing expectations:

"Mr. Vice President,[5] I think you have a real opportunity to give a truly hysterical speech."

Oddly, this remark drained the nice-to-meet-you smile from his face. His head tilted toward the heavens, or at least to the ornate forty-foot ceilings of the OEOB, and he took in a deep breath. Then he brought his eyes down to mine, his face redrawn with no-nonsense purpose:

"You have *no idea* how much I want to knock this thing out of the park."

Our eyes locked for a moment as we sized each other up, and our silent, mutual exchange confirmed a shared, if abnormal, seriousness of purpose about a humor speech. Lorraine had found an empty desk for me somewhere on the second floor of the Old Executive Office Building, a gargantuan structure not fifty feet from the West Wing that is home to 95 percent of White House staffers. I plugged in my laptop and got to work. The next few days were filled with the now-familiar prespeech drill, reading every article about the speech-giver I could get my hands on and debriefing staffers in search of resonant themes. I was looking for a way to incorporate Al Gore jokes into Al Gore's speech—and as I continued to study Al Hunt's joke, I realized that one of its powerful elements was the intrinsic comic value of the name "Al Gore." With

---

5. This being the first time I had ever addressed someone as "Mr. Vice President," I immediately experienced a significant drop-off in the thrill of hearing these words as they left my lips, brought on by the addition of the word "Vice" to the sentence. Example: "Cheese sandwiches are quite tasty, Mr. Vice President" just sounds plain silly.

the realization that jokes were funnier when they had the words "Al Gore" in them, I hypothesized that the effect could be magnified by having Al Gore say the words "Al Gore"—and in the case of *"Al Gore is so boring his Secret Service code name is 'Al Gore,'"* Al Gore would be saying the name "Al Gore" not once but *twice!* As I pitched the idea of this third-person approach to Lorraine and other staffers, I was not surprised that everyone found it promising. But I was quietly shocked that each time I repeated the "Secret Service" line that had inspired it, no one mentioned that they'd heard it before. Having failed to mention its origin the first time, I found myself less inclined to mention it each time after that.

By the end of the week, Lorraine was escorting me to Gore's West Wing office to go over the material I'd compiled. On my first trip there, he opened the door of his office and greeted me enthusiastically. "Welcome to the Square Office of the vice president!" he said, inviting me into the nicely appointed (if rectilinear) workspace.

My eye caught the oversized photograph on the wall—the Earth as a big blue marble—and I smiled, because it reminded me of a poster a guy on my freshman hall had hung over his bed. A hard-core biochemistry major, "Wild Bill" would later drop out to devote more time to psychotropic drugs.

"Do you like that photograph?" the vice president asked. "You know, I took it myself. " His straight face eventually gave way to a mischievous smile.

There was more where that came from. In fact, Al Gore was pitching jokes from the moment I entered his office, but the smile on my face and the laughter I emitted were mostly a response to the fact that of the two of us—the second highest-ranking executive officer of the U.S. government and a designated comedy ringer—he was the one breathlessly hoofing it to make the good impression. That made me like him all the more.

When we turned our attention to the pages I'd handed him, he asked, "Do you have any ideas for an opening bit?" Having already seen his stage act, I was only slightly surprised that the vice president had so casually used the word "bit," sounding like a comedy veteran. I hadn't given a "bit" any thought yet, but I was able to respond to his question with a rare off-the-top-of-my-head joke:

"Yeah, we're going to roll you out to the podium on a hand truck."

As I watched Al Gore's face light up at what I thought was just a warm-up joke, my mind struggled to catch up to his. As he shouted out "Oh, I love it!" I was silently processing something like this: *Wait a minute—I must have been serious when I said that. Yes! Let's actually roll Al Gore to the podium in a hand truck! (Good God—I am a genius!)* I had arrived at the joke but Al Gore had beaten me to the idea, and in the moment that I managed to steal it back, the speech's opening bit was born.

Someone more confident than I might have let Al Gore know that he was at the very least the coauthor of a winning gag. But what Al Gore didn't know was that I was every bit (perhaps less obviously) as desperate for him to think that I was hysterically funny. Humor writers are funny people who are constantly in the process of convincing the world that they are indispensably funny—and at the same time quietly trying to convince themselves of the same thing. I was no more or less subject to these governing neuroses than any other practitioner of my trade, and at this moment in my career I lacked the courage to dispel false notions that were serving me just fine.

By this time, I had arrived at a framework for the "Al Gore" jokes that would give Al Gore the license to borrow a stolen joke he need not know was stolen at all. As I sat across from him at his desk, Al Gore was reading the whole routine aloud:

"By now, I've heard them all: *Al Gore is so stiff, racks buy their suits off of him.*"

He laughed at that. So did Lorraine and I, if only to reinforce his laugh.

"Al Gore is an inspiration to the millions of Americans who suffer from Dutch Elm Disease."[6]

Another laugh registered another score. But I held my breath in anticipation of the line to come:

"Al Gore is so boring, his Secret Service code name is 'Al Gore.'"

That one broke him up and generated the loudest and most sustained laughter yet. I was half expecting him to say, "Oh, Al Hunt told me that joke the last time I saw him," or recount how dozens of people had repeated it to him the day it aired on national television. By now, owning up to its origin would have relieved a growing burden on my conscience. Perhaps I might have, if Lorraine had not been in the room and I didn't have to reveal myself to her as a weasel. I was also distracted once again by the impossible thought that neither Al Gore nor his press secretary had heard an Al Gore joke that was broadcast to millions. I began to wonder if I had hallucinated the whole episode—and if I had, isn't that the same as writing it? But this fevered interior monologue was interrupted by Al Gore completing the last line of the "Al Gore jokes" section of his speech:

"And every time I hear another 'Al Gore' joke, I always have the same response: Very funny, Tipper!"[7]

He clearly enjoyed this part of the speech and read it again without the laughter but with perfect comic pitch on the kicker[8]— "Very funny, Tipper"—hitting the consonants in "Tipper" especially hard.

After laughing again, he looked back over the run and picked out his favorite joke of the bunch, you'll never guess which.

---

6. That joke started its life with the punch line "who suffer from rigor mortis," only to be improved immeasurably with an edit from Erik Tarloff.

7. "Tipper" is one of the few names that exceed "Al Gore" for inherent humor content. However, both still fall short of the standard set by my childhood friend Bebe Rebozo.

8. "Kicker" is another word from the parlance of comedy. (I think I learned it from Al Gore.)

Lorraine chimed in. "That's a great joke, isn't it?"

He nodded in concurrence. "These are all jokes that you wrote?" he wanted to know.

Gulp.

All week long, as I shared my draft with his staff, I had been able to maintain the impression that the Secret Service joke was mine without sinking to an explicitly stated lie. I don't think I ever set out to purloin credit for this joke; it happened incrementally, as I let the assumption go uncorrected day after day. But with each passing opportunity to clear up the confusion, I had dug myself in deeper, and now the vice president of the United States had put a question to me directly that required a direct response. Al Gore had just given me my opening to come clean.

"Sir, I am just a ghostwriter. As far as I'm concerned, *you* wrote these jokes."

I am not proud of what I said—except to note that even as I said it, its brilliance stunned me. Deploying false humility to let a falsehood stand was at least as inspired as the joke I was in the process of stealing. (In fact, I might have just invented the nonadmission admission.) Add to that the deft ego-stroking of a comically needy vice president and you have a skillful political maneuver worthy of its surroundings, the West Wing of the White House.

"Good answer!" Al Gore shot back. He didn't know the half of it.

By signing me up months ahead to work on the VP's speech, Lorraine had pulled a deft move of her own on the president's staff. No longer was I available to be at the center of the process that would produce the speech Clinton gave to that very same Gridiron room. Instead, in my conversation with the president's head speechwriter, David Kusnet, I promised to contribute pages of material and to be a part of the team that wrote it. That speech was in its earliest planning stages, and I was asked to attend a meeting in Dee Dee Myers's office to discuss it with a collection of sharp senior staffers. At some point in the meeting, Ricki Seidman, a deputy something, offered up this idea: how about a video where Bill and Hillary spoof Harry and Louise?

Harry and Louise were the characters of a series of ads in an infuriating yet effective ad campaign designed to bring down the ambitious Clinton health care proposal. The ads presented a seemingly thoughtful married couple—he owlish and buttoned-down, she sensible and attractive—sitting around their suburban home reading the serious parts of a serious newspaper and imagining the horror of the Clinton health care plan. The commercials always built to the same earnest plea ("There's got to be a better way!") that belied the fact that the consortium of insurance companies that produced the ads was perfectly happy with the way things were. That being said, in the spring of 1994 the fictional Harry and Louise were in the process of kicking Bill and Hillary's real asses around the block. Ricki's idea was the perfect comic counterpunch, so simple and brilliant a premise that every person in the room was annoyed that they hadn't come up with it first—but none more than me. Sparking to it imme-

diately, I volunteered to try my hand at a draft. At some point, somebody suggested I contact Al Franken to see if he had any ideas.

"You know Al Franken, don't you?" I was asked, and I nodded my head.

I knew Al Franken from 1988. He was a not infrequent visitor at the Chauncey Street headquarters, and I was one of his most enthusiastic greeters. I had always been a fan of his work on *Saturday Night Live* and thought his material was consistently smart and funny. It seemed perfectly obvious to me at the time that as a nationally known political comedian who liked to hang around the headquarters, he would consider me—the laugh riot of the press office—a colleague, and that we would then become great friends. I followed him around a lot, trying to impress him with how funny I was, but I never succeeded. In fact, the look on his face as I approached him was one you might have upon the sight of a garrulous second cousin at a family wedding. If anything, he accurately sized me up as an Al Franken wannabe, but he also seemed to resist the idea that I might be anything more than mildly amusing. Mark Gearan, with his evil genius for interoffice torment, had witnessed one such exchange and began incorporating it into his various routines at my expense, handing me back a page of material and saying, "Maybe we should get Al Franken to write us something funny." Soon the press office staffers who were my peers had picked up on the joke, giving birth to hundreds of references to Al Franken and his inordinate disinterest in me. It was a very funny running joke that lasted many, many weeks, and I secretly enjoyed it, if only because it put my name in the same sentence as Al Franken's. But even five years later, despite our crossing paths several more times, my relationship with Al had never really progressed from there. Let's just say that he'd never taken me to meet Lorne Michaels.

I called Al Franken up in New York, in addition to a good number of other writers I collectively called "The Comedy War Room." He pitched a joke that made me laugh, and my next draft included Al's improvements and suggestions, among those of others, and I delivered it to everyone who needed to see it.

One of the people I visited on my rounds through the OEOB was a speechwriter named Alan Stone, a good guy with a good ear for humor. During one of my first visits to his office, he gave me a piece of advice that has served me well in every speech I've written since: make sure yours is always the most current draft. In the unsurprisingly political atmosphere of the White House, power is never very far removed from the process, and the process is the only access a speechwriter has to the power. "Try to make the changes come to you instead of you having to go to the changes," he said. Once you lose control over that, he warned, you've lost your own speech. Those words were the reason why, for this script and for every speech I would ever write over the coming years, I would jealously guard my role as the keeper of the draft, sometimes deftly, sometimes not. And as the "Harry and Louise" video script made its way through the perilous vetting process of the West Wing, I made certain to be the one who shepherded it from draft to draft until it was finally approved and scheduled to be shot just a day before the Gridiron speech.

Friday morning around ten, the president and the first lady arrived in the small video production studio on the top floor of the OEOB, usually reserved for video messages regarding policy initiatives or for live satellite interviews with high-ranking staff. Aides had brought a change of clothes for them both, so they could switch from their business attire to sensible weekend sweaters that approximated the Harry and Louise look. The room was filled with the many communications aides who had been involved in the planning of the video—Mark Gearan, Dee Dee Myers, Ricki Seidman,[9] David Dreyer, Bob Boorstin—and me, the humor writer and keeper of the draft. I was too junior to be running this show, but I stood off to the side of Mark Gearan, now the White House director of communications, who was in charge. My script was already loaded onto the TelePrompTer and Gearan and I were getting ready to walk the president and the first lady through it when all heads turned to see the unlikely pair who had just walked through the door: Al Franken and Mandy Grunwald.

What the hell . . . ?

Mandy, the no-nonsense media consultant who cemented her tough-as-nails reputation in the legendary Clinton War Room, was waving a stack of pages in her hand. With Al in tow, she strode directly to the First Couple, who were seated on a couch on the stu-

---

9. Ricki, who had generated the idea, had no interest in taking credit for the video and congratulated me on the script. I might have learned a lesson from her but I didn't.

dio set, to present an alternate script that Al had prepared with another SNL writer, Marilyn Suzanne Miller, who entered the room a few paces behind.

Gearan turned to me. "Do you know anything about this?"

I couldn't get out any words at that moment, but my wide-eyed alarm answered the question.

The room waited in silence as Mandy and Al made their pitch directly to the Clintons, while nobody else dared to approach them. My heart sank a little deeper with each loud laugh that greeted a new line. Gearan put a calming hand on my shoulder as we stood just ten feet away from the comedy coup d'état in progress.

The next thing I remember was that Mandy handed a computer disk to the TelePrompTer operator, whereupon my script was taken down and Al's script was put up. Of course she had the script on disk preformatted for the TelePrompTer! We were watching a ruthlessly efficient power play, and suddenly, despite my adherence to Alan Stone's advice, mine was no longer the current draft.

I devoted my full energies to not showing visible signs of distress—only to come dangerously close to tears when Gearan gave me a supplemental *hang-in-there-buddy* shoulder squeeze. (Even he didn't have the heart at that moment to whisper a variant of the Al Franken jokes he once delighted in tormenting me with.)[10] Watching the new script being shot from the back of the room, I took some small solace in the plain fact that Al's script was tighter and funnier than the one I had produced. Words to that effect were all I could think to say when I had my inevitable moment of eye contact with him when the shoot was over and the room emptied out. Al was neither unpleasant nor apologetic, just matter-of-fact as he explained to me the reasons why the script they shot was better, all of which rang true. Later that day, the phone on the desk that was my temporary workplace rang. Mandy Grunwald had tracked me

---

10. Those would come about a day later.

down. Her tone was soft and nearly sweet, which surprised me because it did not correspond to my perception of her.

"Mark, I just wanted you to know that I think you handled yourself very well in that room today," she said. I thanked her for that and took all the comfort it offered. I returned the goodwill by trying to be gracious in defeat, citing the many reasons why the script that was shot was the better of the two, repeating many of the same points Al had made. By this point, the distress of the moment was all but gone. In fact, I had managed to transform the incident into a self-aggrandizing thought: having my lunch eaten by Al Franken and Mandy Grunwald in a room full of senior White House staff and in the shadows of the First Couple only proved that I was playing in the big leagues. I also found in it a darker impetus, and I got back to work on Al Gore's speech, all the more determined to knock this damn thing out of the park.

By the time of the Saturday night dinner of the Gridiron Club, I was much more invested in the vice president's speech than the president's, and part of me secretly hoped that Al Gore's speech would do to Bill Clinton's video what Harry and Louise were doing to his health care plan. At the vice president's insistence, we had rehearsed the speech many times—including at his residence that Saturday morning, when he came into the room holding a fax from none other than Johnny Carson, who had given the speech his blessings and added a joke or two at the margins. Al Gore had not been kidding when he told me how important this was to him. From what I saw, I'd say it ranked right up there with NAFTA.

Some time around ten on Saturday night, the president of the Gridiron Club announced the evening's next speaker. The lights dimmed but for a spotlight on the far side of the room tracing the slow path of Vice President Al Gore being carted out to the podium on a sturdy hand truck, as though he were a cigar-store Indian. The person delivering him was an advance staffer (ex-Dukaki Dennis Alpert) dressed in a brown UPS uniform, who presented him to the president of the Gridiron Club, Walter

Mears of the Associated Press, and silently asked for a signature on a clipboard. Al Gore had not yet said a word but had already earned crackling laughs and a sustained ovation. As for what came next, here is how the *Washington Post* reported the evening on the front page of its much-read Style section:

AL GORE, BORE NO MORE!

Somewhere, down in paragraph eight or nine, was the account of the president's Harry and Louise spoof. Heh, heh, heh.

I never got to see Al Gore in the aftermath of the speech that night, because he was whisked off following dessert to leave for a trip to South America. A week later, I was back in New York when the phone rang at the Institute. It was Lorraine. The VP was coming to New York for a fund-raising event, and he had asked to see me.

That evening, I put on a suit and tie and went to the Essex House Hotel on Central Park South. Upon stating my name at the door, I was escorted to a VIP holding room filled with a handful of others waiting for a semiprivate audience with Al Gore. I went to the bar to get a glass of white wine and was bold enough to introduce myself to the guy standing in front of me, the actor Richard Dreyfuss. I spent the next few minutes flattering him about his performance in one of my favorite movies, *What About Bob?* When Al Gore entered the room, he headed straight in the direction of the movie star—only to throw his arms open as he set to embrace the starstruck fan at his side. In that moment, I shifted the glass of wine to my left hand and extended my right hand, but that maneuver underestimated Al Gore's enthusiasm. He wrapped his arms around my torso and lifted me off the ground—a flying bear hug—exclaiming the words "Hey! Hey!" My wine splattered over the both of us, but he paid the mess no mind.[11] He wanted to talk about

---

11. Upon recounting this story hundreds of times over the next few months, I added the line "Right then, a Secret Service guy dove in and took the stain."

the Gridiron speech, and suddenly we were doing a line-by-line recap of the shining moment as if it had all taken place not five minutes ago. After two or three glorious minutes, the VP briefly greeted his other guests and left the holding room to speak to the larger audience awaiting his remarks. Before we filed out, Richard Dreyfuss turned to me. "I'm sorry—tell me who you are again?"

I told him my name and kept to myself what I was thinking: I was the guy who knocked Al Gore's speech out of the freaking park. I'm the guy who knocked Al Franken's video off the front page. Who am I? Who am I? I am the guy who wrote the line "Al Gore is so boring, his Secret Service code name is 'Al Gore'"!

* * *

Endnote: In the process of writing this chapter and owning up to a dark secret I've kept for years, I called Al Hunt to admit my transgression and learn the true origin of a truly great joke. His response: "Jeez Mark, if someone had asked me who wrote the line 'Al Gore is so boring, his Secret Service code name is "Al Gore,"' I would have told them, 'Mark Katz wrote it.'"

CHAPTER ELEVEN

A Wet Hacking Cough
on the Presidency

BY THE SEVENTH OR EIGHTH TIME I'D WATCHED A NETWORK NEWS anchor say the word "Watergate" when he meant to say "Whitewater," it occurred to me that I might not be the only one experiencing vivid Nixon flashbacks. Watergate still ranked high among my most cherished childhood memories, but in the spring of 1994—exactly twenty years since my brother Robby and I had bounced on the couch screaming "Nixon is a crook!"—this high-stakes showdown between a determined press corps and a recalcitrant White House was a lot less fun than I'd remembered. Maybe the decades in between had turned me into a partisan flack, but I failed to see the corruption or the cover-up in the Clintons' third-rate land deal.

The aftermath of this real estate venture gone bad kept getting worse, and it soon surpassed the health care proposal as the impossibly complicated topic crippling the White House. Whitewater had been on the back burner of simmering Clinton disasters since the '92 campaign, but its sudden seriousness was hard to miss as I rushed to catch another train back to D.C. on the first Monday in

April. On the newsstand at Penn Station was the new issue of *Time* magazine with an ominous black-and-white Oval Office photo on the cover. The headline read "Deep Water: How the President's Men Tried to Hinder the Whitewater Investigation"—a winking, gleeful Watergate redux[1]—only instead of Richard Nixon and H. R. Haldeman, it was Bill Clinton and George Stephanopoulos. I bought the damn thing and raced for the train.

Until now, I had never successfully reached the end of an article about Whitewater. As a *New York Times* subscriber, I had encountered breathless front-page stories about it on my doorstep each morning for the past few weeks,[2] but each time I tried to read one of them, the mind-numbing details made my eyes glaze over, and by the fourth paragraph, my mind had strayed to tangential topics, and the next thing I knew I had skipped to the sports page to read about the Knicks. But this time I focused on the *Time* magazine article as though it were the reading comprehension section of the SATs, and before the train arrived  at Philadelphia I had filled two pages with good-humored things George might say on what had to have been a really bad day. Upon arriving at Robby's apartment for my second extended stay of the spring, I plugged my laptop into the phone jack and faxed the material to George's office, pleased to be able to offer my help to someone who had helped me so often—and

---

1. "President's Men"—as in *All the President's Men*—is political code word for "Nixon goons."

2. There is a standing working assumption by media-savvy politicos that the *Times*, scooped by the *Washington Post* on Watergate, has since vowed never to let itself be caught napping on a White House scandal, whatever it may be, again.

just as thrilled to be able to use the modem port of my new $2,500 supercomputer.[3]

The assignments that had brought me back to D.C. were the president's upcoming appearances at the Radio and Television Correspondents' Dinner and the White House Correspondents' Dinner, nearly identical annual humor events just nine days apart. But in the weeks since the Gridiron dinner, Clinton's already-strained relationship with the political media had taken a turn for the worse. The thought of him giving even one speech like this was hard enough to imagine, let alone two.

A year after I'd first passed through the West Wing gates, I was still experiencing the Clinton White House as the joyous epilogue to my denied Dukakis dreams, but it was becoming clear to a lot of people like me that this was not the White House we'd long hoped for. The Clinton administration had managed to follow up its difficult first year with a pronounced sophomore slump, the collective litany of which went something like this: gays in the military, a defeated economic stimulus package, a defeated energy bill and a budget bill that raised taxes[4] without a single Republican vote. There was a separate category for the truly tragic: the raid near Waco, the suicide of a distraught White House counsel and the brutal deaths

---

3. In the interim, George had left a message on my answering machine requesting suggestions for things he might say at a public appearance he was making that week. On the pages I'd sent, there were a few lines that George found funny ("Jeez, I really need a haircut!" and "There are better ways to get on the cover of *Time* magazine. Jeffrey Dahmer comes to mind.") and one he found useful: "Jay Stephens has nothing to worry about: I don't get even, I just get mad." To explain its context would be to walk you through two pages of mentally exhausting details about the Whitewater investigation and nobody wants that. Suffice it to say that it was one of those "You had to be there" jokes that make you regret that you ever had to be there at all. Masochists can refer to Chapter 10 ("The Weekend I Was Haldeman") of George's *All Too Human*, especially page 263.

4. It also reduced the deficit, but tax hikes—even one on the richest 2 percent—are the stuff that attack ads are made of. Also, reducing the deficit is a laudable act of fiscal discipline that has little or no political reward. (Just ask President Paul Tsongas.)

of eighteen American soldiers on the streets of Somalia. This year had brought a violent reaction to a mammoth health care proposal and now the boomerang of a real estate venture from the Reagan eighties. There was also a long list of silly stuff that had happened since Inauguration Day that set off disproportionately serious media firestorms—a $200 haircut on the LAX tarmac,[5] the inept firing of a competent White House travel office, an unsuccessful attempt from the East Wing to evict the press corps from the West Wing, various snafus that undid the hiring of women with unlikely names (Zoe, Kimba and Lani) to high-profile posts, and Bobby Ray Inman's Ross Perot–style emotional meltdown in the process of not becoming America's secretary of defense. Add to that an unflattering and widely reprinted picture of the beefy president in jogging shorts, which launched yet another thousand late-night jokes about a Big Mac–eating Bubba-in-Chief, and you have fifteen months of a presidency that might have made William Henry Harrison realize he'd gotten off easy.[6]

Given the unsettled atmosphere in the White House these days, I did not take it personally when, as I walked the halls of the OEOB, people responded to the sight of my now-familiar face with greetings like "Oh my God—are we really doing a humor speech *now*?" But each time I heard it, I became more energized about the task before me. The opportunity to write humor in the midst of a crisis was a fantasy scenario for someone like me. By now, I was something of a

---

5. It was reported at the time that the haircut, administered by the Hollywood hairstylist Christophe, had held up flights trying to take off from LAX that day, a charge vehemently denied by the White House and backed up by the FAA. If you don't believe me, ask Bill Clinton about it and he'll bend your ear for the next forty-five minutes. (I know. I once had to listen to it.)

6. "I'd rather be dead!"

(Also, in February 1994, the name "Paula Jones" first came to public attention as a result of the many press conferences she was holding to announce that her first name—but not her last name—had been besmirched in the pages of the *American Spectator*, a little-known right-wing fringe publication read mostly in Little Rock and at the Heritage Foundation.)

humor evangelist, espousing to anyone who would listen a variant of the Twelve Step philosophy: things are only as bad as the stuff you can't joke about. I was eager to play high-stakes humor, and all of my instincts—the same instincts I shared with every humor writer who ever walked the earth—told me that humor's biggest payoff can come at the hour of maximum danger.

That night, over Chinese food on Connecticut Avenue,[7] Robby and I talked it out in the shorthand of practically twin brothers, and our conversation only charged me up more. Robby understood my brain and my mission as no one else could, and he exhorted in imperative tones the very thoughts I was in the process of arriving at. This was a defining moment, he implored. After all, wasn't this why we were Democrats? Wasn't the reason we always wanted to win the White House so that the fluffy-haired cool guys who could laugh at themselves could take over the offices of the button-downed stiffs with Republican hair and let them go where they truly belonged—the private sector—where they could engage in the kind of sweetheart land deals where people actually *make* money? Maybe on the long list of reasons why Whitewater was not Watergate was that this guy, this president, could stand up in front of three thousand rabid reporters and show the courage to laugh at the very idea.[8]

---

7. On the way in, Rob directed my attention to a plaque on the wall that indicated that this restaurant, the Yenching Palace, had been the site of another urgent and historic mealtime conversation, where an emissary of the Kennedy White House and a Russian KGB agent hammered out the fine print of the deal that ended the Cuban Missile Crisis. My conversation with Rob felt all the more consequential because we requested their table. (Unfortunately, the waiter could not recollect what they had ordered.)

8. **MEMO TO PRESIDENT NIXON**
   From: The Sound Bite Institute
   Subj: Recommended Watergate jokes

   • I will not be giving a speech tonight. I had eighteen and a half minutes of killer material and somehow it got erased. (Isn't that right, Rose Mary?)

The next morning, after setting up the Comedy War Room in an empty office on the first floor of the OEOB, I pulled out my laptop and set out to write the draft that would make the case. As always, I picked up the phone and dialed around to funny friends and colleagues to think out loud about the avenues of humor that seemed most fertile. The night before the speech, we sent a draft to the president; the night after that, a tuxedo-clad Bill Clinton took the podium to address the same Washington journalists who had recently made "Whitewater" a household word[9] and opened with a geographic-specific version of a time-honored line:

> I am delighted to be here tonight. And if you believe that, I have some land in northwest Arkansas I'd like to sell you.

The room laughed well at the joke, partly in relief that the obvious subtext of the speech they were about to hear was not going to go unspoken.

The speech went on to enumerate Clinton's underreported accomplishments[10] in his first full year in office, a self-effacing run

- I want you to know it took Henry Kissinger nine weeks to negotiate the shape of tonight's dais.
- Haldeman! Ehrlichman! Go see if anyone from the White House is sitting at the *Washington Post* table.
- What did I know and when did I know it? I know absolutely nothing and the time now is [check wristwatch] . . . 8:45.
- Okay, which one of you is Bernstein? Don't try to hide—I'll get Fred Malek to find you in no time!
- This has been such a bad week, the best part about it was the phlebitis!
- Spiro Agnew couldn't be here tonight but he asked me to forward his fondest felicitations to you, the fair-weather-philistines of the fourth estate.
- [A saver for a joke that dies]: Forget that joke. It's inoperative.

9. Just that week, *ABC World News Tonight* had devoted seventeen of its twenty-two minutes on air to the topic.

10. "Since I've taken office, millions of Americans feel better about how they look in jogging shorts. There is an increasing awareness of the information superhighway. Today, 72 percent of Americans are in favor of the idea, provided the rest stops are clean. Not only do we have an administration that looks more like America, but one

of jokes that earned him more applause and laughter. His biggest laugh came during a litany that contained his most forthcoming joke of all, given his antagonistic relationship with the press and the widely reported ire he felt about the treatment he'd been receiving:

> Some say my relations with the press have been marked by self-pity. But I like to think of it as the outer limits of my empathy. I feel my pain.
> . . . Despite what is being reported now, I think history will show that, in fact, I had a very good relationship with the press. And if it doesn't, I'll complain like hell to the historians.

Having taken his self-administered medicine, Clinton clearly savored the opportunity to deliver a broadside at those who had spent the last few months poring over his financial records:

> I don't want to alarm any of you, but it's three days before April fifteenth, and most of you have spent more time with my taxes than your own.

And then in a gently taunting, singsong voice he said: "Many happy returns!"

Clinton was plainly enjoying himself at that moment, an unlikely accomplishment given how much he must have regretted having to do these dinners in the first place. But the most memorable moments of the night were yet to come. The traditional format of

---

that changes jobs and careers at the same rate as the American workforce. We established the first smokeless back room of American politics. My vice president has made great strides in his first and most daunting assignment, Reinventing Al Gore. We've created 2.3 million new jobs. Nearly half of them in the health insurance lobby. Over the last eight months, this administration has brought in some very good people to get me over the bumps of my first year. Because I still believe in a place called 'Help.'"

these live-on-C-SPAN dinners has the president's speech followed by a professional entertainer, most often a late-night or political comedian. But on this night, Clinton shared the bill with one of the best-known voices of NPR, Garrison Keillor, whose erudition and professorial tone made him an unlikely choice for this event. Upon taking over the podium, Keillor picked up where the president had left off:

I didn't want to come down here and talk about Whitewater, but as long as the president has brought it up . . . All I know is what I read in the papers, so Whitewater is a complete mystery to me, as is most of what goes on in Washington. But one can get along pretty well in this country without knowing much about Washington.

Rush Limbaugh voted in a presidential election for the first time in his life in 1988 when he was forty-seven years old. I'm amazed by that fact. I guess it took him a while to figure out what he thought, and if I thought what he thought, I'd still be puzzled by it. It must be fun to say what Rush Limbaugh says, but imagine having to believe it and base your life on it . . .

Whitewater is their kind of scandal. It's carbonated, and it's less about what's real than it is about perceptions. It's all surface. But people of my generation are into surface.

Nobody blames the press for enjoying its work, or for enjoying stories about an administration in panic, White House staffers thin-lipped and pale in public, all because of hard-hitting reporting, though the stories may not be exactly true. I'm not saying you do this, but you may have gone to school with people who do.

Sometimes, in the news business, people create cliff-hangers where there are no cliffs and write about events in a tone of urgency that has no basis in fact. I'm not saying that you do this, but you may know people who do.

There is a great danger when the press wanders from the facts. If you do, you will be held to a different standard than the one you're used to. Journalists are held to a standard of truth, which is demonstrable, at least over the long run. But when you slip into the field of fiction and entertainment, then you will be expected to be fascinating. This is going to shorten your careers. Nobody can be fascinating for long, but people can be accurate and responsible for an entire career. And I wish all of you long and distinguished careers.

There was no bigger smile in the room than the one pinned to the face of President Bill Clinton. Each time he slapped his hands down on the dais, he seemed that much closer to shouting out the words "FUCKING-A RIGHT!" This was hardly a surprise. But Keillor's truly remarkable speech did have a truly remarkable result: the room full of Washington journalists also seemed to be absorbed and eager to receive its message. The laughter and applause and full attention of the room suggested a genuine, if fleeting, repentance.

I watched the speech from a perch on the side of room, and I was thunderstruck. Never in my life had I seen humor used to construct such a powerful argument, and by the time they were over, the remarks had expanded the boundaries of what I thought a humor speech could be. Keillor's words also shook me in a way I was not prepared for, reminding me of the fervent and idiotic delight I once took in Watergate. (Okay, maybe I did take too much juvenile enjoyment in the sport of destroying a self-destructive presidency—but in my defense, at least I *was* a juvenile at the time.) Garrison Keillor's speech was so exquisite that later that night I found myself gushingly describing it to Rob as "exquisite"—an adjective I have never used to describe anything before or since.

*   *   *

After a morning of reading the generally positive reports of both speeches from the night before, I began the first draft of the second speech with the leftover material from the first. The prevalent themes remained intact: Whitewater woes and the openly contentious relationship between the White House and the press corps. I had pages and pages of material on these topics and another full week to compile even more. On Wednesday of that week, I was scheduled to meet with the president to go over the material and a few "bits" that used other comedic devices—telegrams of support from friends during trying times,[11] rejected magazine covers even tougher than ones that actually ran,[12] and heartfelt advice from the president on how the press might improve its public image.[13]

Needless to say, days that I knew I would be meeting with the president were red-letter days on my calendar, an occasion to put on my sharpest suit and favorite tie and brag to anyone I encountered that I would be "playing the big room." I arrived at the waiting area outside the Oval Office, where the president's secretary, Betty Currie, sat. Betty was an elegant woman with an effusive charm who remembered me from her days answering the switchboard on the Dukakis campaign headquarters in Boston.[14] Now she was the president's secretary—the Rose Mary Woods of the Clinton White House—and the unofficial greeter to those who entered the

---

11. "'Remember, it's never too late to pull out of the '92 election.'—Ross Perot."
"My pollster, Stan Greenberg: 'I don't have a clue what people want from you. Trust your instincts.'"
12. *Consumer Reports:* Rating the Clinton Nominees (Bobby Ray Inman on the cover).
13. "Do not borrow money; do not lend money; do not make money; and for goodness' sake, do not lose money. Remember the beauty of the barter system. Also, you are never too busy for a good haircut."
"If you really want a friend in this town, get a dog. I wish somebody had told me that before I showed up with a neutered cat."
14. I never admitted this to Betty, but I did not remember her from 1988. Upon asking other Dukaki, I found her story checked out.

inner sanctum. For the second week in a row, upon looking up to see me, she welcomed me by exclaiming "Funny man!"

Escorting me into this meeting were a team of high-ranking communications aides who traditionally briefed the president on his speeches, including Mark Gearan, George Stephanopoulos and Don Baer, the newly appointed director of speechwriting. As we stood outside reading over the draft material, one of them turned to the other and asked, "Did you hear what the president said at the MTV event this morning?"

A knowing grimace was the response.

Before I could inquire about the details, the door to the Oval Office opened to reveal the president of the United States.

"Come on in, guys."

This was my third trip to the Oval Office, but I was still holding my breath as I crossed its threshold. Gearan began the conversation by asking a question to which he already knew the answer.

"How did the MTV event go, sir?"

"Fine," he replied.

Long pause.

"I guess I shouldn't have answered that question about my underwear," the president added.

What?

"Yeah, I think that might have been the way to go," Gearan got in, with a mischievous smile on his face. Clinton surrendered a chagrined laugh. But I still had no idea what the hell anyone was talking about.

Did he say "underwear"?

"I'm sorry, sir, you answered a question about what?" I did not want to say the word "underwear" in the Oval Office, even if it had already been introduced.

Gearan relieved the president of the task of explaining the circumstance. "He did an MTV event this morning and one of the questions he got from the audience Q&A was about whether he wore boxers or briefs."

Given what I'd been able to piece together, I figured out that the president had offered a specific response to the question—but at that moment, I was the only person in the room who did not know what the president was wearing under his slacks. I thought it best not to put that question to him again. However, I did realize that one way or another, we had another fertile topic for his speech on Saturday night.

Clinton liked the material we presented, and I promised him an updated draft before the week was out. On the other side of the door, in the hallway of the West Wing, Gearan filled me in on the incident. As I walked back to the OEOB with marked-up drafts in my hands, I was already imagining the ways in which one could incorporate undergarments into a presidential humor speech. I went out to grab lunch with some OEOB friends, and by the time I got back to my desk I found that someone had already beaten me to it.

Gary Ross is an early riser, a fact I learned from our many conversations when I was working on the Dukakis campaign. (Also, his movie *Dave*, about an unknown taking up residence in the White House, ironically was a catalyst for my own White House career.) He had already heard about the event, written up an idea and faxed in material that, even as I read it, I knew would bring the biggest laughs of the president's speech.

I'd like to take this opportunity to come clean on a statement I made earlier this week. At an appearance on MTV, I was asked a question about my undergarments. More specifically, whether I wore boxers or briefs. I answered I wear briefs—which is a true statement that speaks to the current facts. However, it is also true that for a short time during my youth, I did in fact wear boxer shorts. It was actually a "brief" period of time and this semantic coincidence may have been the source of my confusion.[15]

---

15. This material was not only brilliant, it was prescient.

The number of boxers totaled six pairs in all: three white, two
striped, one baby blue with a Razorback motif and little red hogs . . .
I was reminded of this fact while reading a passage in my mother's
book about doing our laundry.

I am taking this opportunity to make a full and complete disclo-
sure. I have turned all of my underwear over to Mr. Fiske's office—
including the receipts from their donation to charity and the tax
deductions I took for them in 1962: $3.38. I am also making copies
of my underwear available to the news media. Naturally, since the
special prosecutor has all of my current underwear, I will need to buy
some more. I will keep all of you apprised as to the type, size, brand
name, national origin and fiber content.

I have no further statement at this time.

It was perfect as it was, and I retyped it word for word into the
next draft—a task that was, on some level, bittersweet. There was
no getting around the fact that what was sure to be the funniest,
timeliest and most salient satire in the president's speech had
come from a pen other than mine. That being said, as one still
quietly working through the distressing aftereffects of stealing
the funniest joke in the Al Gore speech, I made a point of mentioning Gary's name to every person who read a draft of the
speech from that day forward, often more than once. But beyond
that, I was thrilled that the speech the president was about to give
was shaping up to be equal to the speech I'd hoped for from the
outset.

But one more shoe would drop before this speech was put to
bed. On Friday, April 22, 1994, Richard Nixon died. The news
was stunning, surprisingly sad and just a little weird for my having
learned it in the halls of the White House itself. Nixon was many
things to many people, but his career was seminal to almost everyone in politics and the political media. Even in his last months,

he had maintained a palpable presence in Washington, as the parallels to Watergate intruded upon Whitewater in ways both obvious and undetectable. This was the day that Nixon had so obviously dreaded, when the clock had finally stopped on his tireless efforts to rehabilitate the image that he would leave behind. And I knew that for me, Nixon had as much to do with the fact that I was standing in the White House at that moment as any person I'd ever encountered.

There was talk in some West Wing circles that Clinton should not give a humor speech so soon after the passing of a president, but (thankfully) that first reaction was reconsidered. Instead, the next evening Clinton returned to the podium of the Washington Hilton and opened his remarks with a thoughtful and generous remembrance of Richard Nixon, recalling his resolve and quest for redemption:

> The thing that impressed me about him was that he had a tenacious refusal to give up on his own involvement in this country and the world and his hopes for this country and the world. And he continued it right down to the very end, writing me a letter a month to the day before he died about his recent trip to Russia and his analysis of other places in that part of the world.
>
> I say that because I think we should all try to remember when we are tempted to write off anybody because of our differences with them that we share a common humanity, and we all have the capacity of doing better and doing more.

This was a lot to take in. Bill Clinton—a president immersed in his own watery scandal—was paying tribute to Richard Nixon before some of the same Washington journalists who had successfully chased Nixon from office. From there, the president segued to a lighter tone and set out to win over the room full of would-be Woodwards and wannabe Bernsteins with, of all things, humor. I was proud that Clinton had the courage to make light of something his audience took so seriously while quietly making the case that it was they who had lost their perspective. Those who confused Whitewater for Watergate were genuinely confused. Deep Throat would have to wait another day to try to take down this White House.

CHAPTER TWELVE

The Way of the Spork

PRIME-TIME PRESIDENTIAL NEWS CONFERENCES TRADITIONALLY AIR live on the networks, but in the spring of 1995 ABC, NBC and Fox declined the White House's request for a spot in the prime-time lineup. I was among the small minority of viewers who chose to watch Bill Clinton on CBS over *Home Improvement, The John Larroquette Show* and *Not Without My Daughter,* the Fox movie of the week. As it turned out, the denial of a larger audience on this Tuesday night five months after the midterm elections proved to be a blessing in disguise for Clinton. Halfway through a news conference that no one was watching, the president was asked a question that might make one wonder why CBS even bothered to put it on the air in the first place:[1]

QUESTION FROM JUDY KEEN, *USA TODAY*: President Clinton, Republicans have dominated political debate in this country since they took over Congress in January. And even

---

1. Answer: CBS, a distant third in the network ratings, would otherwise have aired *Diagnosis Murder.*

tonight, two of the major television networks declined to broadcast this event live. Do you worry about making sure that your voice is heard in the coming months?

In his answer, the president felt it necessary to justify his existence:

> The Constitution gives me relevance. The power of our ideas gives me relevance. The record we have built up over the last two years and the things we're trying to do to implement it, give it relevance. The president is relevant here, especially an activist president . . . The question is, what happens now?[2]

"What happens now?" was the incredibly relevant question that Washington and the world had been asking since the stunning 1994 midterm elections, which were as close to a coup d'état as our Constitution allows. The Republicans gained control of the House of Representatives for the first time in forty years and handed Bill Clinton the most unequivocal midterm electoral rebuke since Reconstruction. In the months that followed, Clinton was all but dismissed as a walking political corpse, America's first half-term president—neutered by a guy named "Newt."

As the White House set out to remake itself, the president's first move was the political equivalent of a Steinbrenner managerial change: he fired his pollster. Next the president was quoted as saying that he regretted hiring anyone under the age of forty; soon enough, the "kids at the White House" were being pushed out or aside in favor of people like Leon Panetta, David Gergen and Dick Morris—experienced Washington hands with more moderate instincts and/or disciplined styles. Even George, the archetypal White House kid whose playground was the stratosphere, had a rendezvous with gravity in these dark days, finding himself

2. A recap for *USA Today* readers:

still at his desk but on the wrong side of regime change. Bill Clinton was so open to new ideas from fresh faces that he invited New Age guru Tony Robbins to Camp David to lead a private motivational seminar to awaken the two-term president within.

These new advisors were pushing the president to embrace as much of the Republican Contract with America as he could, and to offer watered-down versions of what he couldn't. As a response, the new and improved Clinton promised a "leaner not meaner" government predicated on the vision of a post-partisan "third way." Rather than universal health care or third-world nation-building, his reinvented agenda included a Republican-lite tax cut, school uniforms and cell phones for community crime watch initiatives. As strategies go, it was probably better than coming out of the gate for a second time with gays in the military.

Historic fiasco or not, the calendar still had its Silly Season, and like everyone else in this administration, the in-house joke writer was in uncharted territory. (Even a self-anointed humor evangelist like me understood that we had arrived at the very limits of self-effacing humor. Brutally honest jokes can make a terrible situation better, but they can't make a terrible situation good.) My first attempt to sway the president toward adopting my confessional comic touch had been an unqualified failure, and as the next speech approached I quietly dreaded the phone call that might inform me that my job had also been reassigned to someone more seasoned: Garrison Keillor, Mark Russell or, God forbid, Al Franken.

Instead, upon returning to this shaken White House, I found myself sitting across the desk from Don Baer, the head of speechwriting, discussing ways to reinvent the Comedy War Room. Don offered two good ideas: first, to construct as much of the humor in the form of stories as possible, because the president had done better with runs shaped in a narrative arc than with one-liners organized by topic; and second, to involve the president in the material earlier in the process, instead of just handing him a speech the night before and saying, in effect, "Here, say this." The egg timer incident was all the proof anyone would need to know that the president thought himself no wordsmith's puppet, even when it came to humor.

Around 11 A.M. on March 14, 1995, I was standing outside the Oval Office with a draft in hand when one of the White House photographers, Barbara Kinney, entered the room. (Almost) every Oval Office meeting began with a few official snapshots, and I sidled up to Barbara and requested she stick around a little longer than she otherwise might. I planned to present an unlikely prop to the president for his speech, I told her, and I wanted her there to capture the moment. Her curiosity aroused, I discreetly revealed to her what I had in the inside pocket of my jacket.

A minute later, I entered the Oval Office with Don Baer and Bill Curry, one of the newly recruited advisors who had such an undefined role that helping to present the president with a comedy speech he had nothing to do with seemed to be a good use of his time.[3] Together we presented a draft for Clinton's upcoming speech to the Radio and Television Correspondents' Dinner, a speech that plowed the comically fertile ground of "reinventing government." Much of the speech was built around a story the president would tell about a fictional brainstorming session on a lazy Saturday morning, with the vice president ambling into the Oval Office after doing some mulching on the South Lawn. The draft read like this:

> Maybe it was because it was the weekend and we were relaxed, but we came up with ideas that had never occurred to us before. Exciting ideas. Breakthrough ideas. Third Wave ideas. Here, let me read you the list:
>
> - Right off the bat, we discovered an extra "C" at the FCC.

---

3. The first time I heard his enthusiastic laughter in response to the president's reading of a joke, I was very glad he was there.

- Quite graciously, the vice president suggested we do away with the White House Christmas Tree and, next year, just hang the decorative ornaments on him.
- We said we could combine the Joint Chiefs of Staff and the Bureau of Indian Affairs. Just call it "Joint Chiefs."
- Leon Panetta heard us talking in excited tones and came in to see what was going on. Then the three of us figured out a way to reorganize the White House staff: replace fifteen thirty-year-olds with five ninety-year-olds. Now we were getting somewhere![4]
- Other people came by. We discussed opportunities for entrepreneurship. We could seek corporate sponsorships for government events. Make February 12 Lincoln-Mercury's Birthday.
- We decided to combine the Bureau of Alcohol, Tobacco and Firearms with both the Bureau of Fisheries and the Interstate Trucking Commission. We'd call it "The Department of Guys."[5]

I sat on the far end of the couch next to the president in his upholstered chair, listening to him read the speech aloud and watching him enjoy the premise and the execution. I stopped him just before he arrived at the end of the run to explain what would come next.

"Sir, before you get to this next line, I need to show you the prop that goes with it." As I reached into my pocket, the snap of a camera's shutter and the whir of its auto-advance filled the room. I presented the prop to the president, announcing it with some fanfare. "A spork."

---

4. This joke was rewritten from its original version, which did mathematical gymnastics involving twenty-four-year-olds. There was sensitivity about making references to twenty-four-year-olds running around the West Wing–even then.

5. Erik Tarloff and I spent a solid eight or nine minutes laughing on the day he called to pitch that joke. He is very good and this was one of his best.

His face lit up at the sight of it.

"Oh man. I've eaten on these things before! . . . What did you call it?"

"It's a spork."

"Is that what they're called?"

"Yes, sir. Spork. Half spoon, half fork." Now I was a presidential advisor on cutlery.

"Spork," he said under his breath. "I've seen these things at the Dairy Queen."

"This one came from Wendy's. Josh King ran over there this morning. They give you one if you order the chili."

That fact seemed to jog memories of a pre–White House world, where he was free to patronize fast-food restaurants without pro-

viding Jay Leno with six weeks' worth of jokes. "I didn't know that—they have chili at Wendy's now? Is it good?"

"I haven't tried it, sir," I said, watching him examine the spork from all angles, perhaps imagining the things he might eat with it. Lunchtime was approaching and he seemed to have lost his appetite for his usual heart-healthy fare.

That Thursday night, the president stood before the supersized ballroom of the Washington Hilton and worked his way through his Third Wave ideas, getting all the laughter I had hoped he would. Then the moment came, and he pulled the spork out of his pocket with a flourish.

> Now, this is the most important thing I'm going to say tonight. I came here to offer a way to make peace with our Republican friends on this heated school lunch issue. Al Gore and I have discovered a reinventing government way, Mr. Armey, to get around this terrible rhetoric we've been flinging at you on school lunches. We have a way to save money through streamlining that does not require us to

deprive our children of food. Instead of cutting food, we're going to cut the cutlery. And here's how—with a spork! . . . I've been eating off these things for years. I never knew they were called sporks. But that's what they are. This is the symbol of my administration. [Laughter and applause.] This is a cross between a spoon and a fork. No more false choice between the left utensil and the right utensil. [Laughter.] This is not an ideological choice. This is a choice in the middle and a choice for the future. This is a big, new idea—the spork.

The president seemed to enjoy both using this new word and this part of the speech, which ended with the room's approving laughter and sustained applause. Before the night was over, the president would return to the podium for an encore photo-op holding the spork. There, he motioned to another person sitting on the dais to come stand with him for the benefit of the cameras. That's when Newt Gingrich—Speaker of the House, architect of the Contract with America and accomplished Clinton antagonist—huddled with the president and joined him in hoisting the spork. As a hundred cameras flashed, I had my one and only truly out-of-body experience. For one powerfully vivid moment, I saw the world through the serrated prong-eyes of a plastic utensil, held aloft by two beefy men awkwardly clutching for the mantle of power.

On the morning of April 19, 1995—the morning after the nationally ignored news conference where the president had pleaded for his own relevance—I was standing in front of the television set, struggling to make sense of the chaos on the screen. It soon became clear that the thick charcoal smoke swelling from the Alfred P. Murrah Federal Building in Oklahoma City had come not from a fire but from a bomb. Each additional detail brought more painful news and unanswered questions. One that sprung to my mind might not have occurred to anyone else on the planet: would the president need funny remarks at the White House Correspondents' Dinner, now only ten days away? That same unfathomable thought must have occurred to Don Baer when he saw my name on his call sheet not long after the dust had settled.

"I don't know what to tell you," he said on the phone. There was no way for Don to know if America would be ready to hear jokes from its president so many days away. He instructed me to come to Washington to work on the speech in the event that it would be the right way to go.

The next morning, I headed down to Washington to write a (contingent) humor speech under circumstances significantly more tragic than the last. In the halls of the OEOB, where my face had become a visual reminder of the occasional respites from the serious work of the executive branch, I practically felt the need to apologize for the fact that I was there at all. That same tentativeness applied to my initial conversations with charter members of the Comedy War Room, and the thinking-out-loud session that always began the process was even more theoretical than usual.

Once ensconced in the limbo of Plan B, my job was exactly the same as always, to produce a funny speech that was the right response to its moment in time. As most others did, it began with the list of unused ideas generated for the last one, and on my notes from a few weeks earlier lay the scribbled words "PBS/Big Bird/New Advisors." This germ of an idea connected the new roster of White House wise men with the impending displacement of the characters on *Sesame Street*. On the list of Newt Gingrich's Contract with America demands—somewhere below disassembling the federal department of education but above actually enacting term limits for members of Congress—was the elimination of federal subsidies to the Public Broadcasting System.

I thought I detected a special glee in Gingrich's voice whenever he talked about taking on PBS, and I suspected that Republicans hated PBS for one of the reasons that I loved it—namely, memories of the daily broadcast of the Watergate hearings that brought the scandal into homes like mine in the decade that preceded C-SPAN. Needless to say, I had become a faithful PBS viewer years before House Judiciary Chairman Peter Rodino's gavel brought the first televised Watergate hearing to order. I can still recall the day my mother told Robby and me about a special program for children that she wanted us to watch. Sitting up on the couch, not knowing what to expect, we were introduced to Big Bird, Oscar, Kermit and, our favorites by far, the comedy team of Bert and Ernie. Now that PBS was in peril, I sensed an opportunity for the Comedy War Room to come to the aid of these lifelong friends in their hour of need, and I set out to find a premise that would bring the president of the United States to their side. After many hours of thinking out loud with people inside the White House and out, an ambitious idea was born.

This idea pushed the limits of any comedy the president had done before, and involved bringing to the stage both eight-foot-tall Big Bird and the larger-than-life purple dinosaur Barney, whose marketing mania in the past two years dwarfed anything ever seen on the streets of Sesame. Slowly, the premise for the appearance of enormous puppets on the podium with the president began to take shape. At an appropriate moment in the speech, Clinton would announce that he was taking on new advisors who suddenly had extra time on their hands. As he read the first name, Barney (the dinosaur) and Barney Frank (the razor-sharp congressman) would enter from opposite sides of the stage, only to meet in the middle for an awkward moment. On the next introduction, Big Bird and Senator Robert Byrd would do the same.[6]

I pitched the idea to Don Baer and he signed off in premise, a protocol that allowed me to start exploring the possibilities. My first stop brought me to the office of Susan Brophy in Legislative

---

6. The idea was borrowed/stolen/inspired by an homage to an opening bit from *Saturday Night Live* in 1988 hosted by Paul Simon.

Affairs, who said she would put out feelers to Barney Frank and Senator Byrd, correctly predicting they'd sign on in a second. Even easier, I assumed, was the task I assigned myself–signing up Big Bird and Barney.

I placed my first call to the Children's Television Workshop in New York. A woman named Allyson called me back[7] and I explained the idea to her.

"It's a fun idea but it will never happen in a million years," Allyson said.

"Why do you say that?" I didn't know this person, but I was hoping she was just being dramatic.

"Big Bird and Barney cannot appear together on the same stage." There was a finality to the statement. This was not just a historical fact or a mere obstacle to overcome. It was a hard and fast rule.

She was surprised that I was surprised. "I guess you haven't spoken to the Barney people yet. They are even more hard-line about this than we are." In the past two years, Barney had exploded into pop culture, becoming to Big Bird what the Beatles once were to Bobby Darin. This probably explained the ill will I sensed on the other end of the line.

I had not called the Barney people yet, for two reasons. First, having grown up on *Sesame Street* characters, I regarded calling the creators of Big Bird/Bert and Ernie/Grover/Oscar-the-Grouch as a special thrill akin to placing a call to my own childhood. Second, as a grown man without children, my experience with Barney was limited to flipping by him on my way to CNN, HBO or ESPN. I hadn't a clue where Barney came from or what he really was, other than a gigantic purple moron. I was pretty sure I didn't care for him and castigated my married friends who let their children waste time watching him rather than *Sesame Street*. The warm

---

7. Bedazzled by the effect that leaving a message from the White House had, I often clocked how quickly my calls were returned. About a third of them were returned inside of a minute; it rarely took longer than five.

and fuzzy Barney seemed decidedly dimwitted, the antithesis of charming Muppets clearly born of clever minds.

"By the way, how do I track down the Barney people?" I asked.

"I can't tell you that." For the second time in our conversation, I caught myself hoping that she might not be serious when, in fact, she was.

Having heard my pro–Big Bird sentiments in this cultural divide, Allyson was willing to help me as much as she could. She closed the door to her office and said in a whisper, "I am not going to give you the number, but call directory assistance in Dallas and ask for the Lyons Group."

A few minutes later, I was talking to a Barney spokesperson with an effusive Texas accent. Her name was Kathy, and she met my pitch for a presidential summit with a similar fatalistic regret, but phrased it more optimistically.

"We would be absolutely delighted to have Barney meet with President Clinton in a venue that does not include any other characters."

Finally, I had a chip to play in this poker game. I called Allyson at *Sesame Street* again.

"You were right about those Barney people," I told her. "They are shrewd bastards. They volunteered to do the event with the president alone."

"That's not what you offered us!"

"That's not what I offered them but that's what they came back with." (Barney may be an idiot, but there was a reason he was eating Big Bird's lunch.)

"You are not going to do it, are you?" she asked.

"It solves half my problem," I said confidently.

"Let me call you back."

Twenty minutes later, I was back on the phone with Allyson and her boss, Michael. They asked me to explain my idea for their character and I presented it again in full. There was a long pause when I finished.

"And Barney's already signed on?"

"They are making plane reservations as we speak," I said, offering as a caveat once more that the speech was contingent upon a White House decision to go ahead with humor ten days after Oklahoma City.

With that bluff, they began to crack as I had hoped: "Are *they* willing to put Barney on the stage with Big Bird?"

"We hadn't got that far," I said. "But let us talk about it right now: what would it take to put Big Bird on a stage with Barney?"

Their hard stance softening, I began taking notes on their concerns, a list that looked something like this:

1. Would Barney and Big Bird be treated as equals by the president?
2. Would they exit the stage together or separately?
3. What, if any, theme music would be played during the skit?
4. Would the president remain in the shot between them or would they be left to interact with each other?
5. In what order would they be introduced?
6. Would Big Bird have his own dressing room? Would it be secure?[8]
7. Would Big Bird be asked any political questions?

The Barney people were not happy to hear that the terms of the debate had shifted back to a joint appearance. But having already imagined their purple marketing-monster in a presidential photo-op, they too were averse to ceding the opportunity to their *Sesame Street* foes. Over the course of the next few days, I conducted long phone conversations with representatives of each camp. Both sides were happy to talk to me but not eager to talk to each other,

---

8. *Sesame Street* goes to great measures to make certain that no child is ever traumatized by the sight of Carroll "Big Bird" Spinney stepping into costume. In that spirit, I ask you to please keep this chapter out of the easy reach of youngsters.

which suited me just fine. My strategy was to play the good cop and let my accounts of the devious machinations of each opposing side function as the bad cop.

The most difficult hurdle involved the logistics of whether the characters would speak at the event. Big Bird is a self-contained unit, in that the person who occupies the suit also provides the voice; Barney the body and Barney the brain (hah!) are two different entities that require careful coordination. This put Big Bird at a tactical advantage in any vocal exchange, and the Barney people insisted that neither character be allowed to speak to the president, let alone each other. The *Sesame Street* negotiators were not happy to cede this advantage, but they did not feel strongly enough to let it get in the way of a negotiated settlement. Before they signed off, the *Sesame* camp had one more question for me: did I know George Stephanopoulos?

"Yes, I do." I told them how we had once shared an office.

"Maybe you can help us with something. We've been dying to get him to come on *Sesame Street* and do a segment with Snuffleupagus. Can you put in a good word for us?"

"Sign off on this event and I will introduce you to him myself at the dinner."

Done!

Josh King, the White House production coordinator tasked to humor speech stunts, began working out the many details. I began the equally important process of bragging incessantly to anyone who would listen about how I had successfully conducted the Barney/Big Bird Summit on behalf of the White House.

Around noon on Friday, I was the first to arrive outside the Oval Office for our rehearsal. Betty Currie greeted me with what was becoming our ritual: "Funny Man!" A moment later, the president popped his head out of the door of the Oval Office to hand something off to Betty and saw me standing there, drafts in hand.

"Hey Mark, do you have a funny speech for me there?"

"Yes I do," I said enthusiastically. I wasn't quick enough to come up with a joke.

"Great, we'll go over it when the rest of the team gets here."

He went back into his office and closed the door. A few pleasantries with Betty later, Don Baer showed up. The pained look on his face suggested I was not going to like what I was about to hear.

"I got bad news for you. It's a 'no-go' on the comedy."

There was a long look as the words set in. As nicely as he could, Don was telling me to beat it. My best suit and sharpest tie notwithstanding, I was not about to "play the big room."[9]

I made my way through the narrow halls of the West Wing and out the side entrance that dumps into the parking lot across from the OEOB. Usually the jolt of a trip to the West Wing sent me racing up the many stairs to the OEOB two steps at a time, but on this trip Don's news had turned my legs into a pair of sandbags. I was lost in self-pity as I slowly climbed the stairs, planning the many calls I would have to make to undo the Barney/Big Bird Summit.

When I got back to the desk that I had claimed for the week, the phone was ringing.

"Is that you, Funny Man?" It was Betty Currie. "The president wants to see you in the Oval Office right away."

I retraced my steps, this time running just fast enough so I would not be out of breath when I arrived. Betty welcomed me back–"Go on in, Funny Man!"–and I walked past her desk without breaking stride. My mind was racing as my right shoe hit the blue carpet of the Oval Office. I had never been invited to this place absent a draft of a humor speech in my hand, and I experienced the room and this moment almost as though it were my first time there. The president was sitting at his desk, with Don Baer and Mark Gearan standing across from him.

---

9. I later learned that this decision was made directly by the White House message maestro in hiding, Dick Morris.

"Hey Mark," the president said. "They told me we weren't going to give your speech tomorrow night but I thought we might just read through it for laughs. You got a minute?"

Did I have a minute? That might have been funnier than anything written on the pages he held in his hand. I sat down in the chair at the side of his desk. The president was about to read me a story, and I was giddy with delight. The only thing that could have added to this delicious moment was if the first lady had walked through the door right then with a plate of cookies and a glass of milk.

For the next ten minutes, the president delivered the speech for the benefit of an audience of one, with Mark and Don helping to fill the room with laughter. Soon enough Betty Currie, Leon Panetta and the director of the president's office, Nancy Hernreich, were standing at the door and offering theirs as well. Yes, it was his pity for me that had brought me to his desk, but I was completely fine with that. What greater pleasure could an emotionally needy joke writer know than to be pitied by the most powerful person on earth? This guy felt my pain and I was happy to let him heal me. On every previous trip to the Oval Office, I had been there to lend the president my humor voice and was rewarded with the exhilarating experience of having material born in my brain fill an auditorium by way of the president of the United States. But now my ears were filled with words spoken for my benefit alone, and I took every ounce of comfort that he offered.

When playtime was over and he walked me to the door, I told him of the negotiations I had undertaken in his name to bring Barney and Big Bird to the same stage.

"If the Republicans keep it up, maybe we'll try it again next year," he offered in consolation. "You know what, this may be my best shot at the Nobel Peace Prize," he joked.

"Correct me if I'm wrong, sir," I said as we got to the door. "I believe it was Henry Kissinger who won the Nobel Prize and not

Nixon."[10] We both laughed—the wiseass was back on the job—and the president turned to Betty Currie saying, "You know, I think Mark's feeling better already." And with that, my extra special trip to the Oval Office was over.

The next night, President Clinton returned to his now-familiar comedy perch at the Washington Hilton. Several days earlier, his words at the national prayer service in Oklahoma City had given eloquent voice to the nation's deep sorrow and collective resolve. Now, after one of the most pitch-perfect weeks of his two-and-a-half-year-old presidency, he was still in the zone.

> The book of Proverbs says, "A happy heart doeth good like medicine, and a broken spirit drieth the bones." And I believe that. But I think you will all understand that—and I hope my wonderful comedy writers will understand—if I take a few moments tonight not to be too funny here at the end because of the tragedy in Oklahoma City, which has captured us all and which still is the focus of our efforts, for understandable reasons, tonight, as the rescue workers are still laboring and as the law enforcement officers are still working.
>
> Now, folks, that is the real America. Sometimes all of us forget it a little bit. Sometimes all of us are too bound up in what we are doing. But this country is bound together in a way that the people like those who committed those crimes in Oklahoma can never understand. And I know our government is not perfect, and I know it makes mistakes. But this is a very free country and a very great country. And a lot of the people who are out there complaining about it today would not even be able to do what they do in the way they

---

10. As I was mining the comic possibilities of successfully completing these historic negotiations, I had asked a speechwriting intern to bring me a list of Nobel Laureates and took special note of that fact.

FYI: Last sitting president to win the Nobel Peace Prize—Woodrow Wilson.

do it in most of the other democracies in the world today. And we should never forget it.

As this story unfolds, I would ask you to continue to return to Oklahoma City, to update our country on how the families who have suffered so much are rebuilding their lives, and to remind us about the countless heroes we have all seen there.

The terrible people who did this thing do not deserve to be celebrities, although they will become famous. But the victims and their families and the people who have labored, they don't deserve to be forgotten. [excerpted]

This was a president at the top of his game, giving a comforting speech against a backdrop of adversity and despair that summoned all of his best instincts and extraordinary skills. This was a president who—maybe just that week—had fully grown into the largeness of his office. Before he was done, he even found it in himself to commend the work of the press corps in the past nine days, no small gesture from such a vocal media critic and target.

Bill Clinton had delivered his second pitch-perfect speech in a week and the room could hardly have failed to notice that the man at this podium was not the president who had already been written off by many. Seated at a table in the midst of the crowd and feeling painfully irrelevant, even I could see that, finally, the Clinton presidency was starting to make sense.

*   *   *

Endnote: After that hopeful moment passed, the Barney and Big Bird camps retreated to their pre-1995 borders. Barney and Big Bird have never appeared together at a public event, but I stand ready to help close the breach.

You don't make peace with your friends. You make peace with your enemies.—Yitzak Rabin

CHAPTER THIRTEEN

Ghostwriter Overexposed

LIKE SO MANY TALES OF EXCESS, THIS ONE STARTED MODESTLY enough. Every person who has ever been handed a plaque at a Rotary Club believes news of the accomplishment is worthy of coverage in their hometown paper or college alumni newsletter. After all, what's the point of attaining success if not to flaunt it to the people who populated your past? Once I had secured my role as the official jokesmith and designated humor speechwriter for the president of the United States, I was ready for my close-up in the pages of *Cornell* magazine.

Rather than call up the magazine and say, "Hey, you ought to do a story on me," I called Helmet Head, my college cohort, to suggest that he call them up and say, "Hey, you ought to do a story about him." Twenty minutes later I was talking to the magazine's managing editor, who wanted to write a profile of the government major from the Class of '86 who went on to write jokes in the White House. I pretended to think it over.

A month later, on my next trip down to D.C., I was the subject of a photo shoot, a self-satisfied portrait of the luckiest wiseass in the world sitting on a lawn chair a hundred yards from the White

House's picturesque North Portico. Sans tie and cloaked in my favorite "I am a writer" tweed blazer, I stared over my cherished laptop and into the camera, addressing it with a cocksure smile as I imagined who might see me: former professors, former classmates and former girlfriends. Especially former girlfriends.

To be sure, I had one particular former girlfriend in mind—and oddly enough, I was imagining not only *her* reaction to this article but also her mother's. Beth had been my girlfriend during my senior year of college and the following year and still holds the single-person record for number of times breaking up with me—three. Our sometimes torrid/sometimes tortured relationship also overlapped with the years I was still wringing my hands over law school, and her mother was one of the people giving me a hard time about my professional procrastinations. Scared as I was of becoming a lawyer to please my own mother, I was horrified at the thought that I might do it to please someone else's. As the shutter clicked and the flashbulb popped, I remembered that Beth's parents, former Cornell college sweethearts, kept recent issues of the alumni magazine on their living room coffee table. The sly smirk captured on film probably corresponded to the thought I was sending out for Beth's mother to consider as she arrived at my page: *Hey lady—flip through the rest of this magazine and see if you find any full-page photos on $200/hour corporate goddamned lawyers.*

Dee Dee Myers had done a nice turn for me when she approved the photo shoot, which took place on the lawn outside her West Wing office. Getting ink as a political underling can be tricky, but generally speaking no one bats an eye at the "local boy makes good" stories that service microconstituencies. Articles like these are deemed to be "under the radar," a minor indulgence on a scale too small to raise eyebrows. But the situation is different on the other side of that threshold, a lesson that I needed to learn and that began with a message on my answering machine from a *Wall Street Journal* reporter, Dana Milbank, who said he wanted to write a profile on me.

I knew that an article in the *Wall Street Journal* was potentially a big deal and/or a big problem. At the very least, I knew this could be a much bigger deal than *Cornell* magazine and quickly assembled a mental list of the people—old advertising cohorts, other women who had spurned me (and some of their mothers too)—who I hoped might see it. Before I called the reporter back, I called Mark Gearan and he filled me in: a *Wall Street Journal* profile meant the middle column of the front page, arguably the best-read article of the best-read newspaper in the world. Just in terms of visibility, the middle column was to the *Journal* what the pullout was to *Playboy*.

I had arrived at the staffer's conundrum. The political handbook states that your job is to make your boss, and not yourself, look good; as a rule, attracting attention to yourself is frowned upon. Of course, it is also illegal to double-park in New York City, and a rule like that often clashes with human instinct. The perennial profiles you see of up-and-coming political staffers are case studies in trying to have it both ways, as limelight-seeking underlings atone by spending the interviews talking up the virtues of their boss. Even I knew that if I were a full-time White House speechwriter, the answer to this reporter's query would have been a no-brainer: *NO!* But my status as an outside consultant was also an escape clause, Gearan pointed out, and I was glad to hear him say that. Forty-four weeks of the year I was a freelance writer in search of assignments, clients and opportunities. That said, he also let me know I was playing with fire. "This is a big deal. Be careful," he warned.

In the days before the interview, the Sound Bite Institute was busy churning out sound-bite talking points for me—cautious, credit-deflecting, ass-covering squawks like this:

- The president has a great sense of humor and these speeches are a great showcase for him.
- A lot of smart and funny people are involved in this process—most importantly the president.

- People inside the White House and out participate in the process of generating funny material. These speeches are the work of the White House Comedy War Room.
- Helping the president prepare for his funny speeches is a serious honor.

On a Tuesday morning, I buzzed Dana Milbank up from the lobby and invited him into the one-bedroom apartment that was the Sound Bite Institute—which, on this day, was significantly tidier than usual. After ten minutes of Milbank taking in everything there was to be seen—a television tuned to C-SPAN, a wall covered with Oval Office photographs, a lot of Ikea furniture and a desktop computer that kept me connected to the embryonic Internet at 14.4 bps—we left for a booth at the Omega Diner. Over the course of our two-and-a-half-hour visit, I regaled him with my well-rehearsed, carefully constructed sound bites that explained who I was, how I got here, what I did and how I did it. Before he left, he asked me to send a photograph to the *Journal*'s art department that would be used for the pen and ink rendering of me that is the newspaper's signature style. He also promised to call to give me a heads-up on the day the piece would run.

When the call came, on December 12, I was down in Washington writing material for a congressional roast.[1] The next day I was

---

1. • Capitol Hill is a very cold place these days. This morning I saw a few of my Republican colleagues huddling around Bob Dole for warmth.
   • The proposed Medicare/Medicaid cuts are the work of the Congressional Ways to Be Mean Committee . . . Remember the good old days when the Republican party just *ignored* the poor?
   • The behind-the-scenes battle between Dole and Gingrich is one of those classic struggles between bad and evil.
   • Has anyone noticed that all the pro-choice Republican presidential candidates have been terminated in the first trimester?
   • If you don't like the way things are going on Capitol Hill these days, don't complain to me. Call your local lobbyist.

off Robby's couch by quarter after six and walking briskly down
Connecticut Avenue in sweatpants and overcoat to the 7-Eleven
on the corner. I had been holding my breath for the better part of
a city block as I stirred the jingly chimes of the door marked IN.

I had spent many hours fretting about the contents of the article, but with each step I took toward the newspaper rack by the
register I realized I had never spent a moment thinking about my
likeness. There, on the top copy of a dozen freshly printed *Wall
Street Journals*, was a representation of my face that hit me like a
punch in the nose.

I had a high school gym teacher whose nickname for me was
"Joe Willie," because my face reminded him of Joe Namath, but
no one else ever made that connection. Once—and only once—
someone said I looked like George Clooney, but even I will admit
that comparison is more than charitable. Far more common is Jay
Leno, as my thick hair, prominent jaw and baby face conjure his
likeness to some. But somehow the perfectly nice picture I submitted to the *Journal*'s art department had been transmogrified
into something worse than I looked on my worst day: Fred Flint-
stone with impacted wisdom teeth. The sketching process not
only reduced the photographic details of my face but seemingly
subtracted chromosomes from my genetic makeup as well. The
sour taste of stomach enzymes pasted my mouth before I could
even take in the headline: "When Democrats Need to Lighten
Up, He Has Laugh Lines."

By the third or fourth paragraph, even I could see that the article itself was a thing of beauty, an approving portrait of an "imp-
ish" thirty-one-year-old who was the "modern-day court jester" of
the Clinton White House. The piece incorporated many of the
funny lines from White House humor speeches (including my
signature bon mot: *Al Gore is so boring, his Secret Service code name is
"Al Gore"*), as well as my best Oval Office anecdotes. Best of all (I
thought) was that the article plugged the project that had kept me
busy for the previous sixth months. I had just finished a humor

book to be released later that year, a collection of self-invented quotes assigned to historical and contemporary figures, and the article was the print equivalent of a sixty-second Super Bowl ad. My cringe-inducing likeness was a small price to pay for the professional bonanza that was about to unfold.

As someone who had spent the previous two years compulsively checking my answering machine three times an hour, this was the day I dreamed about when I closed my eyes at night. Over the course of this day and into the next, the Radio Shack minicassette recorder that had served as the secretary of the Sound Bite Institute was flooded anew with messages left for me in the time that it had taken me to return the last ones. On this fantasy-scenario of a morning, I sat at Robby's kitchen table and filled up page after page of a legal pad with the names and numbers of people I needed to call back.

BEEP Hey Mark, it's your friend Dave Leavy. I got in early to the White House press office and saw the piece on you in the freakin' *Journal*. Awesome, man. BEEP . . . Hi Mark, this is Tina Marcus calling from WFYI in Stamford, Connecticut. I'm a producer on *Bill & Ed in the Morning* and they LOVE Bill Clinton and they would LOVE to talk to you this morning . . . BEEP Hi Mark, this is Laura van Straaten and I'm a producer from *Dateline NBC*. I saw the piece about you in the *Wall Street Journal* and want to talk to you about a possible segment we want to do about you . . . BEEP Hi Mr. Katz. My name is Diana Lewis from *The Late Show with David Letterman*. I read the article about you in today's paper and was curious to know if your dog Wally is still alive—and if so, does he still play the piano? . . . BEEP Hi Mark, my name is Stan Something from *Cigar Aficionado* magazine. I saw the article about you and was wondering, are you a cigar smoker? If you are, would you please call me at . . . BEEP Hi, it's Mom. Remember how mad you were about what I said to the president about spanking you? Well, if it was so terrible, why are you repeating that story to reporters? Oh, wait, are you at Robby's? I'll call you there . . . **BEEP** Hey Mark Katz, this is Dandy Dan Harris live on the air from the Morning Zoo on KROX in St. Louis, Missouri, calling to talk to the funny man of the Clinton White House. Pick up if you are there . . . Okay, he's probably out walking Socks the cat, or something. Now here is Jessica McVicar with the KROX Accu-weather forecast for the tricounty area . . . **BEEP** Hey little bro. It's Bruce. I am looking at today's *Wall Street Journal* right now. I am on my way into court, and if you want, I could file the papers for the dot matrix slander that's been committed against you. I say we take drastic action . . . **BEEP** Good morning. If this is the same Mr. Mark Katz who was written up in today's *Wall Street Journal*, would you be so kind as to call the office of U.N. Secretary General Boutros Boutros-Ghali at your earliest convenience . . . **BEEP** Hi Mark, it's Rabbi Frishman. Your mom called to tell me about the article and I just wanted you to know there wasn't anything in there that was funnier than the joke you made at your bar mitzvah speech about how you use horseradish as bait to catch gefilte fish! Happy Hanukah! **BEEP** Hi Mark, it's your Aunt Doris. Your dad told me you were in the *Wall Street Journal* today but your Uncle Stanley is at work already and my Volvo is in the shop and I can't leave the house to get the paper, so would you mind faxing it to me? The fax number here is . . . **BEEP** Hi Mark. This is Sigourney Weaver. Gary Ross gave me your number. I'm being honored as the Woman of the Year at the Harvard Hasty Pudding Club and I was wondering if you had time to . . . **BEEP** Mr. Katz, I'm calling from the office of Congressman Jack Kemp. He wants to know: do you ever write for Republicans? . . . **BEEP** Hi Mark, I am calling from Gemini Productions in Hollywood. We're putting together a show

for pilot season that is an update on the old *What's My Line?*
and we thought that you would be a great guest. Are you coming to L.A. any time in the next week? . . . **BEEP** Hi Mark, it's
your sister, Ruth. Congratulations. I am so, so proud of you
. . . Uh, have you put on weight? . . . **BEEP** Hey Mark Katz—
it's Ted from *Ted & Andy's Morning Madness* on KQXR in
Sarasota, Florida. We want to pitch our favorite Bill Clinton
jokes to you live on the air and you can tell us what you think!
How about this one: "I did not inhale that cheeseburger!" . . .
BEEP Hey Mark, it's Andy Rosenbaum. You know, I spent
every other weekend hanging out with you in the Hamptons
last summer and I have to say, I had absolutely no idea that
you were funny . . . **BEEP** Hi Mark, it's John Kennedy. You
may remember we played football last fall in Central Park. I
saw the article about you in the *Journal* today and I've been
talking to some people about a political magazine and if you
have time to talk . . . **BEEP** Hey Katzie, this is Ira Gerzog.
That's right—"Big Ig" from your Israel teen tour. Well, I am an
actuary now for Coopers & Lybrand and I just picked up my
morning *Wall Street Journal* and I said, wait a minute, I know
this guy! . . . **BEEP** Hi Mr. Katz, my name is Fred Bruntrager
from the National Right to Life Foundation. We saw today's
Wall Street Journal and I was calling to inquire if we might get
a copy of the picture they ran to use in our brochure about
the horrors of partial birth abortion.[2]

About a third of the calls that day were from news organizations that wanted to arrange an interview with the White House
joke writer. The pages of sound bites that I had written for my
Wall Street Journal interview served me well in the days and weeks
ahead, as I stuck mostly to my own script when I called into radio
shows in eight major markets. Before the week was over, I was

---

2. Fisher!

mouthing some of my sound bites into a television camera during a hastily booked interview on the set of CNBC's *Equal Time*, a *Wayne's World*–style political chat show that marked my very first appearance on television without a toy poodle. (The show was cohosted by my friend Dee Dee Myers, who had landed on her feet after leaving the White House.)

On New Year's Day of 1996, three days after I turned thirty-two, I sat in the New York studio of CNN, staring into a camera as Bernard Shaw—the same guy who put the "Kitty Question" to Mike Dukakis—was asking me questions via an earpiece about how I went about making Bill Clinton so funny. And with every question put to me, I came back with some answer that tried to make the president look good. By the time I got back to my apartment there were more messages on my machine with more invitations to do more interviews or field other stray opportunities. As a result of one call I got that day, later that month I flew first class to Chicago on someone else's dime, checked into a suite at the Four Seasons and gave a speech at some kind of corporate seminar to a roomful of people eager to hear me explain who I was and what I did, at the end of which someone handed me a check for $6,000. Nineteen ninety-six was shaping up to be a very good year.

The $6,000 check had not yet cleared before I plowed a good chunk of the money back into capital improvements to the Sound Bite Institute: three new suits, a $200 first-generation digital answering machine for when opportunity rang while I was away, and my second $2,500 supercomputer, this one six times faster than the last (100 MHz!) and capable of surfing the still-new Internet at a rate of 28.8 bits per second. This was the seven-and-a-half-pound hand tool I needed to write the funny speeches for the president that the spring calendar would call for.

Once again I returned to Washington to find the jokes that would help the president navigate his political circumstances, battling a Republican Congress while laying the groundwork for his reelection campaign against an opponent yet to be determined. In January 1996, the turf battles between Newt Gingrich's Contract with America Congress and Clinton's back-from-the-dead White House were waged over the new year's budget, a standoff that led to the shutting down of the federal government. Clinton opened his Alfalfa speech with this: "Five years ago, we were all glued to CNN as the American government brought Iraq to its knees. These days, we've been watching C-SPAN as the American government brings the American government to its knees." The White House had skillfully cast Gingrich as the Grinch who closed down the government, and the impression stuck. It was the latest and most severe of Gingrich's many self-inflicted wounds, and enabled Clinton to rise from the ashes and appear to be a credible—and increasingly likely—two-term president.[3]

Later in the spring, Clinton was as strong as he had ever been as president, beating the Republicans at their own game by co-opting some of the popular parts of their message in a way that made them look all the more radical for holding out for the rest.[4] With reelection just a few months away, his speech to the Radio and Television Correspondents' Dinner attached a personal post-script on the Gingrich revolution. ("A year later, it's fair to ask: how is the Contract with America doing? Well, great as far as I'm concerned!") The Gridiron Dinner nine days later was an opportunity yet again for Clinton to use the mean-spirited Republican Congress as a made-to-order foil: "I have a message from the kitchen staff: 'We have a list of all the senators who voted against the minimum wage bill. And a seating chart. Hope you enjoyed

3. Of course, the law of unintended consequences that had governed the Clinton-Gingrich drama was quietly generating yet more irony to be reaped at a later date: as a result of the Gingrich-induced government shutdown, informal West Wing commingling brought a pizza and a Gap-clad thong-wearing intern into the Oval Office. See the Starr report.

4. In fact, 1996 was the reversal-of-fortune year when Clinton neutered Newt. If you don't believe me, go back and watch Gingrich's face at the 1996 State of the Union address when Clinton declared that "the era of big government is over"!

the soup.'" The White House Correspondents' Dinner speech in the first week of May offered a chance to address comically an issue the White House had been reluctant to address politically: return fire on the presumptive GOP presidential nominee, Bob Dole, who had just recently stepped down as Senate majority leader to devote his full time to taking on Bill Clinton.

Early in April, Dole had trotted out his first clear shot across Clinton's bow, working into his stump speech a barely concealed ad hominem attack on the president's character that came in the form of this question: *Who would you rather have babysitting your children, Bob Dole or Bill Clinton?*

At first I thought the question was a joke. Bob Dole was a celebrated Washington wit, and I held him in higher regard than most Republicans if for no other reason than that.[5] But when the punch line never came, I realized he intended that as a serious question, and it made me angrier every time I heard it. Dole was dressing up a personal attack as a self-evidently ridiculous matter of public policy—as if Article II of the Constitution assigned to the executive branch the duty of watching the kids whenever a citizen wants to catch a movie. Even a midlevel political operative like me could tell that it was a line handed to him by some pollster who'd discovered that the question worked well in focus groups and was clumsily translated into a campaign "wedge issue." My year on the Dukakis campaign had sensitized me to outrageous, insidious and coded tactics, and even one as stupid as this made my blood boil. Before I sat down to write a word of the speech, I knew it would have to offer a retort as strong and funny as I could fashion:

---

5. Among other devastatingly caustic remarks, he is the author of a line that has been enshrined in the Gridiron Hall of Fame. Acknowledging fellow dignitaries Jimmy Carter, Gerald Ford and Richard Nixon on the dais, Dole remarked: "There they are: See no evil. Hear no evil. And evil."

It's too bad Senator Dole couldn't join us tonight, but thank goodness one of us is free to watch the kids. But this babysitter debate raises only one of many pertinent questions that voters have to ask themselves before they choose the next president. For example, let's say you were going on vacation for a couple of weeks. Who do you trust to water your plants? Bob Dole or Bill Clinton?

And suppose you were too busy shaking hands tonight and you didn't get to eat. And you go home tonight and you decide to order a pizza. Who do you trust to select the toppings? Bob Dole or Bill Clinton?

Or what about this scenario? Bob Dole is on a train headed toward Spring Valley at 65 miles an hour. Bill Clinton is traveling by car from the opposite direction at 35 miles an hour. Given the fact that the train has twice as far to travel as the car, who do you trust to arrive in Spring Valley first? Bob Dole or Bill Clinton?

Now, if you don't think these questions are relevant—I ask you, who are we to question the wisdom of Senator Dole's focus groups?[6]

My draft of the White House Correspondents' Dinner speech also set out to settle another score, this one my own. The professional comic who would entertain the audience that evening was none other than Al Franken—the same Al Franken who swatted me away like a fly back on the Dukakis campaign and squashed me like a bug during the making of the "Harry and Louise" video. The formula for these speeches always had the president acknowledging

---

6. There are two postscripts to this response. (1) Never again did Bob Dole raise the "babysitter question." And if that weren't satisfaction enough, (2) the following week's issue of *Time* magazine actually commissioned a poll that brought back a result I'd suspected was out there: By a margin of 2:1, respondents preferred to have Bill Clinton select the toppings on their pizza.

the evening's entertainer with a joke specific to that person, and it was always kind or flattering in some way. Except this time. Early in my drafts, I wrote down this joke: *Al Franken and I both had a terrible 1995. I had Newt Gingrich's 105th Congress—and Al Franken had Stuart Saves His Family.*

At each meeting where my collected material was vetted, I kept waiting for this line to get killed, for someone to ask the obvious question: Why would the president take a shot at Al Franken? After all, not only was Al the president's most high-profile comic defender, he was also the archenemy of Clinton-archenemy Rush Limbaugh. To my amazement, no one ever crossed out that joke. Even in the Oval Office meeting with the president, that line on the very first page was never so much as debated. On the night of the dinner, as I sat in my annual spot at the *Vanity Fair* B-table, I continued to be amazed that the line had made it through even as the president said it out loud. The laughter in the room was muted at best, perhaps because no one had even heard of Al's ill-fated movie, or because they were pondering the very question a person at my table put to me: Why is the president taking shots at Al Franken? As it happened, I was the only person in the room who knew the answer, but I just smiled and shrugged my shoulders. (Later in the evening, during the awards presentations, my wandering mind began writing other score-settling jokes that would have the president of the United States gilhooly others who had crossed me.)

I was standing on the top step of the OEOB late in the afternoon, taking a break from making mirth for the last humor speech of the season and taking in the sights of the White House compound. As I sipped the last of my diet soda, a black town car pulled up to the western door of the West Wing and out of it stepped George Stephanopoulos. He caught my eye as he stepped out and from fifty feet away said, "Hey Katz, nice pencil!"

I immediately understood his seemingly cryptic comment as a jab about another highly visible article about me. Throughout the spring, reporters who had read about the White House jokesmith contacted me in hopes of doing a story of their own. Balancing my un-Amish instincts for publicity with the perils of being too visible, I said okay to a few and "no thank you" to most. But there was one request over which I had no control. In the spring of 1994, *People* magazine had *almost* run a story on me but for some reason changed their mind after the article was written and the photos were shot. A year later, the editors saw the *Journal* piece and changed their minds. In the first week of April, they published a one-page piece that was two-thirds photograph—me hanging off an oversized prop of a pencil against the backdrop of the U.S. Capitol. (The only restraint I demon-strated was refusing to do it in front of the White House.)[7] Upon return-ing to Washington to work on the White House Correspondents' Din-ner, I knew I was going to get grief— some good-natured, some not—and George was only the latest to poke me about the preposterous pencil photo-op.

I hustled down the staircase to get in some quick face time with George. As it happened, I had been meaning to get into his office to have a conversation with him on this very topic. My book of

---

7. This article generated its own slew of follow-up phone calls, 95 percent of which went to my father. That week he fielded calls from forty dentists who had just flipped through the most popular magazine on their waiting room shelf. If the *Wall Street Journal* is "the daily diary of the American dream," then *People* magazine is the guilty pleasure of the American dentist.

fake quotes[8] was due to be published in the middle of June, and I knew that upon returning to New York I'd direct my attention to trying to promote it. He was as savvy as anyone in the building about the political media and had been the subject of more profile pieces in the past few years than Al Gore. When I told George I wanted his advice on how to handle my upcoming media tour when he had a few minutes to talk, he said, "Follow me."

Just like that, I was walking into the West Wing, something the visitor's pass around my neck would not allow me to do without an escort. Normally, West Wing meetings had me putting on my suit jacket. This time, I could only unroll my shirtsleeves and tighten my tie to look more appropriately dressed. As George picked up his messages and had me follow him back to his tiny office on West Wing Players Row, I experienced a powerful déjà vu of the first time I entered the Clinton Little Rock headquarters on his heels. After he returned a phone call or two as I checked out his CD collection stacked by a mini–boom box (on his recommendation I purchased a Cranberries album that went into heavy rotation on my stereo for that entire summer), George turned his attention back to the topic on which I sought his advice: how to tiptoe through the pitfalls of the press I hoped might come my way in the months ahead.

He asked me to recap my exposure to date and I ran down the

---

8. A free sampler of a book that hundreds and hundreds of people once paid $8.95 for:

- Albert Einstein: "I first realized I was blessed with above-average intelligence when my classmates began referring to me as 'Einstein.'"
- Karl Marx: "From each according to his ability. To each according to his needs. Plus tax and tip." (splitting the bill with friends at a restaurant)
- Queen Isabella: "A crueler, more gentile nation." (announcing Spanish Inquisition)
- Clarence Thomas: "I'll have what Scalia is having." (decision on lunch)
- Francis of Assisi: "Who are you calling Assisi?"
- Napoleon: "Curse that Count de Custarde! I must invent a dessert of my own!"

list: *Wall Street Journal*, *People* magazine, *USA Weekend*, *CNN Inside Politics*, the *Guardian* of London, the *Los Angeles Times*, *Cornell* magazine and a dozen morning zoo radio shows in medium-sized cities across America. At that moment I was embarrassed by the garishly long list I presented, but George mulled it over and then said this, "You are doing just fine, and from what I've seen, you are saying all the right things." His hands clasped together, he put his index fingers to his lips and added, "Just do yourself this favor: stay out of the *Washington Post*."

Phew. I had been half certain George was about to counsel me to seek help for my need for public attention. His mild caution felt to me like I had gotten off easy.

I returned to New York on Sunday after the Correspondents' Dinner on Saturday night, my head still spinning in the annual glory of the *Vanity Fair* party, which never broke up before 3 A.M. and which I never left before 4. By Tuesday morning I was unpacked, fully rested and back at the helm of the Institute, thinking about ways to inflict my humor book upon the world[9] when the phone rang.

"Hi Mark, my name is Laura Blumenfeld and I am a reporter with the Style section of the *Washington Post*."

Uh-oh, did she say the *Washington Post*?

"I understand you have a book coming out and I wanted to talk to you about a profile piece I want to write about you."

Then I gave the response that I was incapable of not giving: "Great!"

Of course I remembered George's advice, but I also knew that my successful navigation of potentially treacherous waters had resulted in the perfectly positive wiseass-makes-good pieces that now lined my walls. She told me she was going to be in New York the following week and we put a date on the calendar.

---

9. I would later come to regard these weeks during which I planned the book's rollout as "the calm before the calm."

The day we met began with a quick tour of the Institute, an interview over a sandwich at a neighborhood sidewalk café and then a quick trip to the Barnes & Noble near Lincoln Center to take in the beautiful sight of my shiny book displayed on the "New Arrivals" table. I was very excited about the book, delighted to have something to put my name to without having to back away from its authorship. As for the White House stuff, I gave her all the same cautious, ass-covering quotes about the president's great sense of humor and the many people involved in the process. Before she put her notebook away, I asked her for the same courtesy I had requested of every reporter who was writing about me, to give me a heads-up the day before the story ran. She assured me she would. A few days later, a professional photographer arrived at my apartment to take a photo of me to accompany the article.

On a Monday morning in June, my phone rang sometime around seven. It was my brother Rob calling from Washington.

"What the fuck?" he wanted to know.

"What? What?" My first guess was that he had called to complain about the long-distance charges I'd run up during my last two extended stays at his apartment.

"Have you seen today's *Washington Post*?"

"No, is there a piece about me in there today?"

"Uh, yeah. You haven't seen it?

"No, the writer told me she would call before it ran."

"You mean Laura Blumenfeld?"

"Yeah. You know, I meant to call you. She says she knows you from Harvard."

"You dumb schmuck."

"What? Is the piece bad?"

"Why didn't you call me to tell me she was doing a piece on you? *Yes, it's bad!*"

"Why? Is there a picture of me? How do I look?"

I had been missing the point until Rob made it clear. He read me a few select lines from the article. It was bad. In between reading a few lines that felt like punches, he went back to castigating me and called me a dumb schmuck a few more times.

"I wish to God you had called me," he said. "I would have *beseeched* you not to talk to this person. She is bad fucking news. She is evil."

In all the time I had known Robby—since the day he came home from the hospital and was placed in the crib next to mine— I had heard him describe only three other people as "evil." Richard Nixon, Miss Nussbaum and a girl named Alicia whom I dated one summer despite his heartfelt, hard-learned advice, which I chose to ignore because she was unusually attractive—only to learn the lesson for myself the day she threw my Casio Digital Diary into her parents' pool because it wouldn't stop beeping. Rob went on to tell me a few stories he had collected about Laura Blumenfeld in their days at Harvard that he could recall, so vividly visceral was his response to her. Had I called him, he assured me, he would not have let me get off the phone until I promised to cancel the interview. But now it was too late and all there was left to do was get off the phone, go get a copy of the *Post* and have a terrible day. Over the course of our numerous conversations, it seemed Laura Blumenfeld had forgotten to tell me the premise of the piece she was writing—that for a "ghostwriter," Mark Katz gets an awful lot of ink. My involvement in the piece was little more than a setup, my comments used as a launching point for the barbed, mostly unattributed comments she solicited. One unnamed White House speechwriter[10] described me this way: "I'd say he's more of a *boast*-writer than a ghost-writer." Ouch. Another "seasoned Washington veteran" described my public profile as "unseemly." The only person who trashed me on the record was a Republican joke writer, a guy I'd never met named Doug Gamble, saying if Mark Katz is going to take his bows in public, maybe he should, too. Laura Blumenfeld had

---

10. I know who you are!

coldcocked me with a piece that amounted to snarky payback, a boomerang to what she described as the "lipstick kiss" *Wall Street Journal* and other pieces that up until this very moment I thought I had successfully managed. Ironically, this piece was as ugly as my portrait in the *Journal*, but the irony did not stop there: it was accompanied by an unusually flattering picture, reinforcing the eerie sense that this was the metaphysical negative of the article that had started all this.

The same cordless phone that had been the lightning rod for opportunity over the past six months was dead silent that morning. In those agonizingly quiet hours, as most of Washington turned to the Style section—the well-read sports pages of the city's intramural politics—I was as furious as I've ever been, mostly at myself. Rereading the article felt like perusing my own professional obituary. I could not get through a paragraph without blurting Tourette's-style compound expletives that corresponded to the thought that all I ever had to do to avoid this catastrophe was to heed the thoughtful advice I solicited from a very smart person, or, short of that, just call my brother.

The gentle condolence calls started around noon, one of the first from the man I still regarded as my professional godfather.

"Mark, it's Kirk. Welcome to the big leagues, kid."

In the years since the Dukakis campaign, Kirk O'Donnell had remained a steadfast friend eager to help me any way he could, usually in the form of sage advice. Once or twice per Silly Season, we would go to lunch and I would read him pages of jokes, always taking just as much pleasure in watching him laugh as he did in laughing. But on this trying day, just hearing his voice retightened my throat.

"There's actually some good news here if you want to hear it," he said. "You haven't done anything in this town until people start taking shots at you."

In a subdued voice, I admitted to Kirk what I feared was true, that I had just ended my own too-good-to-be-true White House career, all for the sake of promoting a goddamn toilet joke book. Kirk didn't bother trying to convince me that this wasn't a black eye, but he did set out to convince me it was no more serious than that.

"Listen Mark, for the next month or so, people will know you got your ass kicked on the front page of the Style section. But come the fall, all anyone will remember is that you were on the front page of the Style section. In the meantime, just keep your head down and keep doing good work."

Before he got off the phone, Kirk offered one last piece of advice: "Make a mental note of every person who calls you today to tell you to 'hang in there.' Shitstorms are when you find out who your friends are. Okay, pal?" That lesson alone was (almost) worth the agony of that day, and before it was over I did get a bunch of "just checking in" calls—though maybe not as many as I would have liked.[11] But the greatest kindness may have been the call that never came, the call from George Stephanopoulos to say "See?—I told you so."[12] ("You dumb schmuck!")

My self-inflicted media wounds were not limited to the printed word; I was also making inroads into jeopardizing my career via television as well. *Dateline NBC* had approached the White House press office about a story that would have their cameras following me around as I produced a speech, and Mike McCurry

---

11. I got even fewer calls the following day when the piece was reprinted in the *International Herald Tribune.* But then again, very few of my close friends live in Europe.

12. A few years later, I was walking through the same Barnes & Noble that Laura Blumenfeld and I had visited that day we met. There I saw a book with her name on it. *Revenge* is the story of the year she spent living in the home of the Palestinian terrorist who shot and injured a Jewish tourist years earlier. In making this living arrangement, she evidently failed to mention to her host the terrible fact that the man he had shot was her father—still alive and well—and that it was the premise of a book she was writing. For a moment, I was proud to have helped a young reporter hone her professional modus operandi.

rejected the pitch before the producer got past the "Kuh" sound in "Katz." Soon after that came my clumsiest maneuver of the spring, one that corresponded to what was at the time the most intriguing media parlor game to come along since "Who is Deep Throat?" This time the question was, "Who is Anonymous?"—the well-veiled author of the popular roman á clef about the Clinton campaign, *Primary Colors*. In article after article, dozens of writers with inside knowledge of the campaign were suggested as its possible author. As the list grew and the plausibility of each new suspect declined, I began hoping someone would nominate me. Upon hearing a tip that Larry King had assembled a roundtable on the topic for that evening's program, I called someone I knew who was booked to go on and whispered in his ear that I secretly wanted to join the ranks of suspects.[13] Here is the transcript of what my deft ploy produced:

LARRY KING: Welcome back. We're still on our mysterious hunt. By the way, when we go to your calls, you can have questions of the panelists, you can also have an opinion as to who wrote it. Give us your opinion. Hey, it's all up for grabs here. This is sleuth, tonight.

All right. Begala, from what you read, and what you have learned, who are some of the suspects in your mind?

PAUL BEGALA: Well, I have read a bunch of the reviews and I've seen some of the names. There is one that hasn't been mentioned and that's Mark Katz. Mark Katz is a very funny humorist

---

13. At the White House Correspondents' Dinner in May, Clinton had presciently laid down a marker on his candidate months before the mystery was officially solved: "Joe Klein is sitting at the *Newsweek* table next to his imaginary friend, Anonymous."

and has written a lot of humorous stuff for
the president and for other politicians. He
called me today and asked me if I could
mention that he might have written it.

LARRY KING: [nonplussed] All right. Well . . . Mandy, you
said you were on the plane today with Bob
Boorstin and he said he didn't do it . . .

Granted, this curveball to Larry King and his viewers was just a
momentary embarrassment that only made me cringe. My more
sustained televised failures were to come a few months later—after
the Silly Season was over and the *Post* piece was beginning to
recede into a terrible memory.

In the early summer of 1996, an ambitious all-news network was
just taking to the cable lines. MSNBC was the self-consciously
high-tech, Internet-focused, Must-See-TV-news channel that
hoped to be the CNN of the latte-sipping laptop generation. As
the network was preparing to launch, its producers rounded up
gangs of demographically correct baby pundits who would chime
in during anchor-moderated conversations on current events. The
pile of press clips I had generated in the previous six months had
brought my name to their attention, and having survived a taped
audition in the Rockefeller Center studios of NBC News, I was
signed up to join the crew as a resident humorist. Maybe this was
the opportunity that I had been shamelessly advertising myself for
all along.

By joining this roster of two dozen opinionated, well-groomed
punks, I had found my element. We were a band of hard-core
careerists so eager for public attention that we each signed on for a
sum that—when divided by the hours the part-time job entailed—
approximated babysitting wages. But the fact was, most of us
would have written MSNBC a check for what they were giving us:
our faces on TV.

The premise of these segments was twofold: (1) cheap pro-
gramming over the course of ten hours of daytime news coverage,
and (2) informed discussion and debate among an ever-rotating
cast of spirited colleagues with varied backgrounds and ideological stripes. Three times an hour, a trio of fresh-faced thirtysomethings in Banana Republic urban wear would rush to a set that
looked like a Starbucks on the Mir Space Station. For the next
three minutes, a news anchor would moderate our conversational
opining on the news report that had just run before cutting away
to a commercial for Ovaltine or Gold Bond's medicated anti-inch
powder. As the guy with the words "speechwriter and humorist"
as my identifying credentials, I felt a fair amount of pressure to be
articulate and funny—and I was pretty sure that this was going to
be a problem for me.

What the MSNBC producers did not know when they hired
me was that 99 percent of my "impromptu" humor is actually my
saying something funny I'd thought of earlier. Mine is a *slow*,
sharp wit; I'm rarely quick enough to produce a decent real-time
joke, but I am capable of instantly recalling something funny I
wrote or thought as far back as the ninth grade. (If my brain were
a computer, the specs would be a Pentium I chip with a huge hard
drive and adequate RAM.) For this reason, in the ten to twelve
minutes of advance notice regarding the next roundtable topic—
Clinton's welfare bill, mandatory school uniforms, Roberto Alo-
mar spitting on an umpire, the introduction of blue M&M's, and
so on—I would fill up a page with clever sound bites and/or jokes
and bring them with me to the table, where I would begin the
process of finding an opening to say things I had already written
as though the idea had come to me then and there.

To make matters worse, I soon learned that the red light of a live
camera had a further stultifying effect on my brain. The pressure of
live TV made me nearly incapable of participating in an actual
conversation and left me no choice but to toss in my prewritten
material whether it was salient or not. When absolutely forced to

think on my feet by a question put directly to me, I would begin a sentence not knowing what it was I had to say, sometimes arriving at a cogent thought, other times meandering until I found a place to put a period or just ran out of breath. For the most part, my fellow baby pundits demonstrated generous instincts—helping me out by cutting me off or laughing as though my non-sequiturs were funny—but not always. I had arrived at the inartful conclusion of one such run-on sentence in search of an idea when the person I was responding to, conservative vixen Laura Ingraham, just held her tongue to create a pregnant pause, then said, "Whatever *that* means . . ." If I had a quicker wit, I would have had a snappy reply to that boulder she had handed a drowning man. Instead I looked down at my notes and wished I were dead.

The real fun didn't begin until later that summer, when the pundit squads were dispatched to the political conventions to offer our insta-blather analysis during the long days preceding the scripted events of each night. I had never spent much time around Republicans before, so I approached my trip to the GOP Convention in San Diego as something akin to an anthropology project. In addition to exploring fish-out-of-water humor on the air that week for the many hundreds of MSNBC's viewers, I also got the opportunity to have some jokes published in the *New York Times*. An editor from their op-ed page had tracked me down to ask me to participate in a dueling convention-related Top Ten list with a Republican joke writer, Doug Gamble—the same guy who took a shot at me in the *Post* article. I accepted the assignment and the challenge, determined to best this backstabber I'd never met in a mano-a-mano joke showdown.[14] The next morning, I was up early and waiting in a hotel lobby for the first editions of the *New York Times* to arrive so I could see my jokes on the op-ed page I had long hoped to crack:

---

14. In case you haven't noticed by now, revenge is my most effective productivity tool. Maybe Laura Blumenfeld and I have something in common, after all.

Why Democrats Will Have More Fun at
Their Convention Than Republicans

by Mark Katz

10. Members of 1968 Chicago police force are retired and living in San Diego.
9. Wednesday is "Subpoena Night" at local Bennigan's.
8. Tobacco-free smoke-filled rooms.
7. Loophole in welfare bill: food stamps apply to the purchase of sangria.
6. Gender gap is disaster for G.O.P. Convention Dinner Dance.
5. Al Gore: human limbo stick.
4. Reports of life on Mars re-energize Jerry Brown supporters.
3. G.O.P. concession to Pat Buchanan: ban the Macarena, popular Latino line dance.
2. Let's face it: Bob Dole is not 72 anymore.
1. Even if Democrats don't have more fun, the press will report that we did.

Upon reading the piece, my MSNBC producer thought my one-liners might make for a fun on-air segment if I came on the set and read them ten through one. I was pleased for all the obvious reasons as well as an unobvious one: I would not be required to think of material on my feet, only to read jokes I had already written. The segment went well, and later in the day I got a message from another MSNBC producer, this one from the network's nightly newscast anchored by Brian Williams. They wanted to air a similar segment as well. Getting bumped from daytime to prime time was nothing short of a promotion; between having an article in the *Times* and being showcased on MSNBC, I was enjoying a banner day.

Around five o'clock (8 P.M. back east), I walked onto a remote set on a rooftop against the backdrop of the yacht-jammed San

Diego harbor. By 5:20, I was staring into a live camera, and after being greeted on-air by the anchor, I began to recite the jokes that had made me famous for a day, each typed out against a blue backdrop simulating a Letterman Top Ten list. (TV was stealing back its own format from the *New York Times*.) As I counted down to one, Williams's laughter seemed to indicate he was enjoying the segment, at the end of which he announced he'd have more questions for the Democratic humorist lost behind enemy lines upon returning from commercial break.

What? No one ever said anything about a second segment! I began to panic, as I had no prepared material for the segment ahead. My choices were limited, and fleeing the set felt like a short-term solution at best. As a commercial for Ovaltine played in my ear, I scoured my mind for material I might use when Brian Williams came back from the break to ask me to be funny live on national television. The nervous sweat that was in the process of dampening my armpits actually gave me an idea: undershirts.

Just that spring, during my extended stays in Rob's apartment, my brother disabused me of a long held Katz family prejudice, that undershirts were worn only by Republicans and "goyim"—a distinction barely worth making in our house. Somehow undershirts were assigned overtones that were vaguely Presbyterian and/or proletarian and thus out of tune with suburban, dental-community Jews such as us. But in his time wearing suits every day in Washington, D.C., Rob had discovered their utility.

"We've been all wrong about undershirts!" he said to me with evangelical glee as I got dressed to go into the White House one spring day. "They're great—they keep you warm in the winter and cool in the summer."

As it turned out, Rob was on to something and I was now a convert too. (I had experienced a similar breakthrough years earlier when I developed a taste for BLTs.) As my brain trawled for ideas I would need in a minute and my undershirt absorbed the sweat I gave off, I decided to go with a riff on undershirts, as if I had learned of their virtues from the Republicans all around me. (Now you have an idea of how desperate I was.)

Sure enough, Brian Williams introduced the next segment by asking what a Democratic humor writer had learned while mingling with the enemy, and I launched into my answer.

"Well Brian, I have learned one thing from the Republicans. I noticed early in the week that the Republican men all wear undershirts beneath their dress shirts, and so I went to the store to pick up a pack, and you know what—these guys are on to something. Undershirts keep you cool and dry during the hot days and keep you warm on the air-conditioned convention floor at night . . ."

Odds are, no one was listening to these words, because as I was saying them I had tossed my tie to one side and was in the process of unbuttoning my blue chambray shirt to make my point. Even *I* didn't know I was going to do this as I broached this topic, but clearly I was "committing to the moment"—an expression I once heard from an instructor in an improv class. But even as the unbuttoning bit progressed, I knew the moment was terrible. As my fingers reached for the buttons around my sternum to reveal the white cotton V-neck underneath, I was midway through a Sammy Sosa–size swing-and-a-miss.

Brian Williams was stunned. A man was undressing himself on the evening news. Like me, he had no idea where I was going with this, but his instincts told him to cut me off before I could segue from undershirts to boxer shorts. As my fingers reached my belly button, I heard through my earpiece the reassuring, apologetic words the anchorman offered viewers at home:

"Uh, we are going to let Mark Katz compose himself and put his clothing back on while we cut away for another commercial message."

With that, my segment was over and perhaps my television career as well. Like a person who'd taken a clumsy spill on an icy sidewalk, I got back up, determined not to make eye contact with others. My exposed undershirt soaked in flop sweat, I walked off the set with a shaken expression, the very opposite of the cocksure smirk with which I once stared down the camera lens of *Cornell* magazine.

*   *   *

Postscript: 1996 was a banner year indeed. The New York Yankees won their first World Series since I was fourteen years old, defeating the Atlanta Braves after being down in the series 0–2.

Oh yeah, Bill Clinton also became the first Democrat elected to a second term in office since Franklin Delano Roosevelt.

CHAPTER FOURTEEN

My Thirty-six Finest Hours

THE MORNING OF FRIDAY, MARCH 14, 1997, BEGAN WITH ME HALF dressed in the fresh, clean undershirt of a brand new day, ironing the dress shirt I'd be wearing in the Oval Office later that afternoon. From two rooms away, I heard my brother's clock-radio alarm go off to the soothing tones of NPR. A moment later, Rob called out for me with the standard salutation from our shared youth:

"Hey, Bum!"

This mutual nickname for each other—which dated back to high school days when we foraged through each other's closet looking for something to wear—had a particular significance now that I spent weeks at a time sleeping on his couch and eating out of his refrigerator.

"Yeah?"

"They just said on the radio that Clinton's in the hospital."

I ran to the television, where Matt Lauer soon explained that the president's condition was no more serious than a horribly mangled knee, injured in an improbable set of circumstances. Late the previous night, while staying as a guest at the Florida home of golf pro Greg Norman, Clinton had taken a tumble down a flight of stairs. (It seemed like a weird place for the president to stay over, but maybe the Ramada was booked.) He had spent the night in a local hospital and now was already en route to Bethesda Naval Hospital for arthroscopic surgery.

Having learned that the president was not in grave danger, my concerns turned to things more trivial. Would the crippled president stand up to deliver the Gridiron speech that I had been working on for the past week, now only thirty-six hours away? I finished getting dressed and put on the Oval Office–worthy tie I had already selected for a trip to see the president. There was no telling how this day might play out.

I arrived at the security checkpoint line at the OEOB and crossed my fingers. Upon reaching the front of the line, I received the greeting that began four out of five of my White House days:

"Sorry. Your name is not in the system."

Ugh. I went to the house phone to perform the usual drill, calling the point person of the speechwriting office, Gaby Bushman, and asked her to clear me in again—a process that never failed to take less than fifteen minutes.

As I took a seat on a bench and waited to be rescued, I pulled out the latest draft of the president's Gridiron speech and sighed heavily at the very sight of it. This was without question the most difficult speech I'd worked on thus far, which was no surprise given the impossible circumstances that surrounded it. The giddiness of a second inauguration had quickly given way to the administration's bumpiest spring yet. The year 1996 had been the most zealous political fund-raising period in history (a record that's been broken every four years since George Washington's second term), and 1997 brought its aftershocks. The newspapers were filled with reports of White House "coffees"— exclusive policy briefings with the president where corporate fat cats drank beverages that were not exactly complimentary. Coming after the "Lincoln Bedroom" mattress sale debacle, this was the second well-heeled shoe to drop in the saga of the administration's controversial fund-raising tactics.

Al Gore managed to get his hands dirty in the oily enterprise of political fund-raising, too, somehow finding himself at a Buddhist temple surrounded by monastic celibates in saffron robes and passing his own collection plate, whether he knew it or not. And if that weren't enough, Gore had also admitted to placing a number of fund-raising phone calls from his White House desk, a practice at odds with federal laws. (The many years of Democratic dominance on Capitol Hill and absence from the White House had made our team significantly more adept at spending billions than raising millions.) All told, the media were having a field day. In response, the Clinton/Gore White House had leapt into full damage-control mode, and a Gridiron humor dinner set for the Ides of March made nearly everyone wary.

Five days earlier, I had arrived quietly excited about a comedy speech set against crisis. Tucked away in an empty office, I had worked my way through a stack of press clips, many of which glibly used the term "White House coffees" as a synonym for unseemly quid-pro-quo money-grubbing at the very highest levels. Later, after seven or eight laps around the quarter-mile track that is the first floor of the OEOB, I arrived at the thesis that I thought was a solution: ignore the metaphor. Let coffee = coffee, not $$$. Or, at the very least, obfuscate the difference. Maybe coffee was like cholesterol, in that there can be both good coffee and bad "coffees." I wanted the president to give a speech premised on good coffee–that well-loved, fresh-brewed, aromatic morning beverage. That way, he could give a speech that appeared to be fearless while merely harping upon something patently innocuous–hence the humor! I went back to my office and began to write.

My three-month stint writing ads for an instant cappuccino mix proved to be perfect training for writing jokes with punch lines steeped in coffee culture: non-dairy creamers, Joe DiMaggio, Juan Valdez, El Exigente, General Food's International Coffees, secretly replaced Folgers crystals and, of course, frothy-to-the-last-drop Starbucks *venti* lattes. On the top of the page was an opening joke that had the president complaining about his well-meaning but adamant waiters that evening, who would serve him only tea or cocoa.

This moment of clarity notwithstanding, the speech I held in my hands as I sat on the bench contained none of that material. Over the course of a long, tense editing session the previous Wednesday night, I had watched Don Baer decaffeinate my draft until not a single reference to coffee remained. Don, once the head speech-writer but now the director of communications, was of the unshakable opinion that the word "coffee"—even at its most literal—was too hot for the president to handle. This was also the consensus among the West Wing brass he answered to. He sent me back to my office with unambiguous instructions to produce a speech focused solely on getting the president through the evening alive.

The next day I rewrote the speech, muttering under my breath a question to which I already knew the answer: How could the president knock it out of the park if his speech never took the bat off his shoulders? The draft I held in my hand went to the president on Thursday night,[1] five pages of material on stray topics like the NCAA basketball tournament, a recent Washington snowstorm and a run of jokes and slides about cloning—a topic in the news thanks to a sheep named Dolly. The only section that was politically salient was on the broader subject of campaign finance reform, also carefully childproofed. But at this moment, with Bill

---

1. The rumor mill had generated all kinds of scurrilous scenarios about what the president was doing as he started down those stairs. I was probably the only one speculating that he was too absorbed by a draft of a humor speech he was reading.

Clinton on a gurney on the way into surgery, even those unambi-
tious jokes were in peril.

After twenty long minutes, my name had finally cleared the system. Once on the other side of the magnetometers, I walked
directly into the speechwriting office to see if any new details had
come to light in the hour I had been away from a TV set. Gaby
said the president's surgery was slated for that afternoon but nothing else about his schedule was certain. Eager for additional details,
I set up camp in front of a TV in a speechwriter's office. As I tuned
in to CNN, I heard a familiar voice coming from the other room.

"Has anyone seen Katz?"

Lorraine Voles, the vice president's communications director,
had steered her eight-months-pregnant body into the speechwriting office suite looking for me. I stuck my head out of the office.

"Come with me," she said, with an expression that was either
very serious or the result of severe personal discomfort. Lorraine
already knew what the speechwriting office was anticipating, that
the VP was going to stand in at the Gridiron for the president. I
was being dragooned to produce an emergency replacement for a
speech that had taken me a week to write. The time was a little
before eleven, T-minus 33 hours until the vice president would
take the stage.

Just like that, I was as excited again about this speech as I had
been when I got off the train from New York. Maybe the speech I
couldn't write for Clinton might turn into one I could produce
for Gore, with material that wasn't scared of its own shadow. But
an even bigger maybe remained: could Al Gore, who had been so
savagely self-effacing about his wooden reputation at the Gridiron
three years earlier, summon the same courage with the much trick-
ier subject of semilegal fund-raising? And even if he could, would
it be wise?

As I thought about it, I realized that the stakes were even higher.
Bill Clinton had already won his second term; Al Gore would soon

be seeking his first, but even his unofficial campaign was off to an inauspicious start. Just eleven days earlier, during an impromptu pressroom briefing to White House reporters, the vice president had given a clumsy and tortured explanation of his recent fund-raising activities. (Over the course of ten minutes, he said slightly different versions of this sentence eight times: "My counsel advises me that there is no controlling legal authority or case that says there was any violation of the law whatsoever.") Before leaving the briefing room podium that Monday morning, Gore had both insisted he had done nothing wrong and promised he would never do it again.

At least I had a lot to work with.

Back in Lorraine's office, I began the process of this impromptu Gridiron speech with the instincts of an ardent environmentalist as we rummaged through the president's speech to see what might be recycled. The campaign finance reform material the president had been set to give would be even more appropriate for the VP, and reclaiming the rejected jokes from Don Baer's cutting-room floor would only make it better. Okay, that was a start.

Lorraine told me that the VP had been getting laughs recently with a short opening routine called the "Five-Minute Presidency," which had been written weeks earlier by his pair of sharp speechwriters, Dan Pink and Eric Schnure. The bit took as its premise the few precious minutes on the day of the second inauguration when Gore had been resworn into his office and Clinton had not. It was funny, and it sounded very promising to me.[2] I suggested that we could transpose the material into something more up to

---

2. This run was predicated upon a footnote to history: At noon of January 20, 1997, Bill Clinton's first term in office expired. Like most events of the Clinton administration, the swearing-in ceremony was behind schedule and the vice president was sworn in to his second term at 12:00 and the president at 12:05. According to a strict reading of the Constitution, during the five minutes while Gore was in his second term and Clinton was not, Al Gore was the highest-ranking member of the executive branch and the de facto president of the United States.

date should the president's surgery require the vice president to take over the reins, per the Twenty-fifth Amendment. At this moment Al Gore might have been the only other person in the building silently hoping the president's surgery would involve general anesthesia.

But the speech still needed an idea, an overarching rationale that might set it apart and cast the vice president's words as the perfect and heroic response to a difficult set of circumstances. As he stared down the Buddhists and controlling legal authorities that had come to haunt him in recent days, Al Gore needed lines that would earn him laughter but also respect. Soon enough, I was back pacing the halls of the OEOB, this time outside of the Gore staff's home on the second floor.

Later that afternoon, Don Baer came looking for me, and at the moment I saw him, I feared a reversal of the reversal of fortune I had experienced earlier that day. The president had done well in surgery, he told me, and now there was talk about having him make an appearance at the Gridiron by way of a pretaped video shot at the hospital. He asked me to give it some thought. (Don also told me that Clinton had undergone the surgery under only local anesthetic—meaning the Twenty-fifth Amendment had never been invoked—and looked at me strangely when I seemed crestfallen at the news.)

One of us—I don't remember who, but let's just assume it was me—suggested we put some of the material from Clinton's original speech into use in the video, prefaced with some kind of funny apology for missing the event. The bit that would translate most easily, I suggested, was the one about cloning, which incorporated a series of photographs of various clone-comic scenarios cobbled together in Photoshop.

"Great," he said. "Why don't you write up a script?"

"Sure thing." At T-minus 26 hours, a presidential video had been added to my to-do list.

The timetable and multiplying assignments had me pounding

the keyboard, walking the halls, calling the most reliable Comedy War Room veterans (Erik Tarloff especially) and thinking out loud with Gore speechwriters Pink and Schnure, both of whom had keener comedy instincts than your average White House word-smiths. They were going to put a call in to Al Franken to see if he had any material to add.

"Great," I said, conflicted at best.

The next thing I knew it was 11:30 that night and I was spent, starving and still not done. Before leaving around midnight, I faxed the current draft of the vice president's speech to Lorraine and the current draft of the Clinton video to Don Baer, as I had promised to do.

At dawn (T-minus 14 hours), I was sitting at my brother's kitchen table punching up the Gore speech, tweaking the presi-dent's script and still wearing yesterday's undershirt. By 9 A.M., I was behind the wheel of my brother's car,[3] on my way to the first of two stops: Bethesda, where we were to shoot the president's video message. Lacking White House credentials, I had to wait a few minutes at the hospital for Don to arrive so I could get past the temporary Secret Service checkpoint.

Don's first words to me that day were, "Katz, you are a piece of work." I immediately knew what he was referring to. The draft I sent him the night before had the president expressing his regrets with this: "I wish I could be there right now. Talking with you. Exchanging ideas. Having coffee." I took the fact that he allowed me to enter the building as a sign that line might live. (It did.)

From there we went to a hospital room that was in the process of being transformed into a video recording studio. Michael Sheehan, Washington's A-list director/media coach, was there with his video team setting up shop. In the half hour before the president would arrive, I wrote his lines on oversized cue cards with a thick Magic

---

3. I am a bum.

Marker and quietly traded notes with Sheehan on the specifics of the script.

Just as we were finishing, and without trumpet or fanfare, the president entered the room on *Wheelchair One,* his injured leg perpendicular to the rest of his body. The Vicodin smile on his face quickly morphed into a grimaced yelp when the person negotiating his chair through the entrance smacked the cast leg on the interior of the door. A roomful of people first gasped in horror and then, seeing that he was okay, resisted the urge to laugh; between tumbling down a staircase and having his broken leg banged, this guy's life over the last two days had somehow become a *Three Stooges* short.

Once the president was safely in the room, Don briefed him on the video we were about to shoot. After waiting for the right moment, I walked up and trotted out a joke I had honed to perfection the summer I was a soccer coach for a bunch of injury-prone thirteen-year-olds.

"Good morning, sir. How's your left knee?"

"You mean my right knee?" he asked in a groggy voice.

"No, I know your right knee is terrible. But how is your *other* knee?"

"Fine," he said laughing, "thank you for asking."[4]

Sheehan took over from there, and soon the shoot was under way. The president would offer his apology for missing the dinner and then segue to a narrated presentation of a secret White House initiative on cloning, set against a slide show of poorly Photoshopped sight gags. In all, it was no more or less funny than your average Jay Leno desk piece.

---

4. Actually, this was a scaled-back version of the original, which had me explaining to writhing children that their injured legs or elbows would probably have to be amputated—the shock of which almost never failed to stop the crying. Later that spring, this silly playground joke would lead me to another joke the president used at the Radio and Television Correspondents' Dinner: *C-SPAN came on the air to report on my broken knee, while C-SPAN2 covered my other knee.*

Numerous retakes (attributed to the strong pain medication) pushed us far behind schedule. By the time I left the hospital, I was already forty-five minutes late to the second stop of the day, a noontime prep session for Al Gore's Gridiron speech. Borrowed keys in hand, I raced to Rob's car and headed down the straight shot of Wisconsin Avenue that connected Bethesda Naval Hospital to the VP's home a few miles away.

Not until I was alone in the car did I realize that I was having the time of my life. A quick glance into the rearview mirror revealed me to be practically glowing. Driving from the president's hospital room to the vice president's house had put me right in the middle of the moment I had dreamed about. If I had known this was how the president's accident would play out, I'd have been tempted to push him down some stairs myself. On this day, for these precious hours, I was the one person both these guys really needed to see. Finally, after all this time, I was the undisputed controlling comic authority.

I looked down at my watch to see that I was now an hour late. My beeper was buzzing incessantly, but in these last months before the purchase of my first cell phone, I was powerless to communicate the message that I was only minutes away. I pulled into the driveway of the vice president's residence, gave my name to a guard at the gate and rode up the driveway as if I were pulling into just another nice house on a nice block. I let myself in and followed the sound of voices until I arrived in the dining room, where a meeting was waiting for one last person to show.

"I'm sorry, sir, I have the only legitimate excuse there is: I was with the president."

The look on Al Gore's face suggested that this was not the first time he'd heard that—but in the spirit of good humor, he pretended to be amused. I took a seat at the dining room table with five or six aides, each with marked-up copies of my midnight draft.

Of the many details I had taken in during my first minute in the vice president's home, most surprising was the sight of Al Gore in something other than a dark suit. On this Saturday afternoon, he was comfortably attired in a faded T-shirt and New Age comfort slacks that split the difference between pants and pajama bottoms—not exactly tie-died but certainly not covered in little whales. Strapped to his socks were Teva-style sandals. Seeing him in his native garb made me smile. Now I had a stronger sense of who the real Al Gore was: a guy you might see at a Spyro Gyra concert.

Over the course of the meeting, I got my first glimpse of what a President Al Gore might look like—engaged, decisive, agile of mind and perhaps given to micromanaging. Even with a trained and licensed comedy speechwriter in the room, nobody had any doubt about who was running this meeting. My role was akin to that of a special advisor whose input was more valued than, say, the expert on global warming seated to my right. Before we got off the speech's first page, we found ourselves in the midst of a prolonged roundtable discussion focused on this joke in the "Five-Minute Presidency" bit:

Historians will look back fondly on the Gore administration. I believe that when they write about this period, they will record that during the Gore administration, our country was at peace, at home and abroad. Inflation remained low and the economy boomed—3.1 new jobs. There was less crime on my watch than any other presidency in the twentieth century—Democrat or Republican. We made America's streets safer with two new community police officers, Bob and Duane.

Having delivered this material to big laughs over the past few weeks, Gore was very familiar with it, except for the three new words added at the end. Now he wanted to know, "Can we come up with names funnier than Bob and Duane?" For the next few minutes, he entertained suggestions from the table—a small gang of policy advisors, media gurus and a pregnant press flack—the same way the leader of an improv troupe solicits suggestions from an audience. I didn't hear any I liked better, but having personally added those two names to the back end of Pink and Schnure's material, I have to confess that I was pretty partial to Bob and Duane. After momentarily giving thought to replacing "Bob" with "Stan," the vice president decided to stick with the names he had.

Okay. Now imagine two and a half hours of this—scores of jokes examined with microscopic attention paid down to the last Bob&Duanish detail. (Also imagine the early adrenaline of the day giving way to late-afternoon fatigue.)

The process came to an end around four that afternoon, giving me barely enough time to get to Sauro's tuxedo rental—the only place in Washington that rents the getup of white tie and tails—to pick up the 40-short that Mr. Sauro (my friend of five years) had set aside for me. Upon returning at last to Robby's apartment, I took a short nap and a long shower. While in the midst of bathroom-sink grooming, savoring the anticipation of the evening to come, I heard the telephone ring. Rob picked it up.

"Hello, Mr. Vice President!" Rob said, clearly excited that the second most powerful person in the United States had dialed his number, even if he was looking for me. "This is Mark's brother, Rob."

Rob's attempt to engage Al Gore in telephone chitchat didn't take.

"Hold on, I'll get him."

Wrapped in a towel, I came to the phone.

"Mark, what do you think of the name 'Ted'?"

"Ted is okay."

"Do you like it better than 'Bob'?"

I liked Al Gore. Comedy meant a lot to him and that meant a lot to me. But I needed to finish getting dressed, and Bob was a good name.

"I like 'Bob.' 'Bob' makes me laugh."

"Okay, let's stick with Bob."

Twenty minutes later, dressed and refreshed, I left Rob's apartment and jumped into a cab to the Capitol Hilton, just five blocks from the White House. Somewhere in the back of my mind, I must have realized that this perfectly scripted version of my comedy-writer-to-the-rescue fantasy would eventually have to come to an end. At the very least, I thought I had three or four hours left. But the euphoria ended abruptly as I arrived in the holding room, where I was greeted by a surprise guest.

"Hi Mark."

"Hey Al."

I was shocked to see Al Franken, of course, but found deep within myself the restraint not to ask him what he was doing there. (He was an invited guest of a Gridiron member and had come to the holding room to offer the VP his last-minute help.)

"I read the draft. You did a good job. There is some very funny stuff in there."

"Thank you."

(If only he had given this kind of approval to a Dukakis press office joke writer in desperate need of validation, I imagined, Al and I might have been close friends and true collaborators at that moment.)

"I have a joke I want to pitch to Al when he gets here," he said. Al Franken called Al Gore "Al." I called Al Gore "Sir." Yet another distinction of status between Al Franken and me was now clearly being flaunted in my face.

"Oh yeah? Let's hear," I said encouragingly. At that moment I braced for the joke writer's dilemma: that moment you want a fellow joke writer to offer up a line that is funny but not *too* funny.

"Okay, here's the joke: 'During my weekly lunch with the president on Tuesday, I asked him if he was looking forward to speaking here tonight. He said, "Al, I'd rather fall down a flight of stairs and undergo painful knee surgery . . ." Ironic, isn't it?'"

It was a very funny joke (maybe a notch short of "damn!") and we turned to the draft of the speech to find a place where it might fit.

A few minutes later the vice president arrived and gave Franken a warm hug. We rehearsed the speech once more, this time under Franken's direction. He coached the vice president on delivery and rendered opinions on what worked and what might be cut. Al Franken was generous in his response to the material and even deferential to the person standing next to him, who happened to be the speech's titular author. But all in all, I enjoyed the rehearsal back at the vice president's house just a little more.

Sometime between the entree and dessert of the Gridiron dinner, ten minutes before the evening's speeches were to start, a Secret Service agent came to find me at my table.

"The vice president would like to speak with you," he said, in a very quiet tone.

I looked to the dais and the vice president's seat was vacant. I followed the agent to the holding room behind the stage, where Franken, Pink and Schnure had also been summoned. Al Gore wanted to focus-group something given to him by the person sitting next to him at the head table: a barb directed at Trent Lott.[5]

"I would like to issue a special challenge to Trent Lott on the important issue of money in politics: Senator, we Democrats have upped our standards for campaign finance regulations. Senator Lott, *up yours!*"

---

5. The day before, then-Senate Majority Leader Trent Lott used the occasion of the president's injury to showcase some of the famous impromptu humor that got him where he is today. First this joke at the president's expense: "Somebody said they're going to do fund-raisers by allowing folks to sign his cast." But the joke Al Gore probably had in mind that day was this one: "Mr. President, we also appreciate the fact that you're not going to be put under, because we wouldn't want you to hand off your presidency—even temporarily—to Al Gore."

We all laughed. Then Gore wanted to know what we thought. Al Franken chimed in first: "It's a funny joke."

Dan Pink agreed that it was funny. "You should definitely use it." Eric Schnure liked it too. "Definitely."

I wasn't so sure. First, I had heard this joke before in various incarnations, and that devalued it greatly in my view. Second, the joke at its heart was basically just a more clever way of saying "Fuck you" to the Senate majority leader, and that carried perils of its own.

"The room might give an *ooooh*," I warned, but in the moment after that I had imagined there might be yet another bad turn of events. Even if the room does not object to the joke, I asked, what if Trent Lott does? Then he makes noise about it in the paper on Monday and Al Gore has to apologize for it on Tuesday? Who needs that? I thought the joke had more downside than upside, and all I sensed was the danger it posed for an otherwise winning speech. In the process of sorting out all of these thoughts, I had become convinced. My strong recommendation was "no-go." I was the sole dissenter, and Al Franken was giving me the same look I had given Don Baer earlier that week.

Addressing my concern, Franken pitched a line that might be a saver if "Up yours!" fell flat: "C'mon—the Venerable Master *loved* that joke!"

My reply: "Sir, if the joke needs a saver, you've already lost."

This was a showdown—or at least I thought it was. Whose advice would the vice president take on the matter of the "Up yours!" joke, Al Franken's or mine? I held my breath as he mulled it over. This was far more important than choosing between Bob and Ted.[6]

"I'm just going to play it by ear," the vice president said finally. Our white-tied team broke huddle and headed back to our seats for dessert.

---

6. Thankfully, Duane was never in peril

Like the hand-truck entrance three years earlier, this Al Gore Grid-iron speech opened with a bit of stagecraft. Upon the announce-ment of Gore's name as the evening's next speaker, the house lights went down and a hot spotlight caught Al Gore at his dais seat, a telephone in front of him, its receiver at his ear. On the heels of his fund-raising scandal, that was a punch line in itself, and with his face frozen, he patiently waited for the slow laughs to build. Then, once the laughter died down, he said sheepishly into the phone: "Uh, I am going to have to call you back . . ."

Once again, he earned his first big laugh before assuming the podium and just built on the momentum from there. First, he hit them with the "Five-Minute Presidency" and all the laughs I'd promised him that the name "Bob" would bring. A few strong topical jokes later, Al Gore really took the bat off his shoulder:

I can honestly say that I did not want to be here. Why would I? After the month I've had, I knew I'd be in for a pretty hard time tonight. I could just hear [the Republican speech-giver] Fred Thompson using all his Hollywood skills to cut me down to size. I imagined all the ways the Washington media elite might chew me up and spit me out. I spent some time pondering all the hurtful barbs, the snide remarks, the acid-tongued insults, the shots below the belt. And you all did a pretty good job. But you missed a couple.

Reading off a list pulled from his inside pocket, he continued:

- If Al Gore had only called 1-800-COLLECT, he would have saved Democratic donors up to 44 percent.
- By the year 2000, Al Gore wants to connect all Ameri-cans to the Solicitation Superhighway.
- What's the difference between Al Gore's press confer-ence and Sugar Ray Leonard's last fight? After fifteen minutes, they mercifully stopped the fight.

- How does Al Gore thank Democratic contributors? [Hands pressed in mantra pose] Ohmmmmmm.
- Al Gore would have been here earlier, but his motorcade was speeding—and was pulled over by a controlling legal authority.

. . . God, I miss those stiff jokes.

At that moment, I felt a nearly paternal pride in the fearlessness of my vice president. I only wished Don Baer might have been there to see it, several hundred people cheering Al Gore as he brazenly tackled his most taboo topic. But he was not out of the woods yet. He segued from these jokes at his own expense to the potentially treacherous joke at the expense of Senator Majority Leader Trent Lott. *Oh boy*. I held my breath all the way through to the end of "Up yours!"

Al Gore was so intrepid that night, he had dared to tread where even I had implored him not to go. And he was rewarded with another big laugh, another warm hug of approval from the many hard-boiled journalists dressed like penguins. All I could do was sigh in relief.

Before he was done, Al Gore teed up the president's video, which seemed well appreciated and sufficiently funny. The room's sustained applause at the end of the speech presaged the uniformly positive press Gore would later receive on the Sunday morning talk shows and in the Monday morning papers without any objections from the Senate majority leader.

I was back in New York by then, and I nearly choked on my bagel when reading a very positive account of the night in the *New York Times* that had arrived on my doorstep:

Those who know attributed the [vice president's] material to comedian Al Franken, recruited in the last-minute scurrying

for material to extend Gore's introduction of the president
to a full-fledged comedy routine.

Oh, Jesus.

A few keystrokes into my computer brought me to the story in
that morning's *Washington Post*, which also identified Al Franken
as the vice president's comic Zen Master and revealed the "saver"
line that Gore never needed.

Dear God, please make it stop.

But God had planned one more beat to His practical joke, and
it arrived in my e-mail in-box later that morning, a reply to the
copy of the speech I had e-mailed to friends and family upon
returning from an exciting adventure.

>>>*Very funny stuff, nephew. But I'm confused. Didn't I read that
Al Franken wrote this speech? XO—Aunt Doris*

The last laugh-through-my-tears moment of this day came
when the phone rang with a request for Al Franken's phone number from a *USA Today* reporter with a voice that sounded a lot like
Fisher's.

And yet all of the feelings of aggravating anticlimax suddenly
fell away when a phone call came in during the early afternoon.

"Hi Mark, it's Al Gore."

"Hello, sir!"

"Listen, I just wanted to call and thank you again. You came
through for me in a big way and I want you to know that I truly
appreciate it."

I began to gush about what a thrill that speech was for me, and
I meant every word of it. Before our conversation ended, the vice
president wanted me to know this: "Seriously, I owe you one."

The words "I owe you one" swam in my head for the next
hour or so, because I did not know what that meant. Al Gore

owes me one? Is that code for something? Had I acquired some kind of currency? Could I ask for a favor? And if so, what could that possibly be? Whatever it meant, whether it was a practical, actual offer or just a heartfelt expression of gratitude, I reasoned that this probably wasn't the time to pursue it. No, I decided, it would be much smarter to wait a few years, to hold out until Al Gore became president.

CHAPTER FIFTEEN

Comic Consigliere

OVER THE COURSE OF THE FIRST TERM AND INTO THE SECOND, A good number of Clinton-generated quotes and catchphrases had doubled as templates for self-inoculating jokes.

- "I did not inhale."
- "I still believe in a place called Hope."
- "I feel your pain."
- "It's the economy, stupid."
- "Briefs."
- "The era of big government is over."
- "We must build a bridge to the twenty-first century."

But on the Monday morning that I first heard the most indelible Clinton quote of all, I had a pretty strong sense that this one would not be tweaked into a joke for the Alfalfa Club dinner that Saturday night:

"I did not have sexual relations with that woman, Miss Lewinsky."

This unfathomable moment was no more or less fathomable to those of us who watched it unfold from within the White House.

There, in the speechwriters' suite of the OEOB–the nerve center of the president's State of the Union address just one day away–I stood among a small crowd of dumbstruck wordsmiths staring into a television screen as Clinton issued his third denial of an unseemly allegation. It was the president's most forceful and defiant denial yet, avowed with steely eyes and insistent gestures–a last, best effort to keep the most important speech of the year from becoming the sidebar story of an imploding presidency.

In the past eight days, every previous so-called White House crisis had started to seem like a mere bungee jump compared to what was now an untethered free fall. While testifying in the Paula Jones lawsuit (a troublesome he-said/she-said harassment case that dated back to Little Rock), Clinton was ambushed with prosecutors' questions about an illicit relationship with a specific White House intern that he denied under oath. As the most salacious allegations found their way to mainstream news organizations via backdoor Internet rumor mills, Clinton found himself in the unenviable position of having to deny having sexual relations with "that woman" to live cameras from the Roosevelt Room. Even Nixon's "I am not a crook" (an astounding presidential denial in its own right) never brought to mind an Oval Office occupant anything less than fully dressed–and look what happened to him! At the very least, this was definitely going to be hotter than "coffee."

The speechwriters did not have much to say even after the terrible moment was over, nor did the whip-smart White House interns who answered the phones. (Perhaps they were somehow ashamed that their once-coveted résumé entry was suddenly a synonym for "sexual object.") Besides the obvious dismay, no one wanted to choose between sounding too naïve or too cynical for their own good. Like everybody else, I retreated to my desk and continued to actively ignore possibilities too painful to imagine in favor of a task that was merely impossible: coming up with some jokes for this guy to tell at the Alfalfa Club.

Upon confronting my blank computer screen, I realized that

the rallying cry that had seen me through previous White House flare-ups—*things are only as bad as the things you can't joke about!*— was now more of a grim diagnosis. Although Don Baer had departed the White House earlier that fall, I reluctantly adopted his "coffee crisis" strategy that I had once so actively resisted: get this guy through the evening alive, and let him earn the points for having the courage to show up at all. I had not gotten much further than a possible opening line—"*So, how was* your *week?*"[1]—when the phone on my borrowed desk rang. It was Michael Waldman, the head speechwriter who'd replaced Don Baer.

"You're off the hook. We just canceled Alfalfa."

So much for the courage strategy.

The explanation was self-evident, even though Waldman had no time to give it. He needed to get back to the room where the highest-ranking White House aides were trying to figure out how the guy who had just said *"I did not have sexual relations with that woman"* might segue to *"The state of the union is strong."* Things were pretty tough all around.

For the first time, I found myself feeling relieved to exit the White House, to be on the other side of the  gates. On the train ride back to New York, my mind was spinning like a cyclotron as I tried to separate what I was willing to believe from what was actually believable. Even if I could believe the president's denials—that the charges were false, that he never asked anyone to lie (about what?) and that he knew nothing more than the reporters asking him questions

---

1. Another example of pulling a play from the Comedy Handbook: on the heels of a week worse than Clinton's, Paul Reuben's alter ego "Pee-Wee Herman" arrived at the podium of the 1991 MTV Video Awards and asked: "Heard any good jokes lately?" The sustained applause he received that night still resonated in my head seven years later.

did (prima facie ridiculous)—he'd still acted in a way that gave an *appearance of impropriety* on par with William Howard Taft's appearance of being fat. From Clinton's very first public denial of the charges, in which he insisted to PBS's Jim Lehrer that "there is no improper relationship," experienced Clinton-watchers like me had already begun to ponder what the meaning of "is" was.

Like so many loyalists, I took my cue from Clinton's Elite Democratic Guard—James Carville and Paul Begala, first and foremost—who were on the air and in the papers every day saying the president had looked them in the eye and denied the charges, and that was good enough for them. I tried my hardest to make that good enough for me, but my self-administered brainwash never lasted for more than ten minutes at a time. Each new day seemed to bring another distasteful detail, sometimes broadcast on the most improbable of programs,[2] and pundits were growing more fearless by the hour in their speculation about the imminent demise of Bill Clinton. On the Sunday morning after the abandoned Alfalfa dinner, I watched my former Dukakis campaign bunkmate—the authority to whom I had once looked to tell me when it was "over"—tell me it was over. George Stephanopoulos, now on the roster of commentators at ABC News, was on the air engaged in a roundtable elegy for President Bill Clinton:

> BILL KRISTOL: *He cannot survive, because he's not telling the truth.*
> GEORGE WILL: *He will resign when he acquires the moral sense to understand . . .*
> GEORGE STEPHANOPOULOS: *I'm heartbroken with all the evidence coming out.*
> SAM DONALDSON: *So what does President Gore do?*

---

2. I'm not sure I can define "pornography," but I think I know it when Bob Schieffer says it.

This exchange and others like it raised my cognitive dissonance to new and dangerous levels. Democrats weaned on Watergate cannot dismiss the opinions of the dogged political media as eagerly as Republicans do. I began trading phone calls with those I knew from White House halls that probably felt less hallowed than they had the week before. For all the venom that filled talk radio airwaves and newsgroup chat rooms, those who seethed most furiously at the prospect of what Clinton had done were those who were closest to him, who were thoroughly invested in him. Morality was less at issue than propriety, and making it all worse was his exceedingly inappropriate choice for an inappropriate relationship. Plenty of other presidents found extracurricular activity with Hollywood starlets or attractive ambassador's wives, women who at the very least knew how to keep a secret. But Monica Lewinsky was a joke, the pathetic girl from your freshman dorm who kept offering to give you a back rub until it sort of started to scare you.

What upset me most was what I was able to discern about Clinton's risk/reward ratio. How could he put so much in peril for the sake of something so cheap, knowing full well that a small army of enemies got up every day just to try to bring him down? I remember one day when it wasn't even a dismal report on the television that angered me but the cable box beneath it. Sometime around 1994, I had an opportunity to purchase an illegal cable descrambler. For $300, I could have owned a hand-soldered contraption made by some guy who knew his way around the back wall of a Radio Shack that would unlock every premium channel and Pay-Per-View feature that comprised the other four hundred channels. After thinking about it for a minute, I said "no thanks," the result of a thought process that went something like this: *You know what? I work for the president of the United States. I should really do my best to conduct myself with that in mind.*[3]

---

3. I decided that my radar detector, purchased during the back end of the Bush administration for a long cross-country road trip, was grandfathered in (except in Connecticut and Virginia).

This same guideline saw me through those rare occasions when I found myself in compromising situations. (How could I know if some guy sitting across from me in the limo en route to an Atlantic City bachelor party has a friend who writes for the *American Spectator*? Ergo: "No thanks. I'm cool.") My tenuous connection to the Oval Office was a connection just the same, and Clinton did not lack for enemies eager to take any shot at him they could. I was amazed that a similar thought had not occurred to one so closely connected to the presidency as . . . the president himself. Yet I had denied myself years of unfettered access to the Spice Channel, all for the sake of the man who would become known in the *New York Post* Page Six gossip column as the "Horn-Dog in Chief."

Of course the personal consequences for me were only just beginning, mere ripples of a larger, global crisis, but an unpleasant part of my day just the same. In early February, I got a phone call regarding a possible new project—the kind of call that kept the Sound Bite Institute up and running the whole year round—and promptly scheduled a meeting for later that week, eager for distraction. Upon being introduced to then–Wall Street media mogul Michael Bloomberg as "the guy who writes jokes for Clinton," I was taken aback when he offered this as his "hello":

"Oh yeah? Are you the guy who wrote 'I did not have sexual relations with that woman'?"

Caught off-guard, I offered weakly: "Yeah, that was me." But the remark shook me, flooding my mind with repressed recollections of a thousand exchanges that had me on the receiving end of a Dukakis tank joke, coupled with the realization that a million versions of Bloomberg's crack were headed my way. At the end of the meeting, I quoted Bloomberg a higher price for my services than I originally had in mind. Somebody should pay for the humiliation I was enduring, dammit, and who better than the caustic billionaire who'd inflicted it?[4]

---

4. Had I thought of it at the time, I would have used this bonus to purchase a cable descrambler.

Each day, multiple copies of the same Monica Lewinsky blow-job jokes filled my e-mail in-box, material so widely circulated that its proliferation was testing the infrastructure of the young Internet itself. Yet who could resist the smirking pleasure of forwarding a copy to the Clinton comic? (Certainly no one I knew.) Worst of all might have been when my father told me he'd taken down the Oval Office photos that lined a wall of his orthodontic treatment room. The shots of me with the president that had once served as conversation pieces and guaranteed bragging rights had become a trigger for cheap jokes that were inappropriate for an office filled with eleven- to fourteen-year-olds. My long run as the luckiest wiseass on earth was over. Not only was I the only comedy writer on the planet not writing Monica Lewinsky jokes, but now the Monica Lewinsky jokes were on me.

As March approached, so did another test—another spring's Gridiron Dinner. The White House faced an important choice in response to that annual invitation. To decline would surely invite an onslaught of one of Washington's most cherished clichés, a White House that was "in the bunker." The president's team wisely accepted the invitation, which left me with an important choice as well. Did I want to write it? At the height of my confliction, I was actually thinking about bowing out, declining to participate in something that felt like a lie. Things had gone so far wrong, it was hard to know what was right. Once again, I called my brother Robert, whose Harvard degree in political philosophy made him the closest thing I had to a personal ethicist.[5] Rob, who had left Washington and his job at the Justice Department the previous fall in pursuit of an academic career, responded by engaging me in a Socratic dialogue.

"So you want to resign? Let's see: has the chairman of the Joint Chiefs of Staff resigned?"

---

5. Rob had said "no thanks" to the cable descrambler too, although primarily because he is cheap.

"No."

"Have any of his cabinet members resigned?"

"No."

"Any undersecretaries or ambassadors?"

"No."

"Has his head speechwriter resigned?"

"No."

"Have *any* speechwriters resigned?"

"No."

"How about butlers or people on the maintenance staff?"

I refused to answer that one, as I could sense he was about to administer the mock.

"Bum, you are the *joke writer*. Get over yourself and write this poor bastard some fucking jokes."

My ego adjusted by my alter ego, I resigned myself to returning to the White House to work on the first in a series of humor speeches set against a backdrop of fevered, sordid scandal. *"I am doing this for the presidency"* was the self-aggrandizing justification I gave to myself, the same rationalization that 98 percent of Nixon's staff must have clung to on their way to work for most of 1974.[6]

From the beginning, this speech was different from any other. I had entered the sixth year of my ride along the bumpy sine curve of the Clinton presidency, and for each prior humor speech I had usually just imagined myself in his shoes and lent him the words I might say. But not this time. I knew in my heart that if I were in his shoes right then, I would have resigned within twenty minutes of having the distinguishing characteristics of my penis posted on the Drudge Report. By the time I got to Washington, I no longer wanted to know if Clinton was lying and decided I probably knew too much already.

The good news was that upon walking through the gates and onto the White House grounds, I had arrived at one of the only

---

6. The other 2 percent: "I am doing this for Satan."

places on earth where one could easily maintain such willful ignorance. By the middle of April, this White House had become an asylum for the world's last remaining sexcapade agnostics, a necessary condition that allowed the people who worked there to do their work. In fact, many staffers had even managed to internalize the Clinton legal strategy and kept their mouths shut. Reinforcing the code of silence was the well-known fact that any person discussing the matter immediately became a candidate for a subpoena from a team of prosecutors who clearly knew no bounds.

Most accounts of the president's strategy had the White House divided into two warring camps, the lawyers and the politicos, whose strategies contradicted each other. The political playbook called for Clinton to confess early and on his own terms to whatever transgressions were sure to come to light over time. Some (mostly low-level speechwriters and high-profile pundits) imagined an updated "Checkers speech"[7] set in the White House, while others pondered press strategies that included heart-to-hearts with the likes of Larry King, Barbara Walters and David Frost. The lawyers, meanwhile, seeking to avoid anything that might fortify Ken Starr's perjury case, implored Clinton not to admit anything publicly that contradicted statements he had made under oath to the independent prosecutor. Given the fact that he faced prosecution and not another election, Clinton opted for the legal advice. This had him broadly asserting his innocence, stating that

---

7. NIXON GLOSSARY FOR YOUNG ADULTS: The Checkers speech is political shorthand for a look-'em-in-the-eye ass-saving speech that stems the tide of crisis. In 1952, vice presidential candidate Richard Nixon was dangerously close to being dumped from Eisenhower's ticket over allegations of campaign fund corruption. While addressing the charge of campaign finance irregularities, he attacked his accusers and then launched into a maudlin story about a cocker spaniel puppy, given to him by a well-wisher, that his daughters had fallen in love with. In fact, they had already given it a name. This was where he drew the line: he would not return "Checkers." By the next morning, Nixon still had his spot on the ticket and a little puppy. The maneuver was regarded as nothing less than brilliant.

his lawyers would not let him say anything more than that, while pretending to chomp at the bit of his own gag order.[8]

This was the atmosphere that brought me to an organizing idea for the speech, one that came directly from the realities of the White House at that moment: writing the humor speech as written by a team of lawyers. As unsettled as I was by the circumstances, I was still thrilled to arrive at a promising premise—a response that reminded me that I am a better humorist than moralist. As fast as my fingers could dial, I called my brother Rob again, to pitch him the idea and tap into his law school education. He sparked to it immediately, and what followed was a comic-legal mind-meld a lifetime in the making: we produced the speech's framework and nearly half of its jokes inside of fifteen furious minutes. For a moment, I let myself enjoy the fact that the *markandrobby* tandem that defined my formative days was intact once again, this time applying its collective force for the benefit of the leader of the free world. Before I let my brother off the phone, we'd figured out how to transform the president's remarks into a funny amicus brief.

Writing the draft, as it turned out, was the easy part. What I quietly dreaded was yet to come, when I would have to sit across from the president as we rehearsed it. The very thought of being in his presence made me anxious, as though even that simple act would make me complicit in a lie. Two lies, in fact: (1) his dubious denials, and (2) the implicit lie that I believed them, as my draft and my presence would suggest. For all the obvious reasons, my many hours of hand-wringing and idle speculation about the president could never amount to much more than a subtext during my interactions with him, but I still feared that the undertone would be deafening.[9]

---

8. "If only you knew the truth," Clinton told one reporter.

9. To broach the subject would not only have been as inappropriate as anything mentioned in this chapter, but would also have made me vulnerable to a subpoena and hundred of thousands of dollars in legal bills. If you don't believe me, ask the many subpoenaed White House aides who incurred hundred of thousands of dollars in legal bills.

In my mind, and in my mind alone, my relationship with the president had changed. Every person who interacts with him regularly fancies himself an accredited Clintonologist, and over the previous five years I had cordoned off a part of my brain that allowed me to access his, a catalog of my collected insights into his mental reflexes, poorer instincts and awesome talents. Yet even as I entered the Oval Office for this, the seventeenth speech I had worked on since Clinton had taken office, I wondered what he assumed about why I was there, or whether he assumed anything at all. Honestly, I didn't even know what Clinton knew about me. Did he think I worked on his staff year-round, but that he only saw me in the spring? All I knew of what he knew was that three or four times a year I walked into his office with pages of jokes. Each time, he greeted me warmly and interacted with me in a manner consistent with preparations for an evening of humor.

However dreaded my expectations might have been, I certainly did not anticipate walking into the Oval Office on that afternoon in March to be treated like a returning hero. Our exchange went something like this:

Hey Mark, how ya doing?

Hello, Mr. President. Nice to see you.

I read your draft last night. There is some really, really *funny stuff in here!*

Thank you very much, Mr. President.

You did a great job again! I don't know how you do it . . . Hey, nice tie!

This was easily my most effusive Oval Office greeting from the president yet, complete with his heavy hands squeezing my suit-padded shoulders. In that instant, every angry, negative judgment that had been building inside of me since January melted suddenly away, like ice in August. He had me at *"Hey Mark."*

I didn't doubt for a second that Clinton was happy to see me, and I instantly recognized the extra effort he was making to let me know it. Obviously, this was already his worst year in office, and I reasoned that his response to me might have had something to do

with the fact that his staff was composed of fewer and fewer familiar faces and I had been around since "William Henry Harrison"
and the First Hundred Days. Maybe his greeting was just his
standard-issue sublimated apology to the thousands of loyalists
who had endured these shattering months. Or maybe I was imagining it all, seeking to justify my decision to write this speech by
assigning gracious motives to him. But I don't think so.

My theory acquired more credence in the moments following a
Saturday evening final rehearsal in the White House Map Room,
an antique-furnished chamber located on the first floor of the residence and most famously used as FDR's Situation Room to monitor the Second World War—a humbling reminder that the term
"war room" had not always been a metaphor nor a phrase coined
in Little Rock. These meetings were as much a pregame pump up
as they were an actual rehearsal, attended by those who might
advise him on the speech and/or offer loud, reinforcing laughter
for the jokes he would tell later that night. A podium brought in
for the occasion stood in the middle of the room, and eight or
nine staffers functioned as a chorus that gave him notes and confidence. But despite all of the high-ranking aides in the room, it
seemed to me that the president had chosen me as the person he
wanted to make eye contact with as he ran through the speech.
After the first minute of sustained eye contact during the rehearsal,
I was 99.9 percent certain that I was not just imagining it.

Good evening, distinguished guests and ladies and gentlemen of the Gridiron.
So. How was *your* week?[10]
For 113 years, the Gridiron Club has honored its one
defining rule: "Gridiron humor singes but never burns." You

---

10. This line, written for the aborted Alfalfa, was made relevant again by the
events of this particular week, which included a *60 Minutes* interview with another
alleged Clinton lust-object, Kathleen Willey.

have always maintained that code—and I've got the singe marks to prove it. But tonight, given Washington's current political climate, I'd like to request that the people in this room honor a second rule. And that is: kindly withhold your subpoenas until all the jokes have been told.

This is an . . . unusual time in Washington. Our version of "March Madness." So my preparation for this Gridiron speech was a little different than in years past.

In fact, I wasn't even sure if I was going to come tonight. My political team told me I had to. My legal team pleaded with me not to. So I went to my trusted press secretary Mike McCurry for his advice. And here's the speech he helped me write.

Good evening, ladies and gentlemen of the Gridiron. I have nothing further for you on that. Thank you and good night.

. . . And no, Helen, I will not parse "good evening" for you.

I am honored as always for this opportunity to share a few laughs off-the-record—or, as we now say, "under seal." But this year I offer my remarks with this caveat: they were a lot funnier before the lawyers got their hands on them. This may be the only speech in the long history of this club that has ever been redacted. But the counsel's office did send over some material they deemed funny:

Why did the chicken cross the road?
Res ipsa loquitur.

Why did the chicken cross the road?
Asked and answered.

Why did the chicken cross the road?
Your honor, counsel is badgering the witness!

A lawyer and his client walk into a bar. The client turns to his lawyer and says—No wait. That's privileged!

Knock! Knock!
DON'T ANSWER THAT!

The lawyers also told me that this year I can tell as many Lincoln Bedroom jokes as I want . . . And I just did.[11]

When the president finished his read-through of the speech, most of the staff scattered for their Saturday night plans while Mike McCurry and I, both white-tied and tailed, followed the president, now joined by the first lady, through the door of the South Portico, where a long row of gently idling vehicles awaited.

"Hey Mark, why don't you come ride with us?"

The smile that had broken out on my face remained largely intact even after he added, "Mike, you too!"—and McCurry jumped into the limo as well. For the eight-block drive between the White House and the Capitol Hilton, I got an insider's view of the oddly serene moving bubble that brought the president from place to place in a raucous procession of town cars, mini-vans, ambulances, real and decoy presidential limos and Brinks-built SUVs equipped with mobile rocket launchers. On the way over, I gave the president a rundown of the Gridiron skits that would be performed by a troupe of costumed journalists, infor-mation I'd acquired through back-channel reconnaissance, as well

---

11. Here's a lawyer joke from my draft that was killed by *actual White House lawyers*:

My lawyers also sent along this list of topics I should feel completely free to discuss—like critical infrastructure, the Africa trip, the Millennium Project. Lawyers whose name I can mention: Daniel Webster, Clarence Darrow, Ally McBeal. Recent court cases I can mention: The Beef Industry vs. Oprah. Independent prosecutors whose names I can mention: Lawrence Walsh. People named Starr I can mention: Brenda. Bart. Ringo.

as assurances that the first couple would not be embarrassed by the subject matter of the evening's elaborate skits and parodied songs.

Even though the circumstances of this speech were extraordinary, the drill was familiar. By the time another long Gridiron Dinner had finally ended, Clinton had deftly delivered yet another speech with the full force of his talent. The laughs that he earned from the distinguished fourth-estate elites gave the impression that on this special occasion, it was the president who was granted a pardon—albeit a temporary one.

If this year's trip to the Gridiron was something akin to a white-tie tribunal at The Hague, the next humor event on the calendar was sure to be more like a match at the Roman Colosseum. The crowd at the White House Correspondents' Dinner—an indoor acre teeming with Washington's abundant media class dressed in mere tuxedos—would be much larger, less refined and possibly bloodthirsty. The tables closest to the dais represented Washington's best approximation of Hollywood's Oscars, with brand-name network stars interspersed with the handful of Hollywood celebrities who came as their guests. (Adding to the circus hoopla would be the presence of Miss Paula Jones, the trophy guest of the *Washington Times*'s sister newsweekly, *Insight Magazine*.[12]) This would require a different strategy: if the Gridiron speech had been a nolo contendere plea,[13] this next speech would need to combine a more spirited defense with a textbook Clinton charm offensive.

Late on a Friday afternoon, just as we were putting the final touches to the near-final draft of the president's speech, I received a phone call from the White House social secretary.

"Good afternoon, Mr. Katz. The president of the United States

12. Was this in good taste? I report. You decide.
13. A Latin term made famous by America's first Greek vice president, Spiro T. Agnew.

would like to invite you and a guest to watch a movie with him
this evening at the White House." Having bragged to friends and
family over the previous six weeks about my ride in the presidential limo, I immediately knew that a casual evening watching
movies with the president would be the story that could take me
through the summer. Even as I jotted down the details of when
and where to arrive, I knew precisely whom I was about to call to
invite as my guest.

Phil Rosenthal is the older brother of Rich Rosenthal, one of
my very best friends, and also from my hometown. Since the days
when my buddies and I wasted our precious youth watching TV in
the Rosenthals' den, Phil always made me laugh with the things
that he said and the way that he said them. His obvious gifts gave
him the aura of a star from early on: the buzz that his performance
in my high school's production of *Little Me* created in New City,
New York, approximated what *The Producers* later did for Broadway.
Destined for stages bigger than Rockland County could provide,
he eventually moved to Los Angeles. After many years toiling as
an actor and television writer, he went on to create a sitcom called
Everybody Loves Raymond.[14] In more recent years, on my occasional
trips to L.A., Phil invited me to tapings of the show and to his
home on Sunday evenings for a movie night of his own—a weekly
event with a dozen of his friends, a half-dozen pizzas and a great
movie worth watching again.

As it happened, Phil was in D.C. this week, accompanying his
show's star and namesake, Ray Romano, the professional comedian
who had been hired to entertain the crowd at the White House
Correspondents' Dinner. (In this dicey year, Romano's invitation
was predicated upon the fact that he was not a late-night or hard-
edged comic who might make the president—or his wife—uncomfortable.) Eager to show off for someone I had long idolized, I'd

---

14. You are reading the book of the person who is not even the funniest and most
accomplished comedy writer of his own small hometown. Too late to stop now.

already secured Phil an invitation to come with me to the president's Saturday morning Oval Office radio address, a plum perk of
the job I was almost always able to obtain through the Oval Office
staff. Phil had been so excited about meeting the president in the
first place that I correctly predicted his response to my last-minute
movie night invite: ecstatic babbling. After a question or two that
really just signified his disbelief at the prospect, he asked, "Can I
bring something?" Mrs. Rosenthal had raised her sons right.

"Like what?"

"Like a pizza maybe?"

I immediately knew of two reasons Phil could not bring a pizza
with him to the White House. First, the Secret Service would not
allow it, as it would be considered a security risk. (There were any
number of hate-mongers and third-world despots who'd be
delighted to cater the president's next meal.) And second, "pizza"
had become a whispered word in this White House, evoking as
it did a certain intern/Oval Office delivery girl. Explaining these
things to Phil reminded me once again what a strange world I had
become accustomed to.

From the moment he entered the White House, Phil's eyes
were practically popping out of his head, and I knew I was about
to enjoy this evening all the more for watching him take it in. A
bona fide movie buff, he asked me a question I had neglected to
ask of the social secretary in all the excitement of the initial phone
call itself: what movie was playing at the White House Friday
Night at the Movies? I didn't know, and figured we'd just wait and
see—not that it really mattered to either of us.

Arriving at the theater before our host and most of the other
guests, we both immediately had the same thought, which neither
of us wanted to say out loud. The furnishings, accoutrements and
audiovisual equipment we saw there simply did not measure up
to those found in the Phil and Monica Rosenthal family theater.[15]

---

15. Being a big-time TV producer is a very good job.

This room, seven or eight graduated rows of five or six seats, felt like the product of Mamie Eisenhower's panache. None of this dampened our excitement, of course, and when the president walked through the door everything ratcheted up another notch or two. After thanking the president profusely for the invitation, I introduced him to Phil, who thanked him twice as profusely as I had. I also mentioned Phil's hit TV sitcom, and the president never let on that he had only heard of it for the first time earlier that day, when I had explained the Ray Romano joke in his draft to him.[16] Phil and I took seats two rows behind Clinton for the showing of a film called *Dangerous Beauty*. Neither Phil nor I nor anyone seated in our immediate vicinity had heard of it, but I overheard someone say that the president had selected it himself.

Within five minutes of the opening credits, we learned just about all we needed to know about the feature presentation, which left nearly everyone in the room in quiet dismay. *Dangerous Beauty* is the story of a sixteenth-century Venetian courtesan who not only masters her trade to universal acclaim but also somehow harnesses her remarkable sexual prowess to conduct a foreign policy that saves the city from being wiped off the map—kind of a *Pretty Woman*-meets-Madeleine-Albright scenario. But, unlike the PG-13 sensibility of that other movie with a prostitute protagonist, the feature we were watching in the White House was just a few close-up shots away from something you'd order from the adult menu of a hotel Spectravision. In the 118 minutes that followed, the fifteen or twenty people nestled in to the cozy theater watched these scenes with President Bill Clinton:[17]

---

16. "*Everybody* loves Raymond? I just hate a guy with a 100 percent approval rating."

17. The first lady, thank God, was out of town.

- Opening scene: the topless courtesans of Venice parade down the canals to the bawdy hoots and hollers of the men who are their patrons.
- The courtesan's mother (played by Jacqueline Bisset), once the greatest courtesan in all of Venice, teaches her young daughter the tricks of the trade by performing them upon a naked young man. This scene was shot tastefully from the hips up, with cutaway close-ups on the pronounced facial expressions that registered the ever-quickening pace of his shallow-breath pleasure.
- The courtesan (played by Catherine McCormack, the same actress who practically stole *Braveheart*) demonstrates to the Venetian wives the skills that their husbands find lacking in their marriages, using as her prop a hefty banana.
- At its hour of maximum danger, Venice calls upon its greatest courtesan to practice her brand of diplomacy, which includes a closed-door bargaining session with the King of France where a treaty gets pounded out on a four-poster bed.
- Abundant humping.

For over an hour, Phil and I flashed open-mouthed gapes to each other in response to these scenes and much of the rest of the movie. (I had not been this uncomfortable in a movie theater since the time I went with my family to see *The Jazz Singer*—only to learn that it was sold out, so we bought tickets for *The Blue Lagoon* instead.) All the more incredible was that the president was glued to his seat in the front row, completely transfixed, his attention never wavering except for intermittent trips to the side of the room for another bag of popcorn or can of Diet Coke.[18] The weirdest moment of all came when the movie arrived at its

---

18. This was a humor opportunity undreamed of in the back row of Nussie's class: when the president got up for the third time to get some more popcorn, I muffled through my hand: "Down in front!"

cinematic climax, the scene where the noble libertine is put on trial by a repressed and corrupt right-wing prosecutor. The courtesan is then saved from the gallows at the last hour by the collective protest of the many Venetian men who knew her best.

At the end of this period-piece soft-core skin flick—*Debbie Does Merchant Ivory*—the muscles of my face were nearly in spasm. All of this had occurred in a hypersensitized White House where, just that week, the words "address," "abroad" and "unfettered access" were removed from the president's speeches so as not to elicit audience giggles.[19]

When the lights came up, the president held court for a dozen or so guests, expounding on what he loved about the movie and paying heartfelt tribute to the astounding beauty of the leading actress. ("She sucked the air right out of the room!") He also confirmed one of the movie's underlying historic points, that courtesans were the best-educated women in Europe for many hundreds of years. Bill Clinton loved that movie, and he eagerly discussed its attributes and nuances long after the credits had rolled, either willfully ignoring its subtext or else simply blind to it.

On the other side of the White House gates, Phil and I went out for a bite[20] and retold ourselves the story we had just lived through until we thought we'd exhausted all our laughs. Twelve hours later, we were back at the White House again for the Saturday morning radio address, at the conclusion of which Phil and I got on line to have our picture taken with the president. The pres-

---

19. A partial list of words probably deemed unsuitable for White House speeches circa 1998: interim, my staff, my chief of staff, priming the pump, bring Iraq to its knees, head of state, seat of power, negotiating table, "Don't ask, don't tell," deployment of seamen, missile warheads, the nations of Djibouti, Greece and Liechtenstein, the city of Kissimmee, moniker, Lewis or Clark, Dick Armey, Dick Gephardt, Ambassador to Denmark Dick Swett, the Department of Health and Human Services.

20. Phil is one of the world's great gourmands, with a finely tuned palate and spare-no-expense budget. On this night, the only thing open nearby was a Burger King on K Street, and during the course of our late supper he delivered a heartfelt ode to the undeniable attributes of the Whopper.

ident immediately broke into a big smile at the sight of us and launched back into the topic we'd last discussed.

"That was some movie, huh?" Judging from the president's breathless excitement, the person behind us in line could well have assumed we'd watched the digitally remastered version of *Citizen Kane*.[21]

I specifically avoided eye contact with Phil at that moment, fearing that we might succumb to hysterics yet again. Instead, as the moment came and passed, I found myself marveling at a man whose unabashed enthusiasms and character traits were, in fact, unabashable. Circumstances notwithstanding, Bill Clinton was not afraid to be exactly who he was—and in this case, he was a guy who really loved this movie and didn't care who knew it. As I added this mental note to my Clinton file, I felt like I understood him just a little bit better—and maybe even liked him just a little bit more. Bill Clinton was just like you'd expect him to be—only more so.

Later that afternoon, I returned to the White House in my tuxedo for the final rehearsal of that evening's speech. As I entered the West Wing gate, I saw John King of CNN nearby, just completing a live report on air. I had known John since the Dukakis days, when he was an AP reporter covering the campaign and I was the guy answering the Dukakis press office phones. From ten feet away, he called out to me: "Godspeed Dan Burton!"

I was confused. *Godspeed Dan Burton!* That was a punch line in the president's speech, the draft of which was rolled up in my hand. For half a second, I thought John King had just performed a Kreskin trick. "What did you say?"

"You heard me," King said. "I just reported the joke during my last stand-up."

---

21. My best efforts to re-create this episode notwithstanding, the full measure of these last few pages can only be fully appreciated by those willing to rent *Dangerous Beauty*.

"You're shitting me."

He was shitting me not.

This exchange was a good example of how emboldened the Washington press corps had become circa the spring of 1998. Apparently, reports coming from the White House no longer needed to comply with the ground rules that had been accepted practice for years. In this case, hearsay about the president's jokes had not only been obtained by reporters but had now also been aired live on CNN. In the context of the speech we were about to rehearse, this constituted a small crisis. I went directly to the speechwriting office in the OEOB.

"You are not going to believe what just aired on CNN," Michael Waldman said to me. The gravity of his tone and demeanor might have scared me into thinking there was some kind of national emergency under way had I not already known the answer:

"Godspeed Dan Burton!"

"You know? How could you know? It was just on the air!" For a moment, I topped the list of suspected joke leakers.

"I just saw John King on my way in."

"Oh." My response removed 90 percent of his suspicion.

"Let's go," he said, his back to me and already halfway out the door.

We headed over to the West Wing press office to discuss the matter with Mike McCurry, the White House press secretary. After all McCurry had seen in the past five months, he was bemused by yet another boundary that had been crossed.

"Welcome to my world" was his weary response. Nobody knew better than McCurry that the boundaries of Washington journalism had been deviating downward every day since the third week of January 1998; the fevered pitch of the press corps had at least plateaued in the weeks since the Gridiron, if only because the president had little to say about his legal and political difficulties and had been out of the country most of the time anyway. The White House's rope-a-dope strategy had taken the president on extended trips overseas—and this had actually helped quell some of the clamor.

Waldman and I were still discussing the situation and the options it left us as we arrived outside the Map Room, where our rehearsal meeting was to take place. At the closed door stood a Secret Service agent, who told us the room was still in use and mentioned something about a video being shot inside. Still consumed with the joke leak dilemma, we paid the situation little mind and continued our conversation in a tone of voice maybe a notch or two above a whisper.

Five minutes later, the door to the Map Room opened, and bounding out came Mrs. Clinton. She saw Michael and me and stopped for a moment to give us a warm smile and a kind word.

"Hey! I read a draft of tonight's speech. Really funny. Great work, you guys!"

We were stunned. Had we known the first lady was inside the room, we certainly would have been quieter. The door still open, I peered inside to see who remained. Silhouetted against a southern-exposed window was the back of a man in a light gray suit. The neat, unfluffy hair that tightly tapered to his neck and ears suggested he'd been to a barber as recently as that morning. Although nearly six feet tall, he exuded the pinched stature of a mid-level manager or a high school vice principal. The eyes he kept in the back of his head must have known I was there and he turned suddenly to take me in. That's when my eyes met Kenneth Starr's and in that eerie moment, I thought I knew what it was to be undead.

I dropped my head to the floor as he approached the door to exit the Map Room; the last thing I needed was to register on this guy's radar screen. (So spooked was I by that encounter with an empowered moral missionary, later that day I deleted the porn I'd downloaded to a hidden folder on my laptop.) That night, the first lady accompanied the president to his speech and seemed to enjoy herself throughout the long, joke-filled evening. Each time I looked up at the dais to see her smiling, laughing and waving to familiar faces in the crowd, I imagined how I would have left a marathon four-hour interrogation by a maniacal prosecutor: on a stretcher hooked up to an epinephrine drip.

By 6 P.M., more aides had arrived at the Map Room, all there to help run the pregame drill once the president appeared. Among the assembled staffers were speechwriters Jordan Tamagni and Jeff Shesol, both of whom had played important roles in the process that produced this speech. Jordan, a recovering New York lawyer, was the speechwriter I had worked most closely with day to day since 1996, when she started; she was the point person on the staff for shepherding drafts through the West Wing. Jeff was the speechwriting staff's most recent addition. He had pitched in a handful of jokes for the speech, and a few had lived to see the final draft.

By now, everyone in the room had heard about the joke leak to John King, and the room was brimming with speculation about the leaker's identity. Some thought the joke should be cut as a punishment for whoever had done it, somebody whose sole motivation was clearly self-aggrandizement. Others thought the joke should stay and that we should not let the security breach make the president's speech any less funny. (Besides, everyone in the room was eager to take a shot at Representative Dan Burton, one of the most viscerally disliked Clinton antagonists, most famous for his backyard experiment utilizing a pumpkin and a .22 caliber pistol to "prove" that Vince Foster was murdered.) Ultimately we all agreed to leave the final decision to the president.

At 10:26 that evening, the president arrived at the podium of the Washington Hilton ballroom to entertain the White House correspondents, who for the past four months had done little else besides writing, talking, digging, speculating and entertaining themselves with the details of his private life and public denials. The room greeted him warmly, perhaps an advance on his courage-for-just-showing-up dividend:

Thank you very much. Thank you, Mr. McQuillan, Mr. Powell. Good evening, ladies and gentlemen. As you know, I have been traveling to other lands quite a lot lately, and I just want to say what a pleasure it is for Hillary and me to be here in your country. Since I arrived here, I've been awestruck by the beauty of your landscape, the spirit of your people, the color of your native garb.

Now, the crowds who greet me here are not quite as adoring as in other nations I've visited lately but they seem occasionally friendly, nonetheless. I've even sampled some of your indigenous cuisine. Your hamburgers, quite tasty—sort of a meat sandwich.

It appears that democracy is thriving here. There are regular elections, contested with vigor, honored by some. In the legislature, persistent coup attempts so far have failed to upend the balance of power. You have a lively, independent press, confident in its judgment and bold in its predictions. And persistent, I might add.

Yes, this Washington is a very special place, and Hillary and I will never forget our visit here.

By this time, Clinton had taken over the room and become one with the presidential podium in front of him. His arms resting over the top as he spoke made him look as comfortable as a guy settled into the ass-worn cushions of his own La-Z-Boy recliner. Just as his foreign travel strategy deflected (some) heat, so too did this opening bit that all but acknowledged that strategy itself. One of the striking elements of Clinton's many addresses to the assembled legislatures of these many countries was the contriteness he displayed for past U.S. foreign policies: in Rwanda, he apologized for U.S. inaction during the country's bloody civil war, and in Uganda he expressed regret for the nineteenth-century slavery trade. The press had dubbed his travels "The Apology Tour," sometimes the "Contrition Mission," a characterization the White House did little to rebut. In many ways, his contrition seemed like a surrogate apology for the one he owed to so many but was legally and psychologically unprepared to give. A not-insignificant part of me wanted the president to apologize on this night as well, and the next part of his speech was the comic equivalent of his subtextual mea culpa:

> Now, as I have come to do on these tours, I want to take just a few moments to reflect on our shared history. The past decades, indeed centuries, are filled with regrettable incidents. Mistakes were made. Injustices were committed. And certainly the passive tense was used too much.
>
> Ladies and gentlemen, I regret so much: I regret our long neglect of the planet Pluto. It took until 1930 to welcome Pluto into the community of planets, and that was wrong.
>
> And I am so sorry about disco. That whole era of leisure suits and beanbag chairs and lava lamps—I mean, we all had to endure the cheesiness of the seventies, and that was wrong.
>
> Then there's the Susan B. Anthony dollar. It did look too much like a quarter. And that was wrong. The expression "happy campers." Oh, it was cute the first couple of times, but it got real old real fast. I recently used it at a cabinet meeting, and that was wrong. Pineapple on pizza—some things are just wrong![22]

Having told some self-directed jokes, the president moved on to some new targets. First came the press corps, a group that he could probably only insult by ignoring them altogether:

> I'd also, in this moment of cleansing, like to take just a moment to reflect on past treatment of the White House

---

22. This joke was hotly debated for fear of the word "pizza" but somehow made it through the strenuous West Wing vetting process and got a laugh without repercussions.

press corps. I apologize for the quality of the free food you've been served over the years. At the price, you deserved better. It was wrong. For many years when the space that is now the briefing room in the White House was a swimming pool, reporters had to tread water for hours on end. And that was wrong—sort of.

. . . This is the night I get to poke fun at you. That is my definition of executive privilege.

The roomful of correspondents surrendered their heartfelt laughter and applause to the same man whose real notion of "executive privilege" they spent their collective waking hours trying to expose and undermine. But Clinton's most salient barb was yet to come. The White House's tug-of-war with the political media was always strenuous, but usually fairly evenly matched. Every day in the White House briefing room, Mike McCurry employed artful dodges and semantic gamesmanship more to frustrate his questioners than to illuminate any real kind of answer.

Over the past few months, millions of Americans had flocked to the Drudge Report for their late-breaking news. But in recent weeks, even reputable news organizations had exercised far less caution than McCurry had urged them to take. A number of newspapers, the *Dallas Morning News* most prominently, had printed various stories of specific, salacious details of the president's alleged behavior before they had acquired a second source to confirm it. Days later, those same papers were forced to print retractions and apologize for at least the momentary adoption of less than rigorous standards. These retractions were celebrated as a huge victory in the White House, evidence of an overeager press corps retreating from their front-page falsehoods. I know, because I took heart in it as well and wrote a joke that I was very proud of at the time:

Now, I'm at a little bit of a disadvantage this year. I've been so busy I haven't read a newspaper or a magazine or even watched the evening news since the Pope went to Cuba.[23] What have you been writing about since then? I hardly have any time to read the news anymore. *Mostly, I just skim the retractions.*

Amazingly, the room full of journalists gave the president sustained prolonged applause on this line, which had been written purely to take them to task, and both the president and I basked in it at the same moment. But here's what the president knew right then and there that I did not: some of those retracted stories were (or might as well have been) true. I didn't realize it at the time, but this was the joke that took me over a threshold I had hoped not to cross. For these many years, I had taken a quiet pride that so many of the jokes the president told had allowed him to admit the truths about himself and his circumstance that would otherwise have gone unsaid. *I had a terrible First Hundred Days in office. My State of the Union speech went on a little too long. My thighs are not thin. My health care plan became a fiasco. The Lincoln Bedroom was used as a fund-raising tool. I did serve coffee to people who wrote me huge checks. Etc. Etc. Etc.* These subtextual admissions made him appear all the stronger and his genuine accomplishments all the greater. But now the jokes I had handed him were being used to reinforce lies. Now I was using humor to paint a picture of a plausible story on behalf of a client whom I did not myself believe. Had Bill Clinton succeeded where my parents, my girlfriends' parents and my guidance counselors had failed? With writing these semantic jokes that were narrowly construed to fortify falsehoods, had I finally turned into a goddamn lawyer? *Res ipsa loquitur.*

Had I not been so intoxicated by the room's loud laughter, I might have realized what I had become. Instead, I was busy being

---

23. The Pope arrived in Cuba on the day the Monica story broke in the *Washington Post.*

thrilled with the sight of the president winning over the crowd. Having finished his jokes at the expense of the media, Clinton took careful aim at his other set of eager oppressors, the Republicans in charge of the House of Representatives.

There are barely forty days left in the 105th Congress as of tonight. This is a Congress with nothing to do and no time to do it in. But there will be one news item coming out of Capitol Hill next week. I met with Senator John Glenn recently to decide who should be the next distinguished member of Congress hurled into the far reaches of the universe. And we have our man: **Godspeed, Dick Armey!**[24]

Somewhere in the vast expanse of this room, a high-level White House aide thought: "Hey, that's not the joke that I leaked!" The more observable response was the loud laughter and applause of those who had just watched the president take on himself, the press corps and the GOP Shiites who thought they had Bill Clinton exactly where they wanted him—at their (lack of) mercy. But not on this night. On this night, Bill Clinton owned the room, leaving even the reporters who knew his moves down cold floored by what he'd just accomplished: his first good day on the continent of North America since the Pope went to Cuba.

*   *   *

On Labor Day Weekend of 1998, I was in the Berkshires bike riding with friends, my brother Rob among them. I was two steps from the front door of the famous Red Lion Inn, a picturesque hotel whose

---

24. It is hard to imagine Dick Armey being anyone's *second* most hated person, but that's how deep the House Republican roster was—and he just barely nudged out Tom DeLay and Bob Barr! (By 1998, Newt Gingrich was such an afterthought, he didn't even make this list.)

white painted porch is the region's unofficial epicenter, when Rob, a few steps behind me, grabbed the back of my T-shirt and stopped me in my tracks. Over the shoulder of a man nestled in an Adirondack chair, he had just seen a headline on the obituary page from that day's *New York Times*. Rob's outstretched arm pulled me back to take it in:

Kirk O'Donnell, 52, Lobbyist and an Aide to a House Speaker

My heart dropped like a rock. My brother, his hand now on my shoulder, knew I was taking in the sudden loss of a father figure. The nice man on the porch, sensing his unwitting role as the bearer of bad news, offered his condolences and handed the newspaper to me. I was shaken, saddened and oddly angered at the heart attack that had taken a terrific man decades too soon. I had lost the kind of friend and mentor who comes along once in a lifetime, and even then only to those who are exceedingly lucky. My life would have been very different but for Kirk O'Donnell, and now I would never be able to make good the debt.

On the drive back to New York that evening, I thought about Kirk and all I had gained since the day he came to the Dukakis press office looking for the kid who wrote the jokes. Somewhere on the Taconic Parkway, I let out a good, hard laugh when I remembered that this very day marked the ten-year anniversary of George Bush's misbegotten "Pearl Harbor Day," an unforgettable episode that I'd shared with Kirk and our close-knit team. But from now on, September 7 would be a day that lived in bittersweet memory.

CHAPTER SIXTEEN

Apocalypse Then

MY CLINTON-CAMELOT DREAMS PUT TO REST SOME TIME AGO, I returned to this White House in the spring of 1999 as if I were walking onto the set of *Geraldo!*—a place where anything can happen because it already has. A humor speech on the heels of an impeachment trial? Sure, bring it on!

In contrast to the enervating effects of the sordid scandal itself, the aftermath of impeachment felt liberating, clarifying, energizing! Yes, our guy had conducted his private life appallingly and then proceeded to lie about it under oath. But the first impeachment trial since that of Andrew Johnson (above) mostly left me fuming about those who had administered that oath—loathsome hypocrites eager to put someone else's hand on the Bible. Watching the Republican legislators and their allied prosecutors trump Clinton's reckless personal behavior with ruthless constitutional brinksmanship reminded me why I had signed up with my team in the first place. (Perhaps I had subconsciously processed the vices of JFK and Nixon and made my choice a long time ago.) But having made it through to the other side of this ordeal—for which he was at least half to blame—

Bill Clinton still needed to prove he could joke about it if he was to get past it.

Four weeks after the impeachment acquittal, I returned to Washington to work on not one but *two* humor speeches: the Radio and Television Correspondents' Dinner and the Gridiron, events within forty-eight hours of each other. My first conversation with Michael Waldman that spring set the tone for what was to come. After a few minutes spent hashing out the challenges of this political science-fiction scenario, we agreed that we had more latitude than usual:

"What are they going to do," he said, "impeach us?"

Michael had another idea for these speeches as well. In years past, I had been paired with speechwriter Jordan Tamagni, a talented writer and transplanted Manhattan sophisticate who made no claims upon being a jokesmith. (Instead, she was a combination sounding board/den mother/logistical facilitator, as well as the writer who took the first crack at the speech's loftier concluding thoughts.) This year, Waldman wanted to team me up with Jeff Shesol, a relative newcomer to the staff but one with humor credentials of his own, including a not un-*Doonesbury*-like comic strip called *Thatch* that he penned at Brown and syndicated thereafter. (His other undergraduate accomplishment lived on as well, an honors thesis that became the basis of a well-received book, *Mutual Contempt*, a history of the blood feud between Bobby Kennedy and Lyndon Johnson.) Jeff's arrival midway through the second term bucked the trend of talented people leaving for other pursuits, and his evident gifts quickly made him a rising star. I might easily have felt threatened or unsettled by such an arranged comedy marriage, but the jokes Jeff pitched the previous spring had been good ones that only got better when the two of us worked together to punch them up. Jeff's OEOB office became the Comedy War Room's new headquarters, my new seat the couch across from his desk.

Working together felt instantly familiar for reasons that could only be obvious to me. Jeff was a substitute Robby: a smarter, more accomplished, culturally identical[1] younger brother-in-arms with a penchant for thinking out loud and a natural facility for humor. Our first day working together had us trying to come up with an ideal opening line at a press dinner that was an all-but-formal surrender ceremony of the Monica Media Wars. What might the president say to those at whom he had wagged his finger for more than a year that would demonstrate his contrition while somehow preserving his dignity? *Hmmm. This was a tough one.* But before the day was over, we'd written an opening that neither of us would have arrived at in the absence of the other:

> *Good evening. I want to thank you for your invitation to come have dinner with two thousand members of the Washington press corps. Now, I realize this has been a very serious matter. Let's face it: if the Senate vote had gone the other way, I wouldn't be here speaking to you tonight.*
> *. . . I DEMAND A RECOUNT!*

Jeff and I exchanged high fives, but both of us sensed that we'd stumbled upon a joke more significant than reflexive male ritual could register. In fact, we were taken aback by the joke's admission that the president would have preferred removal from office to this moment of profound humility, and we took a long moment to absorb its full import. What could be more contrite than that? But the more pertinent question was, would Clinton do that joke? Would it even live to see the next draft? To say the least, it would break new ground for presidential humor. (This point was hard to know for certain, as the Johnson administration kept very poor notes.) Later that day, Waldman gave us an encouraging response, repeating what would become a mantra in the Comedy War Room from that week on: *"What are they going to do—impeach us?"*

---

1. Read: Jewish.

Jeff and I found boundless liberation in the postapocalyptic optimism that followed the failed impeachment proceedings, and we took special delight in tossing around ideas that were not necessarily impossible: *Will Rehnquist be there? Maybe we get him to swear in Clinton before he gives his speech? Then let's have him open the* Oxford *unabridged dictionary and have Clinton read the nine different entries for "is." No? How about he parses the meaning of the word "parse"? Is John Goodman available for a Linda Tripp bit? Oh, wait, I got it: A Map Room video testimony blooper reel. No wait—a Marilyn Monroe impersonator sings "Happy Birthday" to Henry Hyde.[2] Okay, ready for this? He tells Tom DeLay to "kiss it." How about this: he walks out to the podium and lights up a big, fat cigar? Okay, maybe not—but at the very least, maybe this can be the year we finally do a joke about the* $200 *haircut on the* LAX *tarmac that was* WAAAAY *too hot to touch in 1993.*

In the frenzy of our free-for-all, we actually came upon another ambitious idea that would not, in fact, get Clinton reimpeached: a parody of a transparent White House ploy, employed frequently during the past fourteen months to restrain the press corps. As Clinton's renewed interest in foreign affairs had grown over the past year or so, so too had the number of joint press appearances with world leaders. The White House clung to the faint hope that the press corps would be less aggressive about asking the president compromising questions as he stood on the international stage.

Our version of this strategy had Clinton calling to the stage the fictional chief executive of a fictional nation, who would provide

---

2. Oh yeah—did I mention that the House leadership was stocked with adulterers? Newt Gingrich, after leaving his post as Speaker of the House, went on to take as his third wife a former staffer he had been dating while married to his second wife. His designated replacement, Robert Livingston, also resigned when his affair came to light. Unlike those who resigned in shame, House Manager Henry Hyde and Congresswoman Helen Chenoweth remained in office in shame.

cover from the press corps on this night as well. Within an hour of hatching the premise, we had fused stray syllables together to create both our world leader's name (Shoreb Arnsvat) and his sovereign state (Karjakistan). The laughter we generated in the process brought speechwriters writing less fun remarks into our den. One of them, Ted Widmer, was a foreign affairs specialist on the staff of the National Security Council, and he loved the idea as much as we did. But he offered this word of caution: making jokes at the expense of foreign nations—even fictional ones—is tricky business. He took a draft back with him to the NSC to run it by some policy wonks. Jeff and I went back to work.

Ted returned later with good news and bad. Concerned that our parody might hit a little too close to home in places abroad, the NSC had decided that we could not use the name "Karjakistan," as it was a pretty obvious slur on the lawlessness of the fledgling breakaway republics of the former Soviet Union. Also, the national security staff was running a linguistic check on the name of our leader to see if it contained any unintentional ethnic or regional ties. ("Shoreb Arnsvat" could be a name right out of the Macedonian phone book, for all we knew.) I was heartened by the NSC's diligence but also quietly enthralled by the idea of writing a joke that set off an international incident.

Ted mentioned one more red-flag issue that needed to be settled as well: in another section of the speech, a joke linked the radical right wing of the U.S. House of Representatives to the radical-right theocracy of Afghanistan:

I was going to make jokes about the House Republicans tonight, about the managers. It wouldn't be fair; they're not here to defend themselves. They're all at the Taliban Correspondents' Association Dinner.

Ted planned to submit this joke directly to Sandy Berger, the White House National Security Advisor, for approval. (How cool was that?) This was a threshold I had never crossed in my many years inside the White House joke-vetting process.

The next morning, Ted returned with bad news: "Sandy killed the Taliban joke."

Jeff and I emitted loud, stereophonic groans.

"He didn't think it was funny," Ted explained.

"Say that again?" I asked.

"He didn't like it. He said he didn't think it was funny."

"Ted, hold on," I said in disbelief. "We need some ground rules here: the National Security Advisor can kill any joke he likes on the grounds that it compromises national security. But he can't kill a joke because he doesn't think it's funny."

The authoritative tone of my voice belied the fact that as the White House joke writer, I was more than a few rungs below the National Security Advisor on the organizational chart. Nevertheless, Ted was sympathetic to my plea and agreed to take the joke back to his boss.

On Ted's next trip back to see us, we learned the unlikely outcome of this unlikely showdown: Sandy Berger blinked. (To his credit, Berger didn't trump up a national security concern to kill a joke that had simply failed to make him laugh.) Ted also had this news to report from the Situation Room: Berger had approved our substitute for Karjakistan, "Karjakador." With the name of his country approved at the highest levels, all Shoreb Arnsvat needed was someone to portray him the following Thursday. Jeff and I got back to writing jokes. Sandy Berger went back to planning the NATO air campaign in Kosovo that would commence three days later.

The weekend prior to the back-to-back speeches found me holed up in my hotel room, racking my brain for all the jokes and premises I could produce to bounce off Jeff come Monday morning. An important part of the process was figuring out which jokes and premises belonged in which speech, as there were significant distinctions between the two. The Radio and Television Correspondents' Dinner was an event that aired live on C-SPAN, and the best handful of jokes would likely be showcased on TV the next day; the Gridiron was an off-the-record event, and its jokes echoed only inside the Beltway by way of a Monday morning *Washington Post* Style piece. A joke that you'd want to be aired on the *Today* show[3] might not be the same one you write with Mary McGrory in mind.[4]

On Sunday, after the beneficial effects of an early morning trip to the gym had been largely undone by a big room-service breakfast, I pulled up a chair at my hotel room desk. For the next few hours, I hammered jokes into my laptop's keyboard to the background noise of the Sunday morning political talk shows. Before the morning was over, I'd watched three or four shows, almost all of which mentioned a story that was gaining currency during the previous week.

On an interview on CNN that Tuesday, in response to a question asking him to distinguish his record from rival Bill Bradley's, Al Gore had made this claim: "During my service in the United States Congress, I took the initiative in creating the Internet." This awkwardly phrased account of a prescient piece of legislation—intended, in its time, to foster an underexplored technology that really did become the Internet—did not even make news on the news program that aired it. In fact, it was all but ignored for the first forty-eight hours, until Republicans on the Hill began mocking the claim. That same day, the right-wing radio talk show hosts also picked up the ball and ran with it. (It was almost as if they were working in concert!) The Republican spinmasters had taken Gore's words, seemingly borrowed from the Book of Genesis, and morphed them into a more conveniently ridiculous form: Al Gore had now "invented" the Internet.

---

3. "I want to thank you for your invitation to come have dinner with the entire Washington press corps. I accepted. If that isn't contrition, I don't know what is."

4. Working title of Clinton's memoirs, *"That's My Story and I'm Sticking to It."*

On Sunday afternoon, a nationally televised Knicks game on in the background and a room-service turkey club sandwich on my desk, I dialed into the Internet (of all things) and found the story running on the AP wires. There could be no more certain sign that Al Gore's allegedly delusional boast would now end up running in any number of Monday morning papers. Clearly, this was spiraling out of control.

Despite the two speeches that needed my attention, I decided to spend the next hour seeing if there might be some kind of comic retort I could write for my old friend Al Gore. About twenty-five minutes into the exercise, I arrived at the line that I thought would do the trick, a self-mocking rejoinder that I could practically hear Al Gore saying with the full force of his comic fearlessness. I picked up the phone and paged Eli Attie, the VP's director of communications. Inside of a minute, my hotel phone rang back.

"Hey Eli, I got the line for the VP to use on 'inventing the Internet.'"

The sigh he let out gave away his feelings about the topic.

"Okay, ready?" I said, to clear the deck for the joke to come: *"I was very tired when I said that. I was up late the night before, inventing the camcorder."*[5]

Eli laughed receptively, but his response conveyed discouraging news: "It's a good line but he won't use it."

Eli explained to me that the joke conceded a fundamental point—that Gore took credit for inventing the Internet—when in fact his statement about the legislation he produced, in the Internet's embryonic days, had been willfully misinterpreted. This was a position that I understood, even agreed with, but I knew that it

---

5. How I knew this was the line that would deliver the laughs: *"Words with a K are funny. 'Pickle' is funny. 'Cockroach' is funny. Not if you get 'em, only if you say 'em."*– Scene Three, *The Sunshine Boys*

was already beside what was now the point: Al Gore was taking on water in a serious way. As a longtime believer in the silver-bullet sound bite, I held out hope that the right line delivered at the right time might kill the story's momentum, and the camcorder joke was my bid to do it. By arguing the merits of his case, Gore remained an open target. But once he comedically conceded the point early, people looking to score easy points or get derisive laughs would just look like they were piling on. Or so the theory went.[6]

"I'll show it to him," Eli said, but he did not sound hopeful.

Oh well. I had done all I could do, and the hour I had put aside for Al Gore was up. It was almost evening, the Knicks game was over and I had many more jokes to write for Clinton before I slept. My last phone call of that long, lonely day of joke writing had me dialing room service and ordering up the red snapper with rice pilaf.

Within forty-eight hours of my conversation with Eli, the Al-Gore-invented-the-Internet boomlet had reached full-blown bonanza, jumping from the realm of Rush Limbaugh to that of Jay Leno. So great was its currency that—all indignations aside—Jeff and I had incorporated it into a premise for Clinton's Gridiron speech:

> *I can't believe the way people are needling the vice president about saying he invented the Internet. I didn't like it, either. I'm tired of him taking credit for my accomplishments.*

6. A more interesting abstract analysis of this circumstance might also consider why a public figure ever had to comically concede something that was actually untrue—in this case, that Al Gore was under the impression that he invented the Internet. The Hill Republicans and their media mouthpieces were enormously effective in generating an entertaining comic premise of a self-delusional pathological exaggerator. But no one (including these brazen misinterpreters) actually believed Gore actually believed he invented the Internet. What to do about this? I don't know—I'm just the joke writer.

By the way, nobody gave Strom Thurmond any grief when he claimed to have invented the wheel.[7]

In his first career as an exterminator, Tom DeLay invented a kind of ideological roach motel. Moderates check in, but they don't check out.

Jeff and I were working on this section of the speech when I had an idea for another joke in this run but then immediately thought better of saying it out loud just yet. This joke connected the Gore theme to another topic simmering in political circles that week, the new book by my old friend George Stephanopoulos.

George had left the White House at the end of the first term—to teach, write his memoirs and then become an analyst for ABC News. The events of January 1998 quickly put George in a very awkward position, under the glare of a white-hot spotlight. His insights into his former boss's situation—especially his dubious distinction of being the first pundit to utter the word "impeachment"—were not uniformly well received in the West Wing, creating a burgeoning rift that the publication of his candid memoirs was not about to heal. While everybody knew that the president was displeased with his former protégé,[8] George still had plenty of friends in the building—and I counted myself among them. But there was also a feeling that George was a big boy who had made his own choices and could fend for himself.

The problem was that the joke swimming in my head was at George's expense. His widely anticipated memoirs were a potato almost too hot for Clinton to ignore, and this joke could allow him to handle it deftly. Though it could be an excellent opportunity, it also put me in the middle of a conflict of interest of my

---

7. By 1999, I could have hardly taken credit for inventing the "Strom Thurmond is old" joke.
8. George *who?*

own making. If I put the joke in the president's draft, I would have effectively ghostwritten a joke at the expense of someone to whom I felt loyalty. (After all, George was the first person to introduce me to Clinton back in Little Rock, a point I doubted the president remembered—and not one I was likely to remind him of, either.) Yet if I pulled the joke, I'd be denying a solid laugh line to the president/my client. Mental hemming and hawing aside, the dilemma only became real if I said the joke out loud and then left it to others to decide its fate; at the present moment, I possessed the power over whether it ever lived at all. I decided to call George to give him a heads-up, but I refrained from telling him that I could make it go away.

"Hey George—I got a joke for the president I want to run by you."

"Run it by *me*?" he asked. Perhaps he thought I'd forgotten that he no longer worked for Bill Clinton.

"It's about you," I told him.

Silence, then: "Okay, let's hear."

I gave him the context first, that the joke was part of a run about what other politicians have invented, building to this line from Clinton's mouth: *For the record, I hold a patent too. I invented George Stephanopoulos.*

After a moment of thought, George said, "That's a good line for him. He should use it."

Indeed, George *was* a big boy who could fend for himself, as his clinical response to a joke at his expense demonstrated. Only after I hung up the phone did I realize something that George may or may not have calculated as well: on some level, this was a good line for him, too. George's book would eventually require a response from the president, and every day that Clinton avoided the matter only raised the stakes. This reprimand was right on point, but it also had an afterthought quality that somehow reduced the temperature of the topic altogether. As spankings go, it was a light one. A few minutes later, I shared the joke with Jeff Shesol, and it went into our draft and never came out.

For nearly a week after Waldman and the other West Wing honchos had signed off on the Shoreb Arnsvat foreign leader bit, we had no one lined up to play the role. Jeff, Jordan Tamagni and I spent a fair amount of time throwing around names *(Dana Carvey! Martin Short! Roberto Benigni!)*. But as time went on, we got more desperate *(Jerry Van Dyke! The guy who played "Balki" from* Perfect Strangers! *John Hart from Intergovernmental Affairs!)*. No one was available or had yet signed on.

Around 9 A.M. on Tuesday, Jordan walked into Jeff's office holding the Style section of the *Washington Post,* which had a feature story on its front page about a local theater director and actor whose work had been well-applauded in D.C. for the past few years. The photograph showed Nick Olcott to be a burly man with a neatly groomed beard, and his impressive credentials gave us reason to believe he would be a better Shoreb than John Hart from Intergovernmental Affairs. Jordan tracked Olcott down and asked him to come to the White House. Two hours later, he was in Jordan's office auditioning for the three of us. (His day on the front page of the Style section of the *Washington Post* was working out a lot better than mine had a few years earlier.) Olcott's on-the-spot demonstration of the Slavo-Nordic gibberish and Mussolini mannerisms he would lend to Shoreb Arnsvat impressed us all. Speaking for the group, I shouted out in Zero Mostel-ish zeal: "That's our Hitler!" When Olcott gave me a knowing laugh, I was all the more certain of our selection. Not only was this guy perfect, he knew one of the funniest lines from *The Producers.*[9] Two days later, when "Shoreb"—wearing a black suit decorated with a red sash and bright medals plucked from a *Wizard of Oz* Cowardly

---

9. In my opinion, it is the second funniest line, right behind "I'm wearing a cardboard belt!"

Lion costume purchased by an intern at a D.C. toy store—got huge laughs as he regaled an actual world leader in an invented language like a long-lost friend, Jeff, Jordan and I shook our heads in disbelief. Dumb luck had rescued this bit from certain disaster. (No offense, John Hart.)[10]

George Stephanopoulos's new book played another, even more important role in the president's speech. It gave us the idea for a memoir theme—a joke breeding ground that Jeff and I found too fertile to ignore. For the better part of two days, we took turns sitting at his computer, trying our hand at a comic preview of the forthcoming Clinton memoirs that would become the premise of his Gridiron speech.

Page 134: "Election night, 1994. A tense and difficult night. In the family quarters of the residence, Hillary and I watched the returns with a few close friends and advisors. Sperling paced nervously. Begala stared sullenly into space while

---

10. THE PRESIDENT: Look, you can probably tell I'm a little nervous, being around all these reporters tonight. So if you will forgive me, I'd like to employ a method that has worked pretty well for me over the last year. ("Hail to the Chief" is played. Announcement is read: "Ladies and gentlemen, the prime minister of the United Republic of Karjakador, Shoreb Arnsvat.")

THE PRESIDENT: Your Excellency, welcome to the United States. The podium is yours.

(The "prime minister" speaks in foreign language.)

THE PRESIDENT: Your Excellency, without my headphones, I have no idea what you just said. But it sounded very much like words of praise. I want you to know that they mean more to me than I could possibly express.

(The "prime minister" replies.)

THE PRESIDENT: I agree with that, as well.

Leon Panetta bit his nails. 'Bite your own nails, Leon,' Begala snapped.

"My own temper flared at the notion of Newt wielding the Speaker's gavel. 'Darn it,' I said, snapping a pretzel stick in my clenched fist. It was a display of anger that startled everyone present, even myself.

"I took a deep breath. I counted to ten. By the time I hit six, word of my outburst had reached CNN. But all of a sudden I knew exactly what to do. I saw it all very clearly, the path to yet another comeback. 'Panetta,' I said, 'take a memo. I want you to book Newt Gingrich a seat on *Air Force One* soon in the back of the plane.'"

Page 319: "I was sitting at my desk reinventing government one day when [pollster] Mark Penn walked into the Oval Office. He was waving a sheet of paper. 'Mr. President, the overnight polls say . . .' I cut him off. 'The polls? Why are you always bringing me polls?' At my strong urging, Mark spent the next six months as an AmeriCorps volunteer."

Now let me read you this from the last chapter, the chapter on 1998. Here it is: "1998. What a year. We saved the surplus for Social Security. Hillary and I took historic trips to China and Africa. I signed the second balanced budget in a row. And in the November election, the president's party gained seats in the House of Representatives for the first time in a second-term off-year election since 1822."

Now, that wasn't an excerpt. That was the chapter on 1998.

Two days later, on the dais of the Saturday night Gridiron Dinner, a white-tied Clinton eagerly presented the poster-sized covers of his would-be memoirs and read the passages that were its supposed "excerpts." He also made some pointed jokes at the expense of those who had devoted all of their energy to removing him from office.

I won't kid you. This was an awful year. It was a year I wouldn't wish upon my worst enemy . . . No, I take that back.

The president was as relaxed as I'd ever seen him, fearless in his self-mockery and brazen in his attitude toward his well-known foes. Smart guy that he is, Bill Clinton probably saw the more-daring-than-usual jokes on the page and thought to himself: *What are they going to do—impeach me?*

*   *   *

Postscript:

A CHRONOLOGY OF HOW AL GORE
INVENTED THE INTERNET

March 9:   Al Gore on CNN: *"During my service in the United States Congress, I took the initiative in creating the Internet."*

March 11:   Dick Armey announces at a Capitol Hill press conference: *"If Al Gore took the initiative to create the Internet, I created the Interstate Highway." (USA Today)*

March 12:   Trent Lott at a Capitol Hill press conference: *"During my service in the United States Congress, I took the initiative in creating the paper clip."*

March 13:   Bob Franken on CNN *Saturday Morning News:* "I invented the Capitol over here, by the way."

March 14:   Mark Katz invents "camcorder" line, goes back to writing Clinton jokes/watching Knicks/ordering more room service.

March 15:   Former Vice President Dan Quayle (!) mocks Al Gore: *"If Gore invented the Internet, I invented spell-check."*

March 18:   *The Late Show with David Letterman* posts this quiz on its Internet website: Who do you think played the biggest role in building the Internet? Pamela Lee (83%) Bill Gates (15%) Al Gore (2%)

March 19:   Comedian Jay Leno: "Al Gore is getting a little loopy—claiming he was the Father of the Internet. He also claimed that he'd grown up bailing hay, cleaning hog manure, plowing land with mules and chopping down trees with a double-bladed axe. A Harvard grad with a pretty, blond wife—wasn't that pretty much the plot of *Green Acres?*"

March 20: At Gridiron Dinner, Bill Clinton jokingly claims to have invented George Stephanopoulos.

Sunday, March 21, 1999

Gore Chuckles at Internet Claim, Says He Was Tired

WASHINGTON (Reuters)—With a few inventive one-liners, Vice President Al Gore ended Saturday an 11-day silence about his much-ridiculed claim that he invented the Internet.

Gore didn't exactly retract his claim, but he did offer an excuse for a possible slip of the tongue in discussing "my role in the creation of the Internet."

"I was pretty tired when I made that comment because I had been up very late the night before inventing the camcorder," Gore told the Democratic National Committee, drawing laughter.

CHAPTER SEVENTEEN

2000 Zero, Zero—
Party Over, Oops, Out of Time!

OF ALL THE FAMILIAR FACES I KNEW ON THE DAY I'D FIRST ARRIVED
at this White House in April 1993, only two still remained by the
first spring of the new millennium: Bill Clinton and Al Gore. In
that time, I had done just about everything I could have hoped
to do on my White House adventure checklist. There had been
dozens of memorable Oval Office meetings, Map Room prep ses-
sions and post-speech congratulatory huddles with the president
of the United States. I had attended eight consecutive annual
Gridiron Club dinners where I was easily the youngest person in
a rarefied room, mingling as best I could among the roster of *Meet
the Press* panelists. Also perfect was my attendance at the White
House Correspondents' Dinner, where many times over I'd experienced the thrill of hearing a packed arena laughing at the president's speech that I'd watched come together from its first blank
page. I had traveled to and fro in countless motorcades, presidential power parades that never seemed to hit a red light. I had
proudly escorted a number of good friends and most of my family to Saturday morning Oval Office radio addresses, where I
could watch their wide eyes soak in the details of living history—

and later introduce them to the president as he draped his arm over my shoulders. (Upon introducing the president to my parents, Clinton launched into a tribute to my comic gifts specifically for their consumption—to which my mother replied: "You just complimented Mark for the same things I used to spank him for.") In late December of '99, I'd brazenly called in a personal favor from a high-ranking aide to attend the White House New Year's Millennial Ball and rang in a new epoch on the Truman Balcony under an exploding fireworks sky kissing the beautiful woman who was my date and then exchanging momentous hugs with our new friend, Bono. And despite the lowest-level "Appointment Pass" credential I was assigned each day by Secret Service gatekeepers, I had once even cracked the innermost sanctum of the fortified West Wing—receiving a dead-of-night guided tour of the White House Situation Room, an unexpected thrill that began with the search for a stapler I needed to submit a *fastened* final draft of a speech to the staff secretary.[1] By the spring of 2000, there was really only one perk for which I still held out hope: a flight on *Air Force One*.

Air Force Two was as close as I'd come—which was, by all reports, not that close. In March of 1998, I was recruited for a covert mission that was, in some respects, Al Gore's very first presidential campaign maneuver. Hoping to best would-be presidential rival Senator John Kerry in his own backyard, Gore accepted an invitation to speak at an annual St. Patrick's Day breakfast, a ritual humor roast held in a

---

1. The details of this incident will remain a secret between me and the high-ranking White House aide who escorted me into this room—mostly just to see the reaction on my face—all under the supervision of a military aide.

South Boston ironworkers' union hall where well-lubricated revelers are entertained with the comic barbs of pandering politicians. By the time Al Gore—his usual earth-tone tie replaced with one of Kelly green—had finished his turn at the microphone, he'd accomplished what he set out to do: win over the room with Irish-themed humor and make Kerry's efforts seem pale in comparison. (This despite the fact that Kerry was definitely from Boston and presumably Irish.) This showdown had been a particular challenge for me, in that my many years of Hebrew school did not prepare me for generating the kind of jokes that make boisterous[2] Irish ironworkers laugh. However, Michael Houley—Gore's street-savvy, Boston-bred campaign ground general in charge of the event—successfully goaded me to meet the task[3] by loudly rejecting jokes too clever by half and dismissing me as "Gridiron Boy," a nickname I secretly liked.

The biggest thrill of the weekend was not the breakfast roast itself but the victory celebration shared with Al Gore and his staff on board *Air Force Two*, en route back to Andrews Air Force base on the outskirts of D.C. (The next day's *Boston Herald* would declare that Kerry "got his clock cleaned" by Gore.) Returning from an Entebbe-style humor mission on a military jet was another milestone on my White House adventure itinerary, and I immediately knew whom I had to tell about it.

Fisher goes through life implacably unimpressed; "not bad" is his idea of effusive praise. This is why I've always taken special delight in presenting my old high school friend and lifelong tormentor with information that leaves him little choice but to be just a little bit whelmed. The first time I ever picked up a White House phone to call Fisher at his law firm desk, his response was begrudging admiration—only to be retracted when his cross-examination unearthed the fact that the Old Executive Office Building was

---

2. Code word: boisterous.

3. "So I've come to be with you today to celebrate St. Patrick's Day, to commemorate the day when St. Patrick drove all the snakes out of Ireland. Unfortunately, many of them found their way to the United States Congress."

across a parking lot from the West Wing and the White House itself. From secured airspace off the coast of New Jersey, I dialed his home number and was delighted when he picked up.

"Hey Fisher!" I said in a voice just loud enough to compete with the jet engines. "You'll never guess where I am calling you from."

The background noise gave him enough of a clue for a first guess: "Atta boy, Katzie!! Okay—now I'm impressed. You finally made it onto *Air Force One!*"

"Uh . . . no. I'm on *Air Force Two.*"

"*Air Force Two*? You interrupted my dinner for that?" Click.[4]

Yet even at the sunset of Clinton's eighth year in office, the horizons for his comedy speeches seemed to be still expanding. Over the course of the 1990s, the Silly Season had become sillier than even *I* might have dared to dream, with escalating expectations and Beltway hoopla that seemed to keep pace with the NASDAQ. For a multitude of self-reinforcing reasons, each humor dinner felt like a bigger deal than the last. High on the list of reasons for this was Clinton himself, who had overcome his disinclination for self-deprecation to see the strategic advantage of tacit comic concessions. Another was the cyclical nature of the "Clinton crises" (everything from gays in the military to guests in the Lincoln Bedroom), which had a habit of cresting each spring, raising the stakes of the president's comic response until it all culminated in a once-in-a-century constitutional trial to remove him from office. (See previous two chapters.) Not to be ignored, of course,

---

4. Later in the flight, I learned that this plane had enjoyed a long run as *Air Force One* during the Kennedy, Johnson and Nixon administrations. In fact, the history of this aircraft included this sad detail: on it, Lyndon Johnson was administered the oath of office as he returned from Dallas on November 22, 1963. A decade later, this same plane also took Nixon (and Kissinger) on historic trips to China and then Russia. As fascinating as this information was to me, I thought better of interrupting Fisher's dinner a second time for fear of a second serving of mocking scorn.

was the time-honored axiom that nothing succeeds like success. Taking victories where they could find them, the West Wing high command placed greater stock in these dinners than any White House had ever before. Consider this little-known fact: each year, only two presidential speeches were rehearsed and polished (usually under the careful direction of Washington's best-regarded media coach, Michael Sheehan), the White House Correspondents' Dinner and the State of the Union.

What I sensed, mostly, was an ever-greater sense of possibility, and each trip to D.C. had me pitching more ambitious ideas. Many were rejected ("Too many moving parts" was the catchall reason I heard most often), but some got through. Over time, Clinton's humor arsenal expanded to include slides, then props, then videos. By the second term, various "bits," stunts and stunt-casting had been added to the menu, and what had begun as a guy in a tuxedo reading jokes off a page was fast becoming more like an episode of *Saturday Night Live* with guest host Bill Clinton. (This was especially true the night of the 1997 Radio and Television Correspondents' Dinner when *SNL*'s Clinton-impersonator Darrell Hammond was enlisted to play the part of Clinton's clone, called in to finish the president's speech when his broken leg needed a rest.)

Of course, the heightening level of humor was not unrelated to the fact that every spring I'd learn the name of another comedy writer or two who was eager to pitch in jokes, resulting in ever stronger suggested material and punched-up drafts coming in via the fax machine. Fellow writers who regularly volunteered their talents—Erik Tarloff, Matt Neuman, Roy Teicher, Alan Mandel, Joel Shapiro, Mark Davis, Cindy Chupack, Phil Rosenthal, Jon Macks, Gary Ross, Evan Schwartz (and even Al Franken!)—were by now decorated veterans of the Comedy War Room; inside the White House, Deputy Press Secretaries Jim Kennedy and Jake Siewert also regularly threw funny lines into the mix. As speeches made their way toward a final draft, I would always make a point of checking in with the administration's sharpest wordsmith, Paul Begala, who tossed in a Texas-twangy bon mot more often than not. As always, these humor speeches were a group effort to which I devoted my full energies, and the spring of 2000 would be the final guffaw.

The political backdrop of the final Silly Season was not any specific political crisis but rather a diffuse condition said to be the accumulation of all of the previous ones: "Clinton fatigue." Most succinctly described in the pages of the *Economist* as "a weary disgust with the whole administration," this syndrome was used mostly to explain why the first lady—now a candidate for a Senate seat from New York—held only a slim lead against a pipsqueak congressman, and why Clinton's vice president was ten points behind a not-especially-accomplished Texas governor living on borrowed name recognition. Predictably, Clinton fatigue was said to affect its namesake as well, as the zeitgeist arbiters declared that America had seen Bill Clinton's act and was ready for whoever was next.

This may or may not have been the reason that White House schedulers cut back the president's appearances at the annual humor dinners to two from the usual four. The invitation to the Alfalfa Dinner, never this president's favorite, was declined for a third year in a row, and the Gridiron Club was given his regrets in favor of a state visit to India. Already in active pursuit of Clinton's job, Al Gore quickly volunteered to take his place. My first trip to Washington that year had me and my latest laptop back on the second floor of the OEOB—my bid to double-down on the "I owe you one" chit given to me by the man I assumed would be the next president of the United States.[5]

---

5. Had the chads dangled another way in the 2000 presidential election, you would have been treated to the tale of yet another memorable Gore Gridiron Dinner that I helped prepare, this one in collegial conjunction with Al Franken. Instead, there's just one joke relegated to the footnotes of history:

- I pledge that under no circumstance will I use the word "risky" in this campaign. Provided that no one proposes a tax scheme that's *really, really* risky.

On a lunch break from the Gore speech, I found my way down a floor to visit Jeff Shesol, my partner from the previous spring, and to muse about the pair of Clinton humor speeches still a pretty long way off. While the usual drill for an upcoming speech had never begun in earnest earlier than two weeks out, our conversation about the president's humor finale was already a few months old. And the topic that had given us our head start was an idea from the first term that I'd long ago given up for dead.

Four springs earlier, in response to Bob Dole's question to kick off his ill-fated campaign—*Who would you rather have babysit your children, Bob Dole or Bill Clinton?*—I pitched to Don Baer a *Home Alone*–style video of President Clinton spending a Saturday night monitoring the activities of a nettlesome child where hijinks ensue. I had gone so far as to flesh out the details of this idea with Phil Rosenthal, my best friend's big brother and the producer of a little-known sitcom that aired on CBS on Friday nights. (See also Chapter 15.) Don liked the idea, but found it more ambitious than circumstance allowed. Once again, I left his office with the words "too many moving parts" ringing in my ears.

Four years later, the *Home Alone* theme resonated anew. With his vice president and his wife barnstorming America with campaigns of their own, the president was increasingly being depicted as the lonely guy left minding the store. In fact, one January morning, a *New York Times* editorial about Clinton's final year in office made reference to Bill Clinton's "*Home Alone* White House," a stimulus that immediately retrieved an abandoned idea from the hard drive of my brain. I put a call in to Jeff to share the idea and he sparked to it immediately (this despite the fact that my call found him exhausted from the process that produced Clinton's last State of the Union address). After a minute of excitedly trading plans for scenes of Clinton's comic desolation, we deemed the idea too good to use for the first of the two dinners, preferring to keep it under wraps and pitch it as a grand finale to those who could green-light it. I called Phil to tell him of the dormant video that might live again, and that had him tossing out new funny ideas and offering to help however he could. Of course, our collective enthusiasm belied the fact that we were still a few months ahead of ourselves; the dinner was at the end of April and the previous weekend had been the Super Bowl.

But before we could pitch our idea for a video finale at the White House Correspondents' Dinner, there was the small matter of the Radio and Television Correspondents' Dinner that preceded it. With visions of videos already unspooling in our minds, and with the president's spotlight on the national stage said to be dimming, Jeff and I tried our hands at a series of commercials that a bored president and political mastermind might produce if given half a chance. Thanks to the assistance of a D.C. video production firm and a voice-over recorded in the Oval Office itself, the president presented the results at his second-to-last press dinner, teeing it up with this:

> I am a strong supporter of the vice president, but beyond that, I'm not going to comment. After all, I'm not running for anything. For the first time in more than twenty years, my name is not on the ballot; this election is not about me. And hey, I'm okay with that. Suits me just fine. It's all of you in the media who keep trying to drag me into this thing. I mean, I don't see how it involves me at all—I'm the commander in chief, I've got a lot of responsibilities. Even if I were inclined to impose myself—which I'm not—I wouldn't have time . . . Except for last weekend, when I did find just a few hours to produce a few campaign ads for Al. I'd like you to take a look at them and tell me what you think.

CLINTON'S CHOICE :30
MUSIC UP: STIRRING ANTHEM
CLINTON VOICE-OVER:

This November, Americans face the future. The stakes are high and the choice is clear. One candidate has worked for eight years with Bill Clinton. He's considered by Bill Clinton to be a close, personal friend, helping make his toughest decisions, a partner in progress as Bill Clinton moves America forward.

SWITCH TO OMINOUS THEME MUSIC:
The other candidate has never worked a day with Bill Clinton. Bill Clinton hardly even knows the guy. And when Bill Clinton first ran for president, he voted *against* Bill Clinton.
   Al Gore—he's Bill Clinton's choice. Shouldn't he be yours?

TOO MUCH LIKE CLINTON :30
When Bill Clinton chose Al Gore as his running mate, the conventional wisdom called it a mistake. They said Gore was too much like Clinton. Too much like Clinton? *Too* visionary? *Too* strong? With a plan that would bring America *too* much prosperity, and the world *too* much peace?
   Bill Clinton stood up to the pundits and stared down the pollsters. Choosing Al Gore was one of his very best decisions. And doesn't that tell you a lot about . . . Bill Clinton?
   Al Gore—too much like Clinton? Good for him. Good for *us*.

STILL FROM HOPE :30
As America's greatest vice president, Al Gore has been a voice for our values, a fighter for our families. More than that, a strong partner to Bill Clinton. Bill Clinton, a small-town boy from Arkansas who dared to dream big dreams. Young Bill worked hard and played by the rules. He went on to lead his country and build a bridge to the twenty-first century. Most important, Bill Clinton

created AmeriCorps. Bill Clinton still believes in the promise of America—and he still believes in a place called Hope.
Al Gore—because there's a Twenty-second Amendment.

The strong laughter may have revealed the oddest symptom yet of "Clinton fatigue"—that Bill Clinton was its own antidote. When the lights came back up, the president concluded his presentation and the humor content of his speech with a heartfelt tribute to the political pundits who populated the room:

> Unfortunately, these ads would be illegal under the vice president's campaign finance proposal. Not because they're unethical, certainly not because they're untrue. Because they're just dumb. Of course, in America, each of us has the constitutional right to silly or dumb speech. I have certainly asserted my right here tonight. But I think we should take another moment to honor that freedom, to recognize that vital principle, by asking the members of the McLaughlin Group to stand.

As usual, the Radio and Television Correspondents' Dinner was merely a warm-up for the other black-tie, live-on-C-SPAN dinner held in the same room—which, to the untrained eye, could easily pass for an identical event. But the White House Correspondents' Dinner, just ten days later, was unrivaled as the premier annual gala of the political media class. This Saturday night affair also begot more buzz with every passing Clinton year, due in no small part to the soaring success of the *Vanity Fair* star-studded after-hours soiree. Minutes after the crowd dispersed from the Washington Hilton, the center of gravity would shift a few blocks up Connecticut Avenue. That's when oversized, clipboard-clutching men manning velvet ropes became the arbiters of who was who in the *Who's Who* of the Washington pecking order. On this one magical night of the year, I made the grade.

With these high stakes in mind, by mid-April the Comedy War Room (née Shesol's office) was humming with a Manhattan Project sense of purpose. Not only did we set out to write a memorable humor speech for the president's parting press corps dinner, but we also had to hone the premise of his video farewell, produce a script that paid it off and pitch the idea to the West Wing powers that be. For me, I knew this would be my Clinton comedy finale as well.

At this point, only two other people had been brought into the confidence of our whispered plan. First was Phil Rosenthal, now the executive producer of the #1 rated comedy show on television (depending on whether *Friends* was a repeat that week). The second was Josh Gottheimer, a hyper-competent twenty-five-year-old pint-sized[6] bodybuilder who, over the past eighteen months, had become the ostensible staff sergeant of the speechwriting office. Despite his young age, underling status and unassuming nature, something about Josh communicated to his fellow staffers that one day we would all be working for him. Plus, given the fact that nothing got done in the speechwriting office that Josh didn't make happen, Jeff strongly hinted that we would be wise to bring him on board early. In the first weeks of April, I introduced Jeff and Josh to Phil by way of a speakerphone.

That's when the process began in earnest, starting with a synopsis of the premise that had been tweaked slightly from the original and made more true to its *Home Alone* roots. Instead of having Clinton babysitting brats in the empty White House, this version had the "leader of the free world" abandoned and all but forgotten by his wife, vice president and the Washington press corps.[7] Already, we had in mind a handful of scenes—some of

---

6. I towered a full two inches over him.

7. The other movie that also presented itself as a perfect prototype was *Risky Business*, but we ignored it for all the obvious reasons, thus depriving the world of seeing the president in his boxers—or was it briefs?—sliding across the Blue Room floor to the sound of "Old Time Rock and Roll."

them placeholders for better ideas to come—that paid off the premise of unbridled chaos: the president raiding the refrigerator, photocopying his ass and tossing around the nuclear football in the backyard with Secret Service agents. Also on the list were downbeat scenes of solitary confinement: clipping the hedges, manning the switchboards, day-trading stocks from an Oval Office computer. We even delved into more wrenching comic pathos, penning a scene that found the famously self-pitying president alone in the darkness of the family theater, weeping inconsolably while watching *The Man from Hope.*[8]

After patiently listening to our mishmash of ideas, Phil prescribed a very simple structure to connect them logically: *Sad President → Pivot Point → Happy President.* The pivot point was whatever it was that would change Clinton's dull desolation to carefree euphoria. That's when Jeff and I assigned ourselves our next task, to take a long walk around the White House and figure out what our protagonist might encounter in the quiet halls of his plush prison to suddenly change his mood. After straightening our ties and slipping on our suit jackets, we departed for a West Wing location scouting expedition that made this abstraction feel suddenly real.

As has been widely reported in every White House memoir written since 1902, the West Wing is smaller and more cramped than its aura would have you anticipate.[9] Perhaps that is why each nook, cranny, recess and alcove feels like it has a historic secret to tell. Jeff, a card-carrying historian, was better prepared than most White House staffers to narrate our tour en route to an unknown destination, his deep voice adding a nice David McCullough touch. In the next hour of this ordinary, if somewhat slow, White House day, we

---

8. It worked for me! See page 150.

9. The West Wing was built in 1902 and its first occupant was Teddy Roosevelt. The first occupant of an oval office in the building was William Howard Taft, and the first occupant of the rebuilt and current Oval Office was FDR.

took in many stray and fascinating details as we walked eastward from the West Wing on: the subtle irony of the Roosevelt Room, where T.R.'s Nobel Peace Prize is displayed directly across from a proud collection of U.S. military service flags emblazoned with battle ribbons. The perfectly flat floors that extend from room to room, modifications made so FDR could wheel himself about freely, decades before OSHA ever existed. The press briefing room built upon what was once the presidential swimming pool, where John Kennedy once splashed about in seclusion with nubile secretaries nicknamed "Fiddle" and "Faddle."[10] A short walk away, the Rose Garden, which separates the West Wing from the White House, the very spot where an overachieving teenager from Arkansas once shook JFK's hand. Under the stairway that leads to the main floor of the residence, a hand-drawn Mason's seal that was the secret signature of those who built an extraordinary building. In a passageway beneath the White House North Portico, we saw black ash scorched on a stone archway, the imprint of the British troops who in 1814 tried to burn this building down.

Eventually we found our way through the labyrinths to the workaday White House residence far removed from the official tour: a kitchen, laundry room, utility closets, storage bins, service elevators and other housework settings interesting only because they existed within an otherwise fascinating house. Our eyes lit up at the gold mine of locales for sad boredom or manic mayhem, and we kept notes of the scenes that jumped to mind. But still no pivot point on which the president's mood might turn.

Proving once again the old adage that you always find things in the last place you look, our White House fun-finding mission ended in a sub-basement of the East Wing, a fluorescent-lit passageway lined with vending machines. Humming loudest was a

---

10. Ironically, JFK never caught any flak for his orgies in the pool, but the occupants of the press office that Nixon replaced it with would chase him from the Oval Office.

stainless steel behemoth that surely had been dispensing ice cream sandwiches since the Cuban Missile Crisis. Jeff and I exchanged hopeful glances; being in the presence of frozen snacks made us feel we were getting warmer in our search.

"What if the president discovered the machine dispensed the ice cream sandwiches free of charge?" one of us asked the other. That idea was all the catalyst we needed. Our leisurely pace picked up perceptibly as we rushed back to the OEOB to call Phil with our report.

Phil confirmed what we suspected: free ice cream was our pivot. With this plot point put to paper, the three of us raced to fill the script with new scenes that would illustrate the "sad president" and the "happy president" on either side of the segue: *Playing Battleship with the chairman of the Joint Chiefs of Staff in the Situation Room! Trimming the hedges of the Rose Garden! Killing time in the laundry room waiting for his clothing to dry! Changing the oil on his* Marine One *helicopter!*

(Also, by now the day-trading scene had expanded sufficiently that we wanted to include a scene with a suddenly famous character from a popular Ameritrade commercial that was running six times an hour on CNN and CNBC—"Stuart," the haphazardly groomed office boy who schools his bosses in the thrills of online stock trading. Tracking down the actor who portrayed him, a college student named Michael Maronna, was Gottheimer's first assigned task.)

With our first draft complete ten days before the dinner, our next step was selling the idea to the powers that be in the building next door. The video gained momentum as our script made its way from the office of head speechwriter Terry Edmonds to press secretary Joe Lockhart, all the way up to chief of staff John Podesta. Soon powerful West Wing players were e-mailing ideas for additional scenes, some of them good. Upon learning that OPERATION HOME ALONE was a "go"—and that he had been given the nod to direct it—Phil booked a flight to D.C. and a room for the week at the Hay Adams Hotel. As Jeff and I pumped our fists in excitement, Gottheimer began assembling a list of the million details he would have to attend to.

Tuesday, April 25, 2000

From my days in advertising, I knew that the role of a writer on a shoot is marginal at best. Just being present on the day of production is, for the most part, the reward for having written a script that merits being produced. This was the day the footage for our little movie would be put to digital video, and I was far more excited than I was needed. Partly to disguise this fact, I'd found a clipboard and clamped the precious script to it, occasionally rewriting lines that had already been polished many times over. In reality, I mostly served as caddy to those who were doing the really hard work under unusual circumstances and considerable pressure: Phil and Josh, along with a small guerrilla unit camera and production crew.

Despite the fact that Bill Clinton was rumored to be home alone with nothing to do, his schedulers could allot us only ninety minutes of his time. In a world where the president's day was planned out in fifteen-minute increments and a major meeting with global imperative hardly ever lasted more than an hour, ninety minutes felt very generous to those who ran his day. But not to Phil. Phil looked at the script in his hand, which contained fourteen scenes shot in eleven separate locations, and knew it did not correspond to an hour-and-a-half shoot. These constraints were taxing Josh's multitasking skills to their limit as he focused on the microscopic details of each precious minute—props, wardrobe, clearing the production crew into the building, arranging the logical order of scenes to be shot, negotiating Secret Service constraints and conducting skillful diplomacy to assuage the head White House usher, who was aghast at our romp through the premises.

Five people were patiently waiting for the president to arrive to shoot the video's very first scene: me, Phil, Jeff, Josh and chairman of the Joint Chiefs of Staff, General Hugh Shelton. Inside a small West Wing conference room just a few feet away from the Situation Room, the president was to engage his top ranking military officer in the board game Battleship. (Diligently trained to take orders from his commander in chief, General Shelton was the only one among us not reflexively checking his watch for each of the forty minutes the president was late.)

When Clinton finally arrived, the two-man cast for this scene was complete and I reintroduced him to Phil by way of the hit TV show Phil had created and a movie they'd once watched together. Having returned as the director of a small, low-budget movie, Phil now found himself in a room with a president and a four-star general, and somehow found the courage to take charge. In his effortlessly comic New York accent, he explained the simple scene they needed to shoot.

"Mr. President, these are your ships here," he said, directing him to his seat. "And the general over there—he's got his ships." That's when the president offered a detail that added another two minutes to the already tight schedule: that he'd never played Battleship before.

Phil was just a sentence into an abbreviated explanation of the premise of the game when General Shelton offered proudly: "I have the electronic version."

Phil then said to the general, "Sir, you have the real version. You put real ships in real oceans."

Both cast and crew had a good laugh and then the actors rehearsed their two lines[11] once more before the cameras would roll. Just before Phil called the first "action!" of the day, he caught the president's eye and nodded in the direction of the

---

11. PRESIDENT: B-9.
    GENERAL: You sunk my battleship!

highly decorated opponent across the table and offered this aside: "Careful. He's probably very good at this." Clinton's loud burst of laughter set the mood for the comic video that was about to commence, and a minute after that, the first of many scenes was in the can.

From there, Phil continued to make maximum use of the limited time, explaining each new scene as he escorted Clinton from the Oval Office to the Briefing Room to the Rose Garden to the laundry room to the vending machine (etc., etc., etc.), rarely asking him to perform the same scene twice. The crowd of West Wing cheeses gathered to witness the spectacle marveled at the ease with which Phil had taken charge of this mobile sideshow—and the degree to which the president eagerly took his directions and laughed at the entertaining way that he gave them. I watched in amazement as well, quietly proud that Phil was there because of me.

For all the intense pressure, the atmosphere was remarkably relaxed, even as we spilled over into the time allotted for whatever was next on the president's schedule. After Clinton's big smile, raucous laughs and full-throttled performances began to indicate that he was enjoying himself immensely, the project gained even more momentum. The scheduling office found another hour to put on his schedule on Saturday morning—the day of the dinner!—when we would repeat the once-in-a-lifetime event, this time shooting scenes with others who had found time for a cameo appearance. (Within a minute of learning that the first lady wished to join the cast, Phil pitched the idea that would become the video's most memorable scene—the president chasing down her departing limo holding her brown-bag lunch.)

Over the course of crazy days that marked some of the most unusual moments ever witnessed at the White House, I was at my most useful when I ran to get Phil and Josh some sodas. But with each new impossible scenario that the president playacted in front of our eyes, Jeff and I remembered the specific conversations when we imagined them, and now we were exchanging grins that silently asked, "How cool is this?"

Saturday, April 29, 2000

The last three days of that week found Jeff and me back where writers belong, at a keyboard, concentrating on the pages that the president would bring with him on his last appearance on a familiar stage. All the while, Phil spent his days in an editing suite in northern Virginia assembling the video bit by bit. At nightfall, for three or four nights straight, Phil took Jeff, Josh and me out with him to the D.C. restaurants we had heard of but never dined at, making us laugh until our stomachs hurt. By early Saturday afternoon, the production team[12] was back in the editing suite transferring additional footage hardly an hour old: the president riding his bicycle, an encounter with actor Kevin Spacey and the scene where Clinton chases down Hillary's limo to hand off her lunch. Racing the clock for the rest of the day, Phil and his team completed the final tweaks shortly before 7 P.M.[13] Meanwhile, on the other side of the Potomac River, I was one among a dozen tuxedoed staffers watching with one eye as the president rehearsed his speech, the other eye anxiously monitoring the Map Room door.

Around 7:30 P.M., all heads turned at the sound of a tentative knock. Phil entered the room in the tuxedo he'd just thrown on and with a still-warm-from-the-Avid videocassette in his hand. The speech rehearsal stopped abruptly in favor of the finished product we all longed to see. As the crowd gathered around a TV

---

12. As long as we are rolling the credits, here are the names of other people involved: editor David Cornman, producer Peter Hutchins, cameramen Al Haehnle and Mike Mayers and deputy press secretary Jen Palmeri. Rich Rosenthal (brother of Phil, good friend of mine and advertising agency producer) came down from New York to help produce this, too.

13. It would have been completed hours earlier except for a video room snafu that caused tempers to flare. Long story. Don't ask.

monitor already placed in the room, I put my hand to Phil's back and pushed him to stand next to the president as the video, now entitled "The Final Days," was presented for the first time, barely two hours before its C-SPAN premiere.

The impact of "The Final Days" in its Map Room debut was great enough to make the nuclear football, somewhere in the presidential motorcade taking us to the Washington Hilton, seem to be the second-most devastatingly powerful item in the president's arsenal. But to eschew hyperbole, it is completely accurate to say that we were very, very excited at the prospect of unleashing the video Phil still clutched in his hands, as well the speech that would incorporate it.

Traveling in the president's motorcade always came at the expense of showing up considerably late, and on this night that meant missing the cocktail-hour schmoozing with the black-tie crowd. In addition to the many high-priest journalists and name-brand pundits was a more abundant collection of Hollywood stars than usual—Sharon Stone, Jay Leno, Spike Lee, John Cusack, Kevin Spacey, one of the Baldwins—plus, disorientingly, the full cast of *The West Wing*, the hit TV show that had just completed its first season. For the first time in eight years, I did not have an assigned seat at the *Vanity Fair* table; the dinner had seen the last of the publication that had all but ruled the roost for the previous seven years. (Instead, upstart Bloomberg News had planned a party to be the night's ultimate destination.) Rather than split up our little team at tables all over the room, Phil, Jeff, Josh and I chose to have our dinner in a staff room and watch the speech from a hidden perch at the side of the stage.

At 10:06 Bill Clinton arrived at the blue podium to deliver his eighth and final humor speech to the White House correspondents who'd covered his administration from the day he arrived in Washington, D.C. In the years since, they'd relayed to the world more about this man than had ever been known about a president, a record we can all hope will never be broken. Yet Clinton never once bowed out of this event, even in his worst days in office, and after saying his good evenings and settling into the room, he noted his uninterrupted attendance:

> In good days and bad, in times of great confidence or great controversy, I have actually shown up here for eight straight years.

That's when the room broke out in a loud, sustained, well-earned ovation, cut short by half a measure by the punch line that followed:

> Looking back, that was probably a mistake.

With a gust of laughter at his back, he moved on to the early jokes of the still-young speech and started to tell a joke about the evening's other speaker—which, with each new syllable, sounded like one that I had never heard before. As was my habit, I held my breath as Clinton launched an unvetted joke, this one all the more perilous because it involved a man who had spent the last eight years making cracks at Clinton's expense:

> This is a special night for me for a lot of reasons. Jay Leno is here. Now, no matter how mean he is to me, I just love this guy. Because, together, together, we give hope to gray-haired, chunky baby-boomers everywhere.

My exhale came in the form of a loud laugh, in concert with a thousand or so others. The draft we'd rehearsed with the president included a Leno joke that was no better than adequate, and this was far funnier, more gracious and self-effacing. My mind flooded with the memory of the many dozens of jokes that I had brought to his office premised in some way upon the fact that he was not a slightly built man, or that he had an appetite for fatty foods—almost all of which were poorly received and quickly crossed-out. Now, on his way out the door, not only was the president amenable to self-effacing jokes about his physical appearance, he was writing them himself!

Atta boy, Prez!

Back to the prepared material, he continued to establish the theme of his comic culmination delivered with a surprising comfort in being his own target. He also acknowledged a fact well known in the room, that the hottest party that night would not be *Vanity Fair*'s but that of blooming Bloomberg News:

> Now, the Bloomberg party is also a cast party for the stars of *The West Wing*, who are celebrating the end of their first season. You'll have to forgive me if I'm not as excited as everyone else is at the thought of a West Wing finale party. But I've got to give them credit; their first season got a lot better ratings than mine did—not to mention the reviews. The critics just hated my travel office episode. And that David Gergen cameo fell completely flat.

After a few more jokes at his own expense, the president had acquired the license to make self-deprecating jokes on behalf of others. The tone in his voice announced that he was up to the task:

> You know, the clock is running down on the Republicans in Congress, too. I feel for them. I do. They've only got seven more months to investigate me. That's a lot of pressure. So little time, so many unanswered questions. For example, over the last few months I've lost ten pounds. Where did they go? Why haven't I produced them to the independent counsel? How did some of them manage to wind up on Tim Russert?

By now, the huge room was in unified rhythm, surrendering loud laughter that the speaker seemed capable of eliciting at will. In our standing-room-only spot off to the side of the stage, the approving nods exchanged among our team confirmed a shared opinion: Bill Clinton's speech was exceeding even our expectations.

> Now, some of you might think I've been busy writing my memoirs. I'm not concerned about my memoirs—I'm concerned about my résumé. Here's what I've got so far. Career objective: to stay president. But being realistic, I would consider an executive position with another country. Of course, I would prefer to stay within the G-8. I'm working hard on this résumé deal. I've been getting a lot of tips on how to write it, mostly from my staff. They really seem to be up on this stuff.
>
> They tell me I have to use the active voice for the résumé. You know, things like "Commanded U.S. Armed Forces," "Ordered air strikes," "Served three terms as president" . . . Everybody embellishes a little. Designed, built and painted Bridge to Twenty-first Century. Supervised vice president's invention of the Internet. Generated, attracted, heightened and maintained controversy.

The speech could have ended right here and been celebrated as an unqualified hit. Instead, the president revealed that with the world moving on and his term dwindling down, a film crew had been capturing how he was filling his final days. And then the lights came down, the video came up on the screen, and the president's farewell gift to the Washington press corps was unwrapped before the eyes of the room and C-SPAN viewers watching at home.

And at least from where I stood, it seemed to be well received. And when the lights came up and the laughter died down, Bill

Clinton rode the wave of laughter into his final prepared joke of the night and offered his own heartfelt conclusion:

Now, you know, I may complain about coming here. But a year from now, I'll have to watch someone else give this speech. And I will feel an onset of that rare affliction, unique to former presidents. AGDD–Attention-Getting Deficit Disorder. Plus, I'll really be burned up when Al Gore turns out to be funnier than me.

But let me say to all of you, I have loved these eight years. You know, I read in the history books how other presidents say the White House is like a penitentiary and every motive they have is suspect; even George Washington complained he was treated like a common thief, and they all say they can't wait to get away. I don't know what the heck they're talking about.

I've had a wonderful time. It's been an honor to serve and fun to laugh. I only wish that we had even laughed more these last eight years. Because power is not the most important thing in life, and it only counts for what you use it. I thank you for what you do every day, thank you for all the fun times that Hillary and I have had. Keep at it. It's a great country, it deserves our best. Thank you and God bless you.

Farewell Party

On a day that I was set to attend a wonderful party, I knew from the moment I awoke that it would be more than a little bit sad. A few weeks earlier, Al Gore had conceded a bitterly contested presidential election, and I knew I was about to spend my very last day in a Democratic White House for at least four years. A few hours later, I returned to the South Lawn for a staff party held for the thousands who had made their way through this place since Inauguration Day 1993.

This was more than just a farewell to a wonderful moment in

time; it was also a celebration of the collective accomplishments of every person who had worked there, from the mail office to the Cabinet Room. Under the canopy of a big white tent, various administration officials took turns on the stage, paying tribute to the president and all those who had devoted themselves to making real his vision. And I don't believe there was anyone there paying closer attention than I was.

A good number of the accomplishments sounded familiar, but I had never had occasion to take them in as a whole. My specific duties in this administration had gotten me in the habit of paying closest attention when things were at their worst, and maybe I was just a little surprised at the record of accomplishment that had accumulated while I was otherwise distracted. Yes, I had written some funny jokes along the way, but watching all this, I was forced to confront my role—and there was hardly any avoiding the fact that on some level, I had failed. In eight years of Clinton stewardship that had been great to America, I had managed to make jokes only about the screw-ups and snafus.

Here is a brief list of jokes I never wrote for Clinton about his accomplishments in office that present the self-evident reasons why such jokes are, by and large, unwriteable:

Sorry I was late, I was off paying the $223 billion national debt of the Reagan/Bush era . . . By the way, does anybody have a quarter for the meter?

By the end of my second term, the number of people on welfare plummeted nearly 60 percent. So many Americans went from welfare to work that just about the only person still on the dole is Elizabeth! [VIAGRA JOKE TK]

The bad news: I broke my leg. The good news: Due to my signing of the Family and Medical Leave Act into law, Hillary can take up to twelve weeks of unpaid leave to care for me.

I almost stole a joke about how America has experienced its longest drop in crime ever and how crime in America was at a twenty-seven-year low. But then I would've doubled the crime rate!

You wouldn't believe the angry letters we got after signing the Hate Crimes Sentencing Enhancement Act in 1994!

GATT and NAFTA and the other 298 trade agreements I signed increased U.S. trade from $4 trillion to $6.6 trillion while I was office. So maybe that "giant sucking sound" you hear is Ross Perot flushing his head in the toilet.

The unemployment rate dropped so dramatically while I was in office, going from 7.5 percent all the way down to 4 percent, that now, at red lights, I have to get out of the limousine and squeegee my own windows.

. . . the unemployment rate is so low that I can't even find anybody to tell me what's happening on The Bold and the Beautiful.

. . . the unemployment rate is so low that most of the people on line at the unemployment office were recently laid off from the unemployment office.

We are in the midst of enjoying the greatest expansion of an economy in recorded history. You know all those sprawling mansions being built in Silicon Valley? I call them "Clintonvilles."

. . . My vice president calls them "Clinton-Gore-villes."

I just built a bridge to the twenty-first century—the nexus between a service-based post–industrial revolution economy and an information-age economy that transcends borders—AND BOY, ARE MY ARMS TIRED!!

My funk started to lift when Fleetwood Mac took the stage to perform a farewell concert, prompting an epitaph punch line to come to mind: *Don't Stop Thinking About Yesterday.* Even so, the day had the bittersweet feel of a graduation party, seeped in the unspoken truth that no one wanted this bash to end and set us all out on our separate ways. Eventually, I wormed my way into the crowd of staffers taking their turns expressing their gratitude and parting words to the president. This was the kind of day where heartfelt sentiments were exchanged with complete sentences and full eye contact, and I already knew what I wanted to say.

"Mr. President, I want to thank you for the opportunity of a lifetime."

Clinton put his arm on the outside of my shoulder and pulled me next to him, an instantly warm gesture that I had earned from him just a handful of times on the heels of a shared victory. Maybe some of those same memories were flashing through his mind when he said in a voice just loud enough for me to hear, "Thank you, Mark. You gave me some of my best moments."

Perhaps for the first time since I'd watched him from the floor of Madison Square Garden, Bill Clinton made me choke up with emotion. His words were so kind, surely too kind, that for a wonderful moment my marginal role in his presidency felt a bit more than trivial. (Had I finally made up for the day I'd failed George McGovern in front of a room of third graders?) I thanked the president one more time and peeled away, knowing that final exchange could hardly be improved.

A day or two later, back in my apartment, I had returned to the familiar morning routines of a freelance writer—reading the paper, watching the *Today* show, checking the early movements of the handpicked stock portfolio (AOL, EMC, AMZN, MOT) that was supposed to secure my eventual retirement—when the telephone rang.

"Good morning, Mr. Katz. I am calling from the White House. The president has asked that we contact those of long-standing service during his time in office who never had an opportunity to travel with him on *Air Force One.* Are you available to join him on his upcoming trip to Minneapolis next Monday?"

This was too good to be true! Even after eight years of parachuting into the White House for the adventures of a lifetime, I'd never landed this paramount presidential perk—and not for lack of trying. Yet despite the peculiar skill set that had first sent me down an unlikely career path, I was never creative enough to imagine a scenario that would earn me a seat on his *primo* plane that was any more realistic than a G-8 summit roast of Helmut Kohl. Even on my last visits through the West Wing, in the immediate aftermath of a winning speech and a comedy video still in heavy rotation on CNN, I had offhandedly mentioned this particular ambition to several high-ranking White House aides, as though I were dropping not-so-subtle gift ideas in the weeks before my birthday.

But now I was back for good in New York and wondering aloud where my career path might take me next. A day trip to Minneapolis on a magic, flying palace was as good an offer as I had at that moment, but to my ear the voice on the other end of the phone had asked an altogether different and unintended question: had the long journey I'd just completed left me any wiser for having taken it? Maybe just a little. With all the nonchalance that I could muster, I gave the caller my reply:

"Hey, Fisher."

Acknowledgments

More than most people you know, I need help. I need feedback, input, and reassurance. At my worst moments, I require actual, physical handholding and—during a particularly stressful period in the making of the book—swaddling. (Thanks Mom.) The fact is, I could hardly be as high-maintenance as I am without the indulgence of others. For eighteen months, I relied heavily upon my friends, family and colleagues and these pages are my best attempt to thank them.

First and foremost, this book would never have existed but for Evan I. Schwartz. In addition to being a noted author—most recently, *The Last Lone Inventor*—he is an extraordinary friend. So great is his friendship that back in 1999 he spent the better part of a day telling me about the book I needed to write and did not stop pestering me about it for the year and a half that I resisted. Evan understood what this book could be long before I did and persisted in explaining it to me—using smaller and smaller words each time—until I relented. Then, through insights,edits and sage advice, he proceeded to make it better at every step along the way. At times, he held Svengali-like powers over me and if you ask me sometime, I'll tell you the story of how he nearly talked me into changing my middle name to "Sebastian."

On the long list of Evan's good turns is introducing me to Elyse Cheney at Sanford Greenburger Associates, the literary agent we now share along with a fortunate few. While exploring this idea, Elyse pushed me farther than I would have gone myself. Like Evan, she had an intuitive understanding of what this book might be and more importantly, knew how to make it happen. Elyse is a wonderful person to have on your team and perhaps the biggest favor she's done for me yet was to bring this idea to Miramax Books.

Without sucking up so loudly as to slurp, let me just say this about Miramax Books: starting on the day I met with Jonathan Burnham, I have watched this small guerrilla unit of smart people graduate from industry upstart to publishing hit factory. And having worked with practically every person on the roster, it now makes perfect sense. These guys are really good. In addition to Jonathan, I owe special thanks to Jaime Horn, Susan Mercandetti and Kristin Powers and each of them knows why.

My good fortune peaked again when Jonathan introduced me to Mark Lasswell, my editor. Mark was coach, task master, sounding board, synthesizer, tweaker, advocate and friend. Most amazingly, in the final stages of the process, he reduced the number of chapters while increasing the book's cohesion. What greater testament could there be for an editor than that?

Another critical day in this process was when I posted an ad for a research assistant on the career site for the Columbia School of Journalism. The most promising candidate was also the most inexplicable. Benjamin Oren was not affiliated with the J-School in any way. Instead he was an under-employed recent Dartmouth grad with well-honed writing and research skills and more importantly, a fertile comedy brain. Ben put countless hours into the many tasks that were generated in the process of writing this book and his hard work is evident on practically every page, sometimes twice. Thanks Ben.

As the book made its way toward its final drafts, another talented person with a very bright future brought his considerable skills to bear. Jeff Himmelman's sharp eye for detail, ear for language and overall good instincts improved this book at its most critical moments, and his enthusiasm for the project bolstered my own as I headed down the home stretch.

Yet I required even more help than all these talented, tireless people could offer. I am especially grateful to a small cadre of friends who were, chapter by chapter, among the most faithful readers and thoughtful first responders: Joel Berg, Harris Cohen, Rachel Kash, Robert Katz, Sharon Krum, James Percelay, Pam Reynal, Laura van Straaten, and Jeff Winikow. Lisa Szarkowski helped me find the courage to sit down and confront the first blank page of chapter one. Fisher called in regularly to remind me of personal humiliations large and small that I needed to include in the book. Rich Rosenthal has read and responded to everything I've written since high school and regularly shared his cruel but insightful comments on this material as well. Cindy Chupack reminded me often that this book was the right project for me at this time even when I doubted it myself, and the mutual encouragement/rivalry of writing our books at the same time added a great new chapter to a treasured friendship. And no one in these acknowledgments expended more red ink on my drafts than Tricia "Eagle-Eye" Summers, who signed on to help during chapter one.

Other people to whom I owe thanks and probably should have found a way to list them higher up: Brian Floca, Timo Lindman, Marty Munson, Rabiya Tuma (& nearly everyone else at 72 Madison), Phil Rosenthal, Bill Novak, Shepardson, Stern + Kaminsky (most especially Lenny). Many of my White House colleagues helped me recollect and make sense of shared experiences: Jeff Shesol, Josh Gottheimer, Michael Waldman, Alan Stone, Don Baer, Mark Gearan, Jordan Tamagni, Gaby Bushman, Josh King, Ricki Seidman, Dee Dee Myers, Eli Attie, Dan Pink, Eric Schnure,

Ken Baer, Jeff Nussbaum, Richard Mintz, Steve "Scoop" Cohen, Patty Solis Doyle, Lorraine Voles, Ted Widmer, Jonathan Foster, Michael Sheehan, and Brandon Moglen. Collaborators from the Comedy War Room (see page 353) made the president's speeches funnier and, in their recounting, also the contents of this book. No chapters were more fun to write than those of my Dukakis days, the best part of which was reaching out to friends I made a long time ago: Andrew Savitz, Michael Peterson & George Stephanopoulos, Wendy Minot, Kim Strama, Sam Buell, Keith Boykin, John Schafer, Steven Akey, Nick Mitropoulos, Matt Tyrnauer, Wendy Smith, Michael Aronson, Jim Steinberg, Dan Sakura, Jill Wilkins, Andrew Frank, Bill Antholis, Josh Levy, Josh Steiner, J.B. Lyon, Bob Boorstin. I'm sure Gene Sperling could have been a big help, had he called me back. Also invaluable in helping me describe my friend Kirk O'Donnell were some of those dearest to him: Mark Shields, Al Hunt, Jack Leslie, Susan Brophy and, of course, Holly O'Donnell.

Wait there's more! Richard Plepler, Jeff Bewkes, Deborah Dugan, Ted Sorenson, Matt Hiltzik, Al Franken, Holly Peterson, Nick Olcott, Tom Allon, Jared Hoffman, Justin Seipel, Michelle Friedman, Karen Salmansohn, Lisa Dallos, Scott Howard, Andy Elkin, Tom Barreca, Dan Kennedy, Rich Albert, Brenda Haas, Karen Sonet-Rosenthal, Bruce Katz, Ruth Katz, Michael Rapaport, Craig Minassian, Scott Krowitz, David Page, Jackie Cooperman, Heather Maidat, Lucille Mazarin, Sharon Hymer, Ed Rader, Michael Kraines, Alan Mandel, Landon Parvin, Bob Bostock, Rocky Botts, Bill Heatley, Maxine Paetro, Doug Patterson, Steve Baer, Roger Poirer, Richard Crispo, Janette Tyson, Curvin O'Rielly, Chris & Mariah Lofting, Adam Turtletaub, Andrew Frank, Brad Mazarin, Warren Zenna, Dana Milbank, Neil Lewis, Chuck Todd (& The Hotline), Wil Saletan, Rob & Julie Khuzami, Steve & Pamela Wells, Michele Melland. Also: my friend Rich Strassberg felt it was important that he be acknowledged and I'm sure he will try to be more helpful should I write another book.

A special note regarding my friends at The Moth: two years ago, Cindy Chupack dragged me to a storytellers' forum in New York City and I've been back many times since. Listening to the extraordinary stories of so many talented people and sharing a few of my own helped me figure out how to tell this story—and not a moment too soon. Thank you Lea Thau, Catherine Burns, Jenifer Hixson and especially Joey Xanders.

No list of thanks would be complete without expressing my love for those nice people who raised me: Mom & Dad. My parents supported me through college and encouraged me every day since—only to be reduced to caricatures of themselves for the sake of cheap laughs. Similarly exploited were my brothers Bruce and Robert and sister Ruth. I suppose I owe an apology to my Aunt Clara as well.

Finally, a word about the man to whom I gave top billing in the title. I hope that my genuine admiration for Bill Clinton and my respect for the accomplishments of his presidency came through in these pages. My gratitude to him bears repeating: thank you sir, for the opportunity of a lifetime.

Mark Katz
New York City
December 2003

Index